Inside Passage
~ Activity Guide ~

Exploring Major Ports of Call
in Southeast Alaska

Nancy Thalia Reynolds

SASQUATCH BOOKS
SEATTLE

Printed in Canada
Published by Sasquatch Books
Distributed by Publishers Group West
14 13 12 11 10 09 08 07 06 05   6 5 4 3 2 1

Cover photographs:
    Mt. Roberts tram over Juneau: 2005©Mark Kelley/AlaskaStock.com
    Ketchikan's Creek Street (top left): 2005©Michael DeYoung/AlaskaStock.com
    Glacier Bay whale-watching (top right): 2005©Mark Kelley/AlaskaStock.com
    Kayaking near the Mendenhall Glacier (back cover): 2005©Peter Barrett/AlaskaStock.com

Book design: William Quinby
Maps: William Quinby
Copyeditor: Kris Fulsaas
Indexer: Miriam Bulmer

Library of Congress Cataloging-in-Publication Data

Reynolds, Nancy Thalia
     Inside Passage activity guide : exploring major ports of call in southeast
Alaska / Nancy Thalia Reynolds.
     p.   cm.
Includes bibliographical references and index.
ISBN 1-57061-449-0
1. Alaska—Tours. 2. Inside Passage—Tours. 3. Cities and towns—Alaska—
Guidebooks. 4. Cities and towns—Inside Passage—Guidebooks. 5. Harbors—
Alaska—Guidebooks. 6. Harbors—Inside Passage—Guidebooks. 7. Cruise
ships—Alaska—Guidebooks. 8. Cruise ships—Inside Passage—Guidebooks.
I. Title.

F902.3.R496 2005
979.8'04--dc22
                              2005052324

Sasquatch Books
119 South Main Street, Suite 400, Seattle, WA 98104
(206) 467-4300 / www.sasquatchbooks.com / custserv@sasquatchbooks.com

CONTENTS

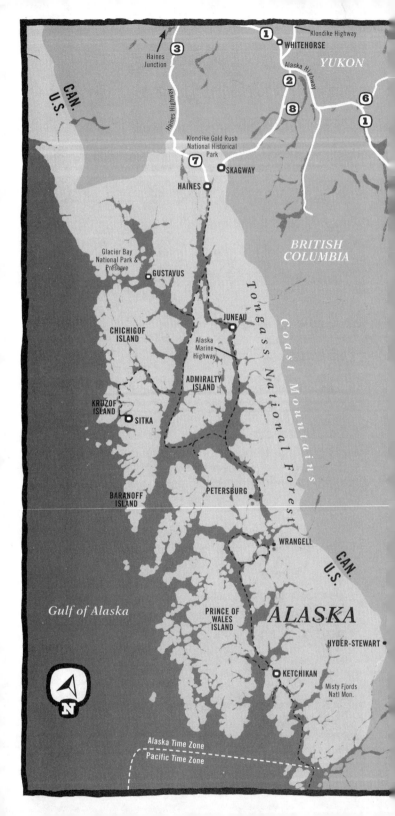

INTRODUCTION

The Inside Passage is the name given to the network of waterways that extend from Puget Sound in Washington State north up the west coast of British Columbia along the narrow Alaska Panhandle, ending in Glacier Bay. Bounded to the west by the islands of the Alexander Archipelago and to the east by the mountainous mainland, Southeast Alaska communities are joined by water, not land. Only a few—Hyder, Haines, and Skagway—are accessible by road. Many—including Ketchikan and Sitka—are on islands.

Because of their isolation from one another, each of Alaska's Inside Passage communities is unique, with a personality and ambience all its own. A visit to artistic, Russian-accented Sitka won't give you a clue about what to expect in the busy working city of Ketchikan. Juneau, the state capital, has the amenities of a large city, along with easy access to the outdoors. Although Skagway and Haines are separated by only 14 water miles, they couldn't be more different: Skagway flaunts its vivid Klondike past, while Haines offers a lower-key, less-touristy atmosphere. The Northwest Coast cultures native to the Alaska Panhandle—Tlingit, Haida, and Tsimshian—and the moieties and clans that comprise them are as varied as the newer cultures that supplanted them.

Each of these destinations along the Inside Passage has something wonderful and unusual to offer—whether you've got four hours or four days to spend, whether you arrive by ferry or air, whether you're traveling with a group or on your own. Your only problem: how to find the time to see and do it all. That's where the *Inside Passage Activity Guide* can help. This book was written to help you organize your time—which may be limited—so you can take advantage of the many things to see and do in Southeast Alaska. (Note that the towns of Wrangell and Petersburg were omitted from this edition because they are less accessible by cruise ship, ferry, and car.)

With a lifetime's worth of exploring to choose from, you'll find it's easy to craft an itinerary that spans a variety of adventures: a historical walking tour, a whale-watching cruise, a road trip by rental car or bicycle, fishing or flightseeing, and more.

This book is intended for all visitors to Southeast Alaska, whether you are traveling by cruise ship or visiting independently. Most tours described in this book are available to anyone. However, a few tours marketed exclusively to cruise passengers have been included. In these instances, the tour provider mentioned offers independent travelers similar tours, which are also described. Tour providers who serve only passengers on cruise ships have been omitted.

Many Alaska tour providers partner with cruise lines to offer tours that can be selected from a cruise ship's shore excursion brochure, which lists a variety of tours offered as add-ons to the cruise. Prices charged for cruise-ship shore excursions are often—but not always—the same as prices charged to independent travelers for the same tour booked directly through the tour operator. Cruise passengers can choose to book a shore excursion or independently. There are pros and cons to each option. Factors to weigh include cost, cancellation policies, how popular the activity it is, and how widely it is offered. Cruise passengers who find a shore excursion is fully booked may be able to book the same tour independently.

HOW THIS BOOK IS ORGANIZED

The guiding principle behind this book is time. Most visitors to Southeast Alaska aim to visit several destinations within a week or two. Managing limited time to maximize your experience of this remarkable region can be a challenge; happily, summer's eighteen hours of daylight extend time for outdoor exploration.

Each chapter opens with an introduction to the destination described, including a quick historical overview, practical tips on getting there and getting around, and a snapshot of the community today.

Activities are grouped in three categories according to the time required to carry them out: Four Hours or Less, One Day, and Two Days or More. Walking tours, shopping, and museum visits fall within Four Hours or Less, as do many of the shorter wildlife and flight-seeing tours. Most road trips fall within the One Day category. Side trips—for example, driving the Golden Circle Route connecting Haines and Skagway—fall in the Two Days or More category.

Where possible, estimates for how much time to allocate to an activity are included. For tours you purchase, such as a kayak trip, times are fairly precise. Many excursions are designed to meet exacting cruise-ship schedules, and operators do an excellent job of ensuring that schedules are adhered to. However, it never hurts to build in time for the unexpected. If possible, leave a half hour of leeway in either direction when setting your itinerary. For activities you organize yourself, from museum going to hiking, times will vary from traveler to traveler; for example, some visitors see all they wish at Sitka's Sheldon Jackson Museum in less than an hour; others need two.

Activities are listed a bit differently within each section. The Four Hours or Less and the One Day sections begin with more leisurely pursuits—walking tours, history and culture, shopping, nature tours, one-of-a-kind activities, and road trips—working from close to port to outlying areas. Then more active recreational pursuits are listed alphabetically: canoeing, cycling, fishing, hiking, and kayaking and rafting. The Two Days or More section starts with general outfitting services followed by active pursuits, then destinations for exploring further.

For all activity sections, length in hours, price, and other tour information in parentheses follow the bold-faced name of the attraction. Names of outfitters and tour operators are also boldfaced, and contact information for these are listed alphabetically in the Outfitters & Tour Operators sidebar featured in each chapter. Organizations, museums, retail enterprises, and the like are also boldfaced, but for these, contact information is in parentheses immediately following the bold-faced name. And in the walking tours, the boldfaced entries indicate that the establishment or activity is described more fully in a later section. Each chapter concludes with sections on Accommodations and Dining, which list some of the options in that community. You'll also find wheelchair icons throughout this book, which indicate at least basic accessibility.

NOTE: Prices for activities are per person, unless indicated—and are subject to change. Unless other-wise noted, prices in this book do not include taxes. Alaska has no statewide sales tax; however, each of the five municipalities covered levies its own sales tax. Expect local sales taxes of about 5 percent on pur-chases along with hotel, tour, and other taxes levied on tourists; collectively, these can add 14 percent or more to items such as accommodations.

THREE-HOUR MUST-SEE ITINERARY

Not everyone has the luxury of time. Ferry and cruise-ship passengers often have just a few hours to explore a stop along the Inside Passage. For you, each chapter includes a short itinerary with a few top choices for getting the flavor of that community. These itineraries build in time for transportation, shopping, and a latte.

ACCESS

Getting to the Inside Passage from the continental United States or Canada can take as little as two hours by air (from Seattle, Washington, or Vancouver, British Columbia) or up to three days by Alaska ferry. A one-way cruise from Seattle or Vancouver to Skagway takes about a week. Nonstop flights from Anchorage to Juneau, Ketchikan, or Sitka take about an hour. Two destinations in Southeast Alaska—Haines and Skagway—are accessible by road (see Golden Circle Route described in the Haines chapter, page 179).

Developments are afoot that will make the region more accessible by road and ferry, including possible construction of a road across Baranof Island from Sitka to the east coast where a new ferry will link the island to nearby communities. Additional fast ferries are planned (see below). The biggest change will be the construction of a road along the east side of Lynn Canal linking Juneau to Skagway. Much of the transportation plan is subject to regulatory approvals, but some elements, such as the fast ferry, are already being implemented.

BY FERRY

Alaska Marine Highway System (AMHS) ferries (800/642-0066; *www.FerryAlaska.com*) serve each of this book's five destinations, with multiple weekly sailings year-round. In summer, they are packed. To secure vehicle slots and staterooms, reservations must be made months in advance. Summer reservations are taken starting in November of the preceding year.

Alaska ferries make the run from Bellingham, Washington, to Ketchikan in 37 hours; from Ketchikan to Juneau is 17 hours; Juneau to Sitka is 8 hours and 45 minutes; Juneau to Haines is 4 hours 30 minutes; and Haines to Skagway is 1 hour. A new faster ferry, the *Fairweather*, has cut sailing times in half. Currently it connects Juneau to Sitka and to Haines and Skagway. In coming years, more fast ferries will be introduced; one will connect Ketchikan to Juneau.

Two- and four-passenger staterooms offer comfortable bunks, peace and quiet, and a private bathroom, though not much more. Many Alaskans forego staterooms, preferring to set up camp on the comfortable reclining deck chairs in the heated outdoor solarium or to pitch a tent in the designated area on deck. Lockers in which to stash gear are available, as well as showers in the restrooms. All ferries have elevators and at least one accessible stateroom for wheelchair users. All

Adventures in Ferryland

Nothing is more Alaskan than the "blue canoes," the fleet of Alaska Marine Highway System (AMHS) car ferries that connect Alaska's coastal communities year-round. Traveling by ferry is not only cheaper than flying or cruising, but it's also one of the best ways to see Southeast Alaska and meet its inhabitants.

Few passengers spend much time in a stateroom when there is so much to see in the observation lounges or on deck: whales, bald eagles, black and brown bears; mountains, glaciers, and rain forest. In summer, U.S. Forest Service naturalists give free talks several times a day on topics such as sea lions, totem poles, or local history. Affable ferry staff contribute to the relaxed and informal atmosphere.

Ferries stop at all major and many smaller ports along the Inside Passage. If there is a downside to seeing Alaska by ferry, it's that stopovers tend to be short and some are in the middle of the night. However, with planning you can devise a terrific itinerary by ferry that allows you to spend a few days in several towns along the way.

the ferries have cafeterias; a few also have restaurants. Food is low to moderately priced and generally good. Small stores sell books, toiletries, and a few toys and items of interest to kids. Onboard amenities include small game arcades, lounges where films are shown, reading and game rooms with puzzles, and indoor observation lounges.

BY AIR

Alaska Airlines (907/225-2145, 800/426-0333; *www.alaska air.com*) has daily flights connecting Ketchikan, Juneau, and Sitka to other Alaskan cities as well as to Seattle, Washington. Smaller charter airlines connect Skagway and Haines to other Inside Passage destinations. Charter airlines play a significant role in linking Southeast Alaska communities. Some offer scheduled service; others serve as air taxis. Many flightseeing tour operators described in this book provide one or both services (see the Outfitters & Tour Operators sidebars in each chapter). For additional options, check with regional visitor centers.

BY CRUISE SHIP

Alaska cruises are among the most popular vacations in the United States, and the trend shows no sign of cooling off. Cruise lines large and small include Alaska in their itineraries each year. In 2004, more than 800,000 visitors came via cruise ship. Most large cruise ships depart from San Francisco, California; Seattle, Washington; or Vancouver, British Columbia. Although round-trip cruises are increasingly popular, many one-way cruises are offered, often in combination with land-based tours of the Alaska and Yukon interior. One-way cruises may head either north or south; the northern terminus is usually Skagway or Seward, or the town of Whittier north of the Inside Passage. Cruises usually run about 6 to 12 days.

Smaller cruise lines with smaller ships also offer a plethora of choices to Alaska. These ships usually lack amenities like swimming pools, spas, and casinos, but are able to get into smaller harbors and visit less-traveled destinations. Some smaller cruises take place entirely within Alaska, often departing from Juneau.

Cruise ships visit Ketchikan, Juneau, and Skagway most days in summer. Midweek is busiest with up to five large ships per destination. Sitka gets a ship or two most days. In 2004, just a few cruise ships stopped in Haines each week.

Large cruise lines sailing to Alaska include Carnival (888/CARNIVAL, *www.carnival.com*); Celebrity (800/722-5941, *www.celebrity.com*); Crystal (866/446-6625, *www.crystalcruises.com*); Holland America (877/724-5425, *www.hollandamerica.com*); Norwegian Cruise Lines (800/625-5306, *www.ncl.com*); Princess

(800/PRINCESS, *www.princess.com*); Radisson Seven Seas (877/505-5370, *www.rssc.com*); and Royal Caribbean (866/562-7625, *www.royalcaribbean.com*).

Smaller cruise lines visiting Alaska include American Safari (888/862-8881, *www.amsafari.com/index.html*); America West Steamboat Company (800/434-1232, *www.americanweststeamboat.com*); Clipper Cruise Line (800/325-0010, *www.clippercruise.com*); Cruise West: (888/851-8133, *www.cruisewest.com*); Glacier Bay Cruiseline (800/451-5952, *www.glacierbaytours.com*); and Lindblad Expeditions (800/EXPEDITION, *www.expeditions.com*).

WHERE TO STAY & EAT

At the end of each chapter, you'll find accommodations and restaurants listed for that community, as well as for some smaller nearby destinations.

ACCOMMODATIONS

Choices range from high-end hotels to rustic hostels. Rates indicate accommodations for two people for one night during the peak summer travel season. All prices are subject to change.

$ = less than $80
$$ = $80–$130
$$$ = more than $130

DINING

Dining options and food quality are good, but prices are somewhat higher than in the Lower 48. In Alaska, children are permitted in bars, provided they are accompanied by parents or guardians. Rates indicate dinner for one without alcohol. All prices are subject to change.

$ = less than $15
$$ = $15–$30
$$$ = more than $30

WHAT TO BRING

When packing for an Inside Passage summer trip, plan for temperatures in the mid-60s by day, dropping to the 50s or even 40s at night. Some rain is virtually certain. However, temperatures have trended upward in recent years; the summer of 2004 saw sustained temperatures in the 80s and 90s, with very little rain.

Alaska weather is notorious for changing suddenly, so when you pack, think "versatile" and "layers." Rain-proof outerwear—hooded jacket and pants—is a must; investing in high-quality raingear can make the difference between a successful trip and a miserable one. Zip-off pants that convert to shorts are space savers. To protect against mosquitoes, bring light-colored cover-ups. In May to early June and September to October, temperatures will be cooler; lightweight long underwear and a warm vest can come in handy.

Whenever you come, bring a hat, gloves, and waterproof boots or sturdy walking shoes. Don't forget good binoculars; although many tour operators provide these, there are rarely enough to go around. Sunscreen and, if you're susceptible, motion sickness remedies are useful. Finally, include a waterproof daypack to store it all in.

SHOPPING

Recreational shopping qualifies as an activity in this book because it's important both to visitors and for the local communities that rely on visitors. These pages feature businesses that are unique to the destination, because what makes shopping on vacation enjoyable is discovering something new that is distinctive to the area you're visiting. Galleries that carry works by local and Native artists are showcased, rather than jewelry-store chains and T-shirt emporiums.

NATURE

Under the heading "Nature" you'll find attractions and undemanding activities that bring visitors in close touch with Southeast Alaska's natural environment and wildlife. Visitors with limited mobility are well served with trips ranging from whale-watching tours aboard comfortable, heated vessels with snacks and restrooms, to small plane and helicopter tours that land passengers right on a glacier or at a prime bear-viewing spot. Not all attractions are wilderness based. Some, such as the Macauley Salmon Hatchery in Juneau or the Alaska Raptor Center in Sitka, are in town. Of these, some require you to join a guided tour; others can be carried out on your own.

BEAR WATCHING

Seeing a bear can be the highlight of an Alaska trip. Of the three Alaska bear species, two live in Southeast: black and brown. (Polar bears live only in the Arctic.) Once considered separate species, Kodiak, brown, and grizzly bears are now grouped as one: *Ursos arctos*. Black bears are smaller and shyer than brown bears, which have distinctive humped backs and are more aggressive. However, many black bears appear brown, and it can be hard to distinguish the two species.

If your introduction to bears comes on a tour, you'll get a safety briefing. But what if you run into a bear while you're out hiking on your own? Here's a primer on preventing surprise bear encounters and how to handle them if they occur.

MAKE NOISE WHEN YOU HIKE. On the "ounce of prevention" principle, it's best to avoid surprise encounters. Bears generally avoid human contact. They have good hearing but poor vision, so it's a good idea to let them hear you coming to alert them to get out of your way before meeting you face to face. Alaska Natives traditionally rattled containers filled with pebbles for this purpose. If you are hiking with a buddy (which is recommended), talk loudly. If you must hike alone, attach a bell to your daypack or test your vocal chords with Broadway show tunes.

LEARN TO RECOGNIZE BEAR SIGNS. Bears love salmon and berries; the presence of either in bear country means bears may be close. On trails, look out for rotting fish carcasses and bear droppings.

DON'T FEED THE BEARS. If you are camping, follow bearproofing guidelines for carrying, storing, and discarding food. After picnicking, pack out your garbage.

KEEP YOUR DISTANCE. Once you see a bear, if it has not seen you, back off slowly. If a bear sees you, do not turn around and run. They can run faster than you can, and running only convinces them that you are prey. Nor should you climb a tree—they can do that, too.

ASSUME ALL BEARS ARE DANGEROUS. Most bears will try to get away from humans, but attacks occasionally occur. A bear may try to scare you by feigning an imminent attack. Stand your ground, yell, and wave your arms, looking as tall as you can, then back off slowly. In most cases the bear will simply leave.

NEVER COME BETWEEN A SOW AND HER CUBS. If you spot a cub in summer, you can be certain its mom is nearby. Back off immediately; do not approach the cub.

IF A BEAR CHARGES YOU: drop to the ground and curl up in a fetal position, arms protecting your neck, and lie as still as possible. If the bear continues to attack once you've assumed this defensive posture, it's time to fight back. A walking stick or daypack makes an impromptu weapon. Bear spray, sold in many sporting goods stores, can be used up to a distance of about eight yards. Note that it is illegal to bring bear spray on a plane.

FLIGHTSEEING

When you're booking an aerial tour, check on cancellation policies in case of bad weather; be sure you can easily obtain a full refund if your flight is canceled. Passengers weighing more than 250 pounds may be required to purchase an extra seat.

WILDLIFE TOURS

The following wildlife can be viewed near many Inside Passage destinations: black bears, brown bears, Dall sheep, mountain goats, porcupines, red squirrels, river otters, Sitka black-tailed deer, and wolves; harbor seals, humpback whales, orcas, and Steller sea lions; bald eagles, golden eagles, cormorants, ducks, great blue herons, loons, murres, marbled murrelets, owls, pigeon guillemots, puffins, ravens, sandhill cranes, and trumpeter swans. Sea otters can be seen in the waters around Sitka, Glacier Bay, and Icy Strait.

WILDLIFE VIEWING PERMITS

To protect bears and their habitat, access to some areas they frequent is controlled. In summer, permits are required to view wildlife at Pack Creek's Stan Price State Wildlife Sanctuary, on Admiralty Island, and at Anan Wildlife Observatory, near Wrangell. Only permit holders are allowed to visit the sites and only for a specified date and time. As a rule, guided tours you book will take care of any permit requirements. However, if you are arranging a self-guided trip, it's up to you to obtain the permit. For Pack Creek permit information contact the **Forest Service Information Center** (8465 Old Dairy Rd, Juneau, AK 99801; 907/586-8800, 907/586-8751; *www.fs.fed.us/r10/tongass/districts/admiralty*). For Anan Wildlife Observatory permit information, contact **USDA Forest Service, Wrangell Ranger District** (525 Bennett St, Wrangell, AK 99929; 907/874-2323).

ROAD TRIPS

One of the pleasures of visiting Southeast Alaska is the speed with which you can get out into the wilderness. The region's highways, while short, are delightful and well worth exploring. Many interesting hikes, awesome vistas, and great restaurants require wheels to get to. Some visitors bring their cars on the ferry, but cruise-ship passengers and other carless visitors can take advantage of local highways, too. Even if you have only a half day for exploration, renting a vehicle for four hours is a great way to get off the beaten tourist path. This book contains road trips for each destination and detailed descriptions of what you'll find along local highways. Short-term vehicle rental information is also provided. Unless otherwise noted, all mileages are round trip, and the times are suggested minimums.

FISHING

Allowing for minor variations by region, the sportfishing calendars shown here indicate peak times for freshwater and saltwater sportfishing from late spring to early fall.

FRESHWATER SPORTFISHING CALENDAR

JAN	FEB	MAR	APR	MAY	JUNE	JULY	AUG	SEPT	OCT	NOV	DEC
					brook trout						
					cutthroat trout						
					Dolly Varden						
					rainbow trout						
					steelhead trout						
						chum salmon					
							coho salmon				
				king salmon							
						pink salmon					
						sockeye salmon					

Year-round: Dolly Varden, grayling, steelhead trout, rainbow trout, cutthroat trout, brook trout

SALTWATER SPORTFISHING CALENDAR

JAN	FEB	MAR	APR	MAY	JUNE	JULY	AUG	SEPT	OCT	NOV	DEC
					cutthroat trout						
					Dolly Varden						
					chum salmon						
					coho salmon						
				king salmon							
					pink salmon						
					sockeye salmon						
						halibut					
					lingcod						
					rockfish						

LICENSES

Sportfishing in Southeast Alaska requires a license for nonresidents age 16 or older, obtainable by mail or online with a credit card from the **Alaska Department of Fishing and Game** (ADF&G Licensing Section, P.O. Box 25525, Juneau, AK 99802-5525; 907/465-2376; *www. admin.adfg.state.ak.us*). A 1-day license costs $10; a

14-day license costs $50. If you're fishing for king salmon, you'll need a king salmon tag ($10 for 1 day; $50 for 14 days). Unless otherwise stated, fishing licenses are available for purchase from fishing tour operators included in this book. Licenses can also be purchased at most Alaska sporting goods stores.

HIKING AND CAMPING

Even a short hike in Southeast Alaska can get you into unspoiled wilderness. Many trails start down-town, within an easy walk of the cruise-ship dock; but signs of civilization are soon left behind, and the visitor is surrounded by beautiful old-growth forest and the creatures who inhabit it. Although urban life may be close at hand, hikers need to prepare for a wilderness experience. Always bring a good map, water and snacks, sunscreen, and bug juice; and let someone know where you're going. Check on trail conditions at the local visitor center. If you're unused to wilderness outings, joining one of the area's excellent guided hikes is recommended. All hiking times given throughout this book are suggested minimums for a round trip, unless otherwise noted.

TONGASS NATIONAL FOREST

Established in 1902, the Tongass is the largest public forest in the United States. Three times larger than Alaska's Chugach, the second biggest national forest, the Tongass could fit the states of Massachusetts, Vermont, Connecticut, and Rhode Island within its 16.9 million acres. The Tongass abuts each destination in this book, except Haines, and shelters much of the world's largest temperate rain forest.

Within the Tongass are thirteen campgrounds, 450 miles of hiking trails, 1,000 miles of logging roads, 150 rustic public-use cabins (see below), and nineteen wilderness areas that shelter abundant wildlife, including about 5,000 brown bears. Visitor centers and ranger stations provide information and resources to visitors.

Forest managers are charged with the task of balancing uses in the forest: providing access to recreation while preserving the natural habitat and animals that depend on it and allowing some commercial uses, including logging, while protecting salmon spawning grounds. Balancing competing interests is an ongoing challenge.

PUBLIC-USE CABINS

The U.S. Forest Service maintains recreational cabins for visitors to use. Cabins are generally in highly scenic locations, but are rarely accessible by road. Some can be reached on foot; others require boat or plane transportation. Some of these cabins are included in this book. Facilities include bunks (but no mattresses or sleeping pads), table and benches, woodstove, cooking area, outhouse, ax, and broom. Water is usually available but must be treated.

Advance reservations are required. Cabins can be booked up to six months ahead; popular cabins are often booked shortly after reservations open up. On average, cabins rent for $35 per night, for up to seven nights in summer, ten nights the rest of the year. Popular cabins may cost a little more and be available for less time. For more information contact **Alaska State Parks** (400 Willoughby Ave, 4th fl, Juneau, AK 99801; 907/465-4563; *www.dnr.state.ak.us/parks/cabins/south/*). To rent a cabin, contact **ReserveUSA** (877/444-6777; *www.reserveusa.com*).

EVERYTHING CHANGES

Although every effort has been made to ensure that information in this book is accurate and up to date, things do change. It's best to verify times and prices before booking.

Is something special left out? Did your experience fail to live up to your expectations? Either way, we'd love to hear from you. At the end of the book there's a feedback form; please fill it out and send it in to Sasquatch Books. We'll consider your feedback for the next edition of this book.

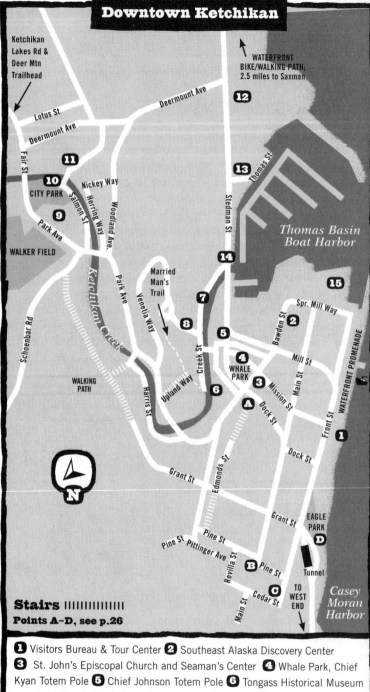

Downtown Ketchikan

Ketchikan Lakes Rd & Deer Mtn Trailhead

WATERFRONT BIKE/WALKING PATH; 2.5 miles to Saxman

Lotus St

Deermount Ave

Deermount Ave

Fair St

11

10
CITY PARK

Nickey Way

Herring Way

Salmon St

9

Park Ave

WALKER FIELD

Schoenbar Rd

Ketchikan Creek

Park Ave

Woodland Ave.

Venetia Way

Married Man's Trail

12

13

Thomas St

Stedman St

Thomas Basin Boat Harbor

14

15

7

8

Creek St

5

Spr. Mill Way

2

Bawden St

Mill St

4
WHALE PARK

3

Mission St

Main St

WATERFRONT PROMENADE

WALKING PATH

Harris St

Upland Way

6

A

Dock St

Front St

1

Dock St

Grant St

Edmonds St

Grant St

EAGLE PARK

D

Pine St

Pine St

Pine St

Tunnel

Pittinger Ave

Revilla St

B

C

Cedar St

Main St

TO WEST END

Casey Moran Harbor

N

Stairs ||||||||||||||
Points A–D, see p.26

1 Visitors Bureau & Tour Center **2** Southeast Alaska Discovery Center **3** St. John's Episcopal Church and Seaman's Center **4** Whale Park, Chief Kyan Totem Pole **5** Chief Johnson Totem Pole **6** Tongass Historical Museum and Ketchikan Public Library, Raven Stealing the Sun Totem Pole **7** Creek Street neighborhood **8** Funicular to WestCoast Cape Fox Lodge **9** Deer Mountain Salmon Hatchery & Eagle Center **10** City Park **11** Totem Heritage Center **12** Sun Raven Totem Pole **13** Stedman-Thomas Historic District **14** Stedman Street Bridge **15** Salmon Landing Market

Chapter 1

KETCHIKAN

Horizontally challenged Ketchikan, Alaska's southernmost city, lies 60 miles north of the British Columbia border at the bottom of the Alaska Panhandle. The city perches on the steep edge of rocky Revillagigedo Island, its ancient and violent geologic history a product of continental drift (two plates converge here), fire, and ice. At first glance, the town appears to defy gravity; picturesque houses cling to the cliffside, connected by rickety staircases and walkways. A tunnel through the black rock bisects the downtown core.

The island was named for Count Revillagigedo, viceroy of Mexico from 1789 to 1794. Residents don't attempt the Spanish pronunciation; they call the island "Revilla," rhyming with "vanilla." More than 13 *feet* of rain per year contributes to the lush rain-forest environment but can stymie visitors who come unprepared. Although summer is the driest season, "dry" is a relative term here.

Whatever the climate, Ketchikan has a way of growing on you. Do as locals do: dress for wet weather, and don't let it keep you from enjoying the outdoors, which has plenty to offer, from beautiful Ward Lake and Totem Bight State Park to Prince of Wales Island and Misty Fjords National Monument. Totem poles old and new grace city streets; historic buildings that once housed shady characters are now light-filled art galleries. And when the sun comes out, take a look around to see why Ketchikaners love their rain-soaked world.

HISTORY

A local joke runs that "Ketchikan" is a Tlingit term meaning "place so rainy only a white man would build a town there." The Tlingit did name Ketchikan, calling it *Kitschkhin*, but the true translation is "where the eagle spreads its wings" or "thundering eagles' wings."

The land around Ketchikan Creek first served as a Tlingit fish camp. It was fish, not gold, that drew others here, as well. The first cannery opened in 1886; within fifty years, Ketchikan was among the world's largest salmon exporters, with more than a dozen busy canneries. Following the 1897 Klondike gold rush, Ketchikan became an important provisioning stop for miners. It was incorporated as a city in 1900. By the 1940s, overfishing had begun to deplete salmon stocks; canneries closed, but not all disappeared. About half of all salmon harvested in the state today still comes from Southeast Alaska.

The timber industry ran a parallel course. The first sawmill opened on Prince of Wales Island in 1898; in 1953, the first pulp mill opened at Ward Cove. Competition and high production closed Ketchikan's last pulp mill in 1997. By the time the timber industry decamped, tourism had become a Ketchikan growth industry. Still, the loss of pulp-mill jobs and the downsizing of the salmon fisheries have presented challenges for Ketchikan. But as government jobs, both state and local, have found their way to Ketchikan in recent years, along with increased tourism, Ketchikan's population is growing again.

KETCHIKAN TODAY

Ketchikan is a busy working town of 7,900, located in the Ketchikan Gateway Borough, which has a total population of 13,300. "Three blocks wide and three miles long" is an accurate description of Ketchikan, which has the traffic and parking challenges of a much larger city. Primary employment comes from commercial fishing and fish processing, government, and tourism. Like Skagway and Juneau, Ketchikan has seen an enormous boom in cruise-ship visits over the past decade, which shows no signs of decreasing. Somehow Ketchikan manages to absorb the daily influx of sightseers and maintain its quirky personality.

GEOGRAPHY

At the same latitude as Moscow, Russia, Ketchikan lies on the southwestern coast of Revillagigedo Island, sheltered to the west and south by Gravina and Annette islands and, farther west, Prince of Wales Island. To the east, Behm Canal separates Revilla from the mainland. Ketchikan is 224 miles south of Juneau and 679 miles north of Seattle, Washington.

CLIMATE

Ketchikan's annual precipitation is 162 inches. Summer is the driest season. In the peak season, Ketchikan's high temperatures average 64°F (June, 61.6°F; July, 65.2°F; August, 65.4°F).

Average Temperatures (°F)

	May–Oct	Nov–Apr
High	60.2	43.6
Low	46.6	32.3

Average Precipitation (inches)

Jan	Feb	Mar	Apr	May	June
14	12.4	12.2	11.9	9	7.4

July	Aug	Sept	Oct	Nov	Dec
7.8	10.6	13.6	22.5	17.9	15.8

Average Hours of Daylight

Jan	Feb	Mar	Apr	May	June
7.75	9.5	11.75	14.25	16.25	17.5

July	Aug	Sept	Oct	Nov	Dec
16.75	15	12.75	10.5	8.25	7.25

ACCESS

Daily Alaska Airlines flights connect Ketchikan to Juneau, other Alaskan cities, and Seattle, Washington; Alaska ferries serve Ketchikan year-round; and all major cruise lines visit Ketchikan (see the introduction, page 7). The Ketchikan airport is across Tongass Narrows on Gravina Island, requiring a 5-minute ferry ride (see Wheels & Keels, below). Ferries connect Ketchikan and Prince of Wales Island daily, year-round (see Two Days or More, page 55).

VISITOR INFORMATION & SERVICES

Alaska Public Lands Information Center, in the Southeast Alaska Discovery Center (50 Main St; 907/228-6220; *www.nps.gov/aplic/*).

Ketchikan Visitors Bureau & Tour Center (131 Front St; 907/225-6166, 800/770-3300; *www.visit-ketchikan.com*).

Post Office: The downtown substation is in Schallerer's Photo & Gift Shop (422 Mission St; 907/225-7678; Mon–Sat 9am–5:30pm).

Alaska Public Radio Network: KRBD 105.9 FM.

Internet Access: Unlike other Southeast public libraries, the **Ketchikan Public Library** (629 Dock St; 907/225-3331; *www.firstcitylib.org*) charges for Internet use; users must first obtain a temporary library card for $5. **Seaport Cyber** (Salmon Landing Market; 907/247-4615; *www.seaportel.com*) has computers with Internet access ($5/hour) and a Wi-Fi hot spot there and at the ferry terminal. **Surf City Internet Café** (425 Water St; 907/225-5475; *www.aptalaska.net*) provides Internet access ($5/20 minutes).

WHEELS & KEELS

With two locations, **Alaska Car Rental** (Ketchikan Airport on Gravina Island, 7am–9pm, and 2828 Tongass Ave, 8am–5pm; 907/225-5123, 800/662-0007; *www.akcarrental.com*) allows you to pick up a car at one spot and drop it off at the other. To drive on Prince of Wales Island, you must rent a sport utility vehicle ($50/day for a compact, $100/day for an SUV). Also with two locations is **Budget Car Rental** (4950 N Tongass Hwy, 907/225-8383, 800/478-2438, 800/527-0700, airport 907/225-6004; *www.budget.com*); prices start at $46.44/day for a compact. Return rentals at the airport (via the airport ferry, see below) or in town. To get to the airport, there's an **airport shuttle** (907/225-5429; $18/person) which also meets all flights.

Downtown Ketchikan is served by **Ketchikan Gateway Borough Transit** (907/225-8726; *borough.Ketchikan.ak.us*; $1.50/adult, $1.25/ages 4–11 and senior, free/under 4), with two routes. Buses run every 15 minutes on Tongass Avenue, Monday through Saturday, with

Ketchikan Three-Hour Must-See Itinerary

- Funicular to the Cape Fox Lodge (30 minutes)
- Creek Street and shopping (55 minutes)
- Totem Bight State Historical Park tour by taxi (1.25 minutes)
- Tongass Historical Museum (20 minutes)
- Refueling stop: **Coffee Connections** (521 Water St)

reduced service on Sunday. The **Blue Line** runs north to Shoreline Drive and the North Tongass Shopping Center (home of Wal-Mart) and south to Saxman Village, hitting the Alaska ferry and airport ferry terminals, downtown, and cruise-ship docks along the way. The **Green Line** runs north to the Alaska and airport ferry terminals and just south of downtown, stopping at the University of Alaska Southeast–Ketchikan campus and making a loop that includes the Totem Heritage Center and Deer Mountain Hatchery, along with downtown and the cruise-ship docks. Pick up bus schedules at the visitor center. **Sourdough Cab** (907/225-5544) provides local taxi service.

Having the airport on another island complicates local transportation. The **airport ferry**, whose dock is just north of the ferry terminal, makes frequent 5-minute crossings to the airport (every 15 minutes before and after flights; $4/adult plus $6/vehicle one way). The **Tongass Water Taxi** (907/209-8294) provides passenger-only transportation to and from the airport and nearby watery destinations.

EVENTS

King Salmon Derby (Ketchikan Visitors Bureau; 907/225-6166; *www.visit-ketchikan.com*): This popular fishing

Ferry Break

Ketchikan's ferry terminal is just 3 miles north of town. With a few hours in port, ferry passengers can walk out to the bus shelter on Tongass Avenue for a quick bus trip into the city (both Green and Blue Line buses stop at the terminal). On your way into town, take a look at the city's residential neighborhoods. Downtown, you can check out the two museums, explore Creek Street, take the funicular up to the Cape Fox Lodge, or shop at Salmon Landing. Or, if you're lucky enough to experience a rare and wonderful sunny Ketchikan day, hire a taxi at the terminal with a few friends to visit Totem Bight State Historical Park, then hike around Ward Lake.

derby, held in late May and early June, is nearly sixty years old and open to everyone. Winners have landed kings topping 50 pounds.

Blueberry Arts Festival (Ketchikan Arts & Humanities Council; 907/225-2211; *www.ketchikanarts.org*): This annual event takes place over three days in early August, with a variety of arts—musical, literary, dance—events, arts and crafts for sale, food, and slug races. The Gigglefeet Dance Festival celebrates the work of local choreographers and dancers.

FOUR HOURS OR LESS

There is much more to Ketchikan than the downtown shopping district and quaint Creek Street, so it's a pity that many visitors don't venture beyond the gauntlet of stores that line the cruise dock. Kayak trips start less than a mile from the cruise-ship dock, and a plethora of guided tours await the adventurous visitor—all doable in a few hours.

WALKING TOURS

Ketchikan Walking Tour *(2 hours)*

Walking through Ketchikan is more a hike than a stroll. Away from the water, within minutes you're huffing and puffing up a vertical hillside, and often, stairs. If accessibility is an issue, consider taking one of the excellent city tours, including one by kayak (see Canoeing & Kayaking, page 40). For walking tour map, see page 16.

1 From the **Visitors Bureau & Tour Center** at the cruise-ship dock (where you can book tours), cross Front Street and turn right on Mill Street.

2 Walk up Mill to Bawden Street; you'll pass the **Southeast Alaska Discovery Center**.

3 Turn left on Bawden and walk one block to Mission Street to see **Saint John's Episcopal Church and Seaman's Center**, the oldest church in Ketchikan, built in 1902.

4 Walk back a half block on Bawden to tiny **Whale Park** (the park's name derives from its odd shape) for a look at the **Chief Kyan totem pole**, carved by Israel Shotridge as a reproduction of a reproduction of a pole first erected in 1897. The pole occupies the site of the summer fishing camp belonging to the chief's clan. The crane at the top represents the chief's wife; the thunderbird, her clan's symbol.

5 Walk through Whale Park to view the **Chief Johnson totem pole** on the far side, another Shotridge reproduction of a pole first erected in 1901. The original can be seen at the Totem Heritage Center.

6 Turn left and walk to Dock Street and the Centennial Building, which houses the **Tongass Historical Museum** and **Ketchikan Public Library**. In front of the building is the **Raven Stealing the Sun totem pole**. Unlike the two chief poles, this one, the work of Tlingit carver Dempsey Bob, is telling a story, not commemorating a leader (see the Reading a Totem Pole sidebar, page 54).

7 As you leave the Centennial Building, turn left (away from the cruise-ship dock) and cross the footbridge over Ketchikan Creek to **Creek Street**. (In late summer, pause to watch—and smell—salmon flopping and leaping upstream.) Picturesque, colorful buildings on pilings line the creek, connected by boardwalks. Once the city's red-light district, whose history is recounted at **Dolly's House**, Creek Street is now home to galleries and shops, many owned by local artists (see Art, page 32).

8 Follow the boardwalk to the **Cape Fox Funicular** (when cruise ships are in, a $2 fee is levied) and ascend to the **WestCoast Cape Fox Lodge**. There's a great view from the hotel lobby, which is a showplace for Tlingit arts.

9 Leaving the hotel lobby, turn left and follow the signs down several flights of stairs to Venetia Way. From Venetia, turn right onto Park Avenue. (If stairs are a problem, from the lodge follow the sign to the **Married Man's Trail** or take the tram back down and retrace your steps to Bawden Street. Turn right and follow Bawden until it intersects with Park Avenue; turn right onto Park and rejoin the main walking tour.) Park Avenue runs along the right side of Ketchikan Creek and eventually crosses it. Turn right onto Salmon Street and follow signs to the **Deer Mountain Salmon Hatchery & Eagle Center**.

10 Outside the hatchery and eagle center, investigate Ketchikan's lovely **City Park**, through which the creek meanders, a great place for a picnic.

11 Cross the creek to reach the **Totem Heritage Center**; notice the carving shed.

12 From the center, walk out to Deermount Avenue and turn right, heading back to the water. The scenery quickly changes from pastoral to urban. When you reach Stedman Street, turn right. Cross Stedman to take a look at the **Sun Raven totem pole**, another Israel Shotridge replica of an older pole.

13 Following Stedman back toward town, turn left to explore charming Thomas Street, part of the **Stedman-Thomas Historic District**. Ahead is the **Thomas Basin Boat Harbor**. A viewing platform with signage describes the Ketchikan fishing fleet spread out below you. Also on Thomas is the **Potlatch Bar**, a local hangout, next door to one of Ketchikan's two downtown Laundromats (the other is a mile south on Stedman Street).

14 Before you cross the Stedman Street Bridge, notice the historic **New York Hotel** on your right. The bridge is often lined with fishers.

15 Keeping the harbor on your left, turn left and make your way down past the **Great Alaskan Lumberjack Show** to the **Salmon Landing Market**. Then turn right at the waterfront promenade and follow it back to the visitors bureau.

West End Walking Tour *(1.5 hours)*

This walk is recommended to those with an interest in the old Ketchikan cityscape and residential areas. Views are magnificent, but hills are steep, and there are stairs. For this tour, see maps on pages 16 and 26.

A From the visitors bureau, turn left and walk up Front Street to Dock Street. Turn right and follow Dock to the foot of the **Edmonds Street stairs**; take the stairs up (and up).

B Cross Grant Street, continue up to Pine Street, and turn left on Pine. While you catch your breath, notice **Monrean House**, a lovely Queen Anne home built in 1904 and listed on the National Register of Historic Places.

C Continue to the end of Pine Street, then turn right and proceed to the **Front Street Overlook**. The view of the city, Tongass Narrows, and Gravina and Pennock islands across the water is spectacular.

D To return to sea level, turn left and follow Front Street to the stairs down to the tunnel. Before you walk through the tunnel, check out **Eagle Park** across Front Street, with the **Thundering Wings** eagle, carved by Nathan Jackson.

E As you emerge from the tunnel, **Harbor View Park** and the boat harbor are on your left. The street name changes from Front to Water and eventually divides into two streets: Water Street veers away from the water; Tongass Avenue follows the waterfront. North of the tunnel on the right is the popular **Burger Queen**.

F For a tad more exercise, take the stairs up **Bayview Avenue** and check out some of Ketchikan's oldest homes, dating from 1910.

G Return to Water Street and take the parallel **Hopkins Alley** to Young Street to see a few older commercial buildings; turn left and return to Water Street.

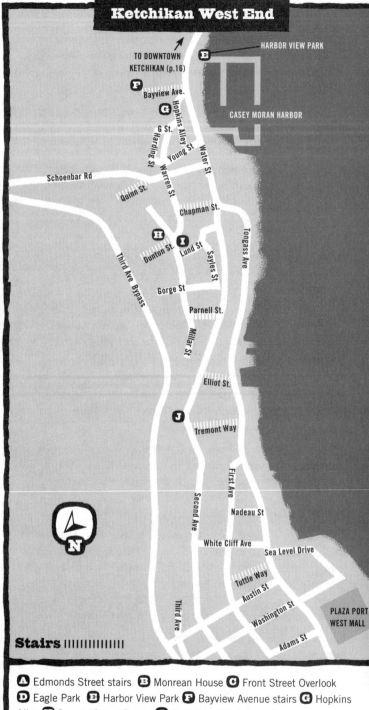

Ketchikan West End

TO DOWNTOWN
KETCHIKAN (p.16)

HARBOR VIEW PARK

CASEY MORAN HARBOR

Bayview Ave.

Hopkins Alley

G St.

Young St

Harding St

Water St

Warren St

Schoenbar Rd

Quinn St.

Chapman St.

Tongass Ave

Dunton St.

Lund St

Sayles St

Gorge St

Third Ave Bypass

Parnell St.

Millar St

Elliot St.

Tremont Way

First Ave

Second Ave

Nadeau St

White Cliff Ave

Sea Level Drive

Tuttle Way

Austin St

Washington St

PLAZA PORT
WEST MALL

Third Ave

Adams St

Stairs ||||||||||||||

Ⓐ Edmonds Street stairs Ⓑ Monrean House Ⓒ Front Street Overlook
Ⓓ Eagle Park Ⓔ Harbor View Park Ⓕ Bayview Avenue stairs Ⓖ Hopkins
Alley Ⓗ Dunton Street Trestle Ⓘ Captain's Hill neighborhood
Ⓙ Third Avenue Bypass

(For sights A through D, refer to map on page 16.)

🔟 Continue down Water to Chapman Street, turn right, walk up yet another flight of stairs, and turn left. Notice the **Dunton Street trestle** ahead, providing an object lesson in the difficulty of engineering a city on a pile of vertical rock.

🔟 Continue on Millar Street through **Captain's Hill**, one of Ketchikan's prettiest residential neighborhoods, with world-class views. Most houses were built before 1925. At Lund Street, turn left and walk down to Water Street. Turn right.

🔟 Continue north on Water Street (its name morphs into Second Avenue) to Whitecliffe Street. The **Third Avenue bypass** above you—another lesson in Ketchikan road-engineering challenges, designed to relieve downtown Ketchikan's traffic congestion—took four years to build. Turn left on Whitecliffe and follow it down to Tongass Avenue. From here, either continue north on Tongass to the **Plaza Mall**, or turn left and follow Tongass south along the waterfront back downtown.

HISTORY & CULTURE

Tongass Historical Museum shares space with Ketchikan's public library in the Centennial Building (30 minutes; 629 Dock St; 907/225-5600; *www.city. ketchikan.ak.us/ds/tonghist/*; May–Sept daily 8am–5pm, rest of year Mon–Fri 10am–4pm, Sat–Sun 1–4pm; $2). This charming museum has a well-chosen selection of Native Alaskan art and artifacts, historical photos, a capsule history of Ketchikan, and temporary exhibits. Kids programs are also offered.

The tour of **Dolly's House** (20 minutes; 24 Creek St; 907/225-2279; $4), once the home of Dolly Arthur, Ketchikan's most famous madam, is *not* suitable for children. Details of the brutal forms of birth control she practiced on brothel residents are alone enough to turn adults queasy. Nonetheless, the brisk tour offered by Dolly look-alikes in garish costume and makeup is fascinating. Dolly had a long and prosperous career in Ketchikan. Arriving in 1919, she worked openly, until prostitution was banned in 1954, and thereafter less openly. During Prohibition, hooch was rowed along Ketchikan Creek at high tide and passed into houses lining Creek Street through trapdoors in the floor;

Dolly made a killing selling shots to her clientele. Tours include her state-of-the-art kitchen and clothes closet.

From Creek Street, a small **funicular tram** runs up to the **WestCoast Cape Fox Lodge**, Ketchikan's spiffiest hotel (see Accommodations, page 57), owned by the native Cape Fox Corporation. When cruise ships are in, nonguests are charged $2 to ride the tram up the steep slope to the hotel. In the lobby, explore an extensive collection of Tlingit artifacts, including exceptionally fine basketry and a beautiful totem screen by carver Nathan Jackson. Don't miss the six totem poles outside the hotel's front doors, carved by acclaimed artist Lee Wallace, who claims Haida, Tlingit, and Tsimshian ancestry. At the front desk, pick up a brochure describing the poles. When you're finished, take the tram back to Creek Street, or follow the Married Man's Trail (see Hiking, page 42) back downtown (45 minutes).

Commercial tours of Ketchikan visit the excellent **Totem Heritage Center**, but you can stroll here on your own. The center (601 Deermount St; 907/225-5600; *www.city.ketchikan.ak.us/ds/tonghert/index.html*; May 1–Sept 30 daily 8am–5pm, Oct 1–Apr 30 Mon–Fri 1–5pm; $5; 30 minutes, plus 30 minutes for adjacent Deer Mountain Salmon Hatchery and Eagle Center) was built in 1976 to display and preserve weathered poles brought from nearby native communities. Carved by Tlingit, Haida, and Tsimshian artists, these poles demonstrate the range of purposes for which poles were created and varied artistic styles. There are mortuary, potlatch, memorial, and heraldic poles as well as house posts. Displays describe how poles are carved and the cultures that created them. There is a large gift shop and bookstore. In summer, watch master carvers at work in the carving shed. A trip here is recommended before visiting Totem Bight State Historical Park.

Beautiful **Totem Bight State Historical Park**, dating from the Great Depression (see the Reconstructing the Past sidebar, below), can be explored quickly, but it's worth taking time to appreciate the totem poles in their extraordinary setting. Visitors make their way along an accessible trail to the clan house and a green open space surrounded with twelve poles; two more poles stand at the start of the path. Paths lead down to a rocky beach of black schist and tide pools. You can take a tour here or drive the 9 miles to the park (see North Tongass

Reconstructing the Past

Totem Bight, along with other restored Inside Passage totem-pole sites, owes its existence to a federal works project during the Great Depression, the U.S. Civilian Conservation Corps (CCC). Its objectives in Alaska were two-fold: to find work for the unemployed and to preserve vanishing Native cultures of Southeast Alaska. To that end, Native and non-Native carvers, under the direction of Native elders, re-created totem poles, using old, disintegrating poles as models. Those less damaged were repaired; others, copied. Wherever possible, carvers used traditional techniques and tools, including paints made with copper pebbles, salmon eggs, graphite, lichen, and clamshells.

The most impressive feat was the construction, again using only traditional tools and without using saws, of a large clan house able to house fifty people. The original plan called for the CCC to build a complete native village; however, when World War II broke out, the project was left incomplete. Perhaps the project's greatest accomplishment was to preserve knowledge that was even then dying out. Techniques and tools relied on recollections of Natives who often had only hazy recollections of their parents and elders to guide them.

Hwy, page 39, for driving directions). There is plenty of parking and everything is free. In the summer, a small gift shop in a trailer sells books and gifts. There are interpretive signs and restrooms. Volunteer rangers offer free tours and talks on the park. For program schedules, contact the **Alaska State Parks Southeast Area Office** (400 Willoughby, 4th fl; 907/465-4563; *www.dnr. state.ak.us/parks/units/totembgh.htm;* allow 30 minutes, plus 30 minutes for transportation; &).

Southeast Alaska Discovery Center, the primary visitor center for Tongass National Forest, is a museum, school, library, theater, bookstore, and booking office (45 minutes; 50 Main St; 907/228-6220; *www.fs.fed. us/r10/tongass/districts/discoverycenter.html*; May–Sept daily 8am–5pm, rest of year Tues–Sat 10am–4:30pm; $5/May–Sept, free/rest of year; &). On the main floor are three totem poles, one each in the style of Haida, Tlingit, and Tsimshian carvers. Displays highlight traditional Native Alaskan life in the forest. Interactive exhibits on the ecosystem, economy, and natural resources of the Tongass paint a somewhat rosy picture of the timber and fishing industries. Give the forgettable film showing scenes of Southeast Alaska a miss. More interesting is the extensive library of books and videos for viewing on site and the opportunity to tap staff expertise in planning trips into the national forest, from kayaking to hiking to booking a stay in a USFS cabin. In late summer, naturalists give talks on a variety of topics.

A visit to **Saxman Native Village**, a Tlingit community 2.5 miles south of Ketchikan (see South Tongass Hwy, page 39, for driving directions), is best made on a tour (2 hours; $35/adult, $17.50/child), which includes dance performances by the Cape Fox Dancers and the opportunity to meet with master carvers. Independent travelers can purchase tours directly from **Cape Fox Tours**. (Cruise passengers will find it among shore excursions offered.) Tours, which include transportation from Ketchikan, start with an orientation to Tlingit culture and its complex language, plus a video. Visitors watch dance performances in the Beaver Clan House, then are given a guided tour of the totem poles, some of which are quite unusual—such as the ridicule pole—and the carving shed with carvers in action. Finally, visitors are encouraged to shop in the village store, which contains mass-produced Alaska souvenirs along with some books. If you're interested in authentic Alaska Native art, walk down to the Saxman Arts Co-op instead (see the Good Buys sidebar, page 32).

GUIDED TOURS

Ketchikan's guided tour offerings are as diverse as they come, ranging from an amphibious boat-bus to horse-drawn carriages, vintage automobiles, Humvees, and taxi cabs. For other sightseeing excursions, check with the Visitors Bureau & Tour Center on the waterfront.

Seahorse Ventures Horse-Drawn Trolley Tours has tours (45 minutes; call for pricing). **Alaska Amphibious Tours** will drive you around Ketchikan and *into* the harbor (90 minutes; $34/adult, $19/ages 3–12, free/under 3). **Sourdough Cabs** also offer guided tours by the hour (see Wheels & Keels, page 21).

David Freeman, a fluent Spanish speaker, runs **Tailor Made Tours** ($56/hour, 1–6 passengers). These customized tours range from 1 to 3 hours. To commune with your inner gas guzzler, take a tour with **Alaska Hummer Adventures**.

Classic Tours offers customizable tours (2 hours; starting at $70/person, 2-person minimum) in a **vintage 1955 Chevy**.

Tours with set itineraries include Native-owned **Cape Fox Tours**, which offers narrated city tours combined with trips to destinations such as Misty Fjords National Monument. Their **Ketchikan tour** (3 hours; call for prices) includes a visit to the old cannery south of town. And for those who've fantasized about quitting their jobs and joining a motorcycle gang—or who just want to take advantage of a rare Ketchikan sunny day—check out **Panhandle Motorcycle Adventures**, whose tour (3 hours; $249/driver, $149/passenger) includes Totem Bight State Historical Park. You must be 21 or over, have a valid motorcycle license or endorsement on your driver's license, and be willing to sign a lot of release of liability forms. Tours vary in destination. Summer is road-construction season, and roads may be torn up or muddy. The bikes are Harley-Davidson XLH 883 Sportsters.

SHOPPING

Thanks to the enormous increase in cruise-ship visits, downtown Ketchikan has turned into a veritable den of gift shops. Along with by-the-numbers generic jewelry stores are many high-quality galleries owned by local residents, Native and otherwise.

Good Buys

A marvelous but all-too-often overlooked gallery carrying locally made, traditional Tlingit art is the **Saxman Arts Co-op** (2706 S Tongass Ave; 907/225-4166) in **Saxman Native Village**. Operated as a cooperative that returns a high percentage of profits directly to artists, this unpretentious store sells button-blanket and appliqué wall hangings, jewelry, beaded items and clothing, and much more—at some of the lowest prices in Southeast Alaska. Traditional crafts handed down for generations are on display. Leave your shoe size or foot imprint, and leather moccasins will be sewn and beaded for you. The co-op is closer to the water, down the street from the main Saxman Village store where visitors are usually encouraged to shop.

Art

ALASKA NATIVE ARTISTS: A visit to **Eagle Spirit Gallery** (310 Mission St; 907/225-6626, 866/867-0976) conveys the breadth and quality of Native Alaskan artists. Traditional artworks include button blankets, bentwood boxes, baleen and cedar baskets, and carved wooden masks. **Alaska Eagle Arts** (5 Creek St; 907/225-8365, 800/308-2787) displays the work of Native Alaskan artist Marvin Oliver. Tlingit carver Norman Jackson sells his extraordinary carvings in wood, silver, and gold, including masks, bentwood bowls, bracelets, and rattles at **Ketchikan's Carver at the Creek** (28 Lower Creek St; 907/225-3018). Across from Whale Park is **Crazy Wolf Studio** (607 Mission St; 907/225-9653, 888/331-9653), owned by local Tsimshian artist Ken Decker and also featuring works by other Northwest Coast Native artists.

KETCHIKAN AREA ARTISTS: Maybe it's all that time the artists are confined indoors while it rains, but Ketchikan has a lot of great local art with a decidedly original bent.

Ray Troll, whose work is featured at **Soho Coho** (5 Creek St; 907/225-5954, 800/888-4070), next to Alaska Eagle Arts, is the best known of Ketchikan's local talent. Troll blends his fascination with evolution, fishing, fossils, and the Southeast Alaskan landscape into strange and wonderful art. Browse for T-shirts bearing slogans such as "It's never too late to mutate" and "The data is in the strata" (featuring an "Evolvo" car). Books, decorated baseball caps, and art posters sound the same themes. Works of other similarly inspired Alaskan artists, such as Evon Zerbetz and Christine Elberson, can be found here. In a high-priced city, this gallery has budget-priced items.

Down Stedman Street is Sharron Huffman's **Herring Cove Originals** (229 Stedman St; 907/247-2683), which sells her delicate fish prints in various forms from clothing to wall hangings and linocuts.

Some of the best high-end work by artists and craftspeople across Alaska is on display at **Scanlon Gallery** (318 Mission St; 907/247-4730, 800/690-4730). The gallery carries items ranging from notecards and embroidery kits to sculptures, prints, and paintings, offering a good introduction to contemporary Alaskan arts and crafts.

At the **Exploration Gallery** (633 Mission St; 907/225-4278), antique maps are a specialty; they also sell jewelry, soaps, ties, and low- to moderately priced gifts that won't take up much space in a bulging suitcase or backpack. **Blue Heron Gallery and Gifts** (123 Stedman St, Ste B; 907/225-1982) carries Alaskan artists and a selection of mammoth-ivory jewelry, fossilized walrus teeth, and Alaskan food products.

Books

For all subjects, head to **Parnassus Books** (Creek St; 907/225-7690). Visitors who find their way to Creek Street will discover Parnassus up a flight of stairs, in a crooked warren of small rooms packed with treasures. Alaskana and Pacific Northwest as well as literary titles are strong suits. Longtime owner Lillian Ference has downsized her involvement in recent years, but this Ketchikan institution continues to thrive.

Books of regional interest can be found in the **Alaska Natural History Association (ANHA) Bookstore** in the ground floor of the Southeast Alaska Discovery Center (50 Main St; 907/228-6220; *www.fs.fed.us/r10/ tongass/districts/discoverycenter/*). The **Totem Heritage Center** (601 Deermount St; 907/225-5900) is a good source of books on Alaska Natives. There is a **Waldenbooks** at the Plaza Mall (2417 Tongass Ave, Ste 103; 907/225-8120).

Clothing & Sundries

Given downtown Ketchikan's focus on serving cruise-ship clientele, it can be hard to find mundane items such as underwear. Hidden among the souvenir and jewelry stores are a few options. **Tongass Trading Co.** (201 Dock St; 907/225-5101, 800/235-5102) has two locations close together. The main sportswear and sporting gear store is at the north end of the cruise-ship dock; the **Ladies Loft** is upstairs nearby. For something a bit more dressy and original, try **Alaska Rose** (5 Salmon Landing, Ste 119; 907/247-4755). And of course there is always **Wal-Mart** (4230 Don King Rd; 907/247-2156).

    Schallerer's Photo & Gift Shop (422 Mission St; 907/225-4210) sells and services cameras; there's a post-office substation here. If the weather is too horrible to make strolling in it bearable, two good-sized malls allow you to browse dry: **Salmon Landing Market** (5 Salmon Landing; 907/225-3299) has two stories of gift shops, galleries, cafes, a fish market and convenience store, and a bead shop. The **Plaza Mall** (2417 Tongass Ave; 907/225-7000), a mile north of downtown, has more generic mall stores, plus McDonald's.

Food & Drink

Sam McGee's Taste of Alaska (18b Creek St; 907/226-7267) sells local taste treats, from smoked fish and salmonberry preserves to birch syrup. Test a free sample here before springing for a jar of fireweed jelly. Across the highway from the Alaska ferry terminal is **Alaskan & Proud Market** (3816 Tongass Ave; 907/225-1279), a large supermarket with everything foodies could desire. In the Plaza Mall is a **Safeway** (2417 Tongass Ave; 907/225-9880). Just south of downtown is **Tatsuda's IGA** (633 Stedman St; 907/247-6328).

NATURE

A trip to the **Deer Mountain Salmon Hatchery and Eagle Center** (30 minutes; 1158 Salmon Rd; 907/225-5503, 800/252-5158; daily 8:30am–4:30pm; $7.95) is best combined with a visit to the adjacent Totem Heritage Center. Most downtown sightseeing tours include both destinations, or you can come on your own. Tours through the hatchery allow visitors to observe salmon in successive stages, from egg through fry to adult. Trout are also raised here. The eagle center is part of the same facility; the birds on display were rescued from human predators and are pleasantly housed with their own salmon stream and fed on freeze-dried (and thawed) mice. There is a gift shop.

The **Alaska Rainforest Sanctuary** (2.5 hours, plus 45 minutes for transportation; 8 mi s of Ketchikan on S Tongass Hwy; 907/225-5503; *kris@alaskarainforest.net*; $45; $79 with transportation from Ketchikan), new in 2003, is a work in progress, combining a hike in the rain forest, a stroll past salmon spawning grounds, and a walk through a rusty sawmill. A half-mile wheelchair-accessible trail has been constructed through private rain-forest land at Herring Cove. The tour is fairly basic and goes slowly; it's not recommended for hikers familiar with this part of the world. But for visitors from afar with mobility issues, this is an opportunity to have a guided tour into real rain forest. Bald eagles and black bears are often encountered. The largely intact sawmill offers a rare glimpse of what was once a primary way of life in Southeast Alaska, now almost completely gone. There's a spacious gift shop where you can munch on smoked-salmon snacks, coffee, tea, hot chocolate, and cookies while you look at displays and shop. Visitors here receive a free pass to the Southeast Alaska Discovery Center.

Bear Watching

Although no tour operator can guarantee that you'll see bears, most visitors do see them; when the salmon are running, late July to September, bears bulk up for winter, engaging in nonstop fishing. For prime bear-viewing sites you'll need a USFS permit (see Wildlife Viewing Permits in the introduction, page 12). Trips are by air; flightseeing operators usually provide permits, but be sure to check in advance. **Anan Wildlife Observatory** is north of Ketchikan on the mainland, not far from the town of Wrangell; although black bears predominate, brown bears are seen as well. Also on the mainland, but closer to the twin "cities" of Hyder and Stewart, is **Fish Creek Wildlife Observation Site**, where brown and black bears are on view. **Traitor's Cove** and **Neets Bay**, northwest of Ketchikan on Revilla Island, are home to black bears and abundant wildlife. Some bear-watching tours head west to **Prince of Wales Island**. Trips usually run 3 to 4 hours and are offered only in July and August. Expect to pay $275 to $450 per person, depending on destination and tour length.

Tours to Anan Wildlife Observatory are offered by Carlin Air, Family Air Tours, Island Wings, Southeast Aviation, and Taquan Air. Tours to Fish Creek Wildlife Observation Site are provided by Alaska Seaplane Tours and SeaWind Aviation. Tours to Traitor's Cove or Neets Bay are offered by Carlin Air, Island Wings, Promech Air, and Taquan Air. Alaska Seaplane Tours visits Prince of Wales Island.

Flightseeing

A brief **Ketchikan and Revilla Island flyover** won't get you to Misty Fjords, but it will give you an interesting bird's-eye view of Revilla, at prices lower than most Inside Passage flight tours. Flyovers, running 30 to 60 minutes, are offered by Alaska Seaplane Tours, Pacific Airways, SeaWind Aviation, Southeast Aviation, and Taquan Air. Expect to pay $80 to $125 per person.

Taquan Air also offers a **bush-pilot tour** (1–2 hours), an intriguing opportunity to fly along with a bush pilot to destinations in the Tongass National Forest. There's a four-passenger minimum; call for pricing details.

The most popular flightseeing destination from Ketchikan, **Misty Fjords National Monument,** (1–4 hours) is spectacular from the air. Floatplane flights often include a brief landing along the way for wildlife viewing. However, if you have a whole day, taking a combination cruise and flightseeing tour is recommended (see One Day, page 44). If you have less time, shorter flights can still get you out to the fjords.

Every flightseeing provider listed in the Ketchikan Outfitters & Tour Operators sidebar, pages 46–47, offers one or more of these trips, sometimes combined with a look at nearby glaciers or a brief landing on a mountain lake. When bears are active, bear watching is often included. Prices range from $175 for shorter trips to $325 for longer tours.

Wildlife Tours

Lighthouseexcursion.com offers a **Lighthouse, Totems & Eagles Tour** (3 hours, including transportation; $85/adult, $45/child; schedules vary—call for departure times) that combines a tour of Ketchikan and Totem Bight State Historical Park and circumnavigates the Guard Island Lighthouse from the water. Passengers get a look at Ketchikan's working waterfront, including a floating logging camp and cannery, along with city mansions. Bus transportation to the dock is included. Mostly marketed to cruise ships, the tour is also open to independent travelers. Snacks and beverages are provided; on Fridays, the trip is offered as a dinner cruise. There's an onboard gift shop.

Because of the high volume of summer visitors to Ketchikan, mostly on cruise ships, many more **wildlife and sightseeing cruises** (3–4 hours) are offered to meet the demand. Most include transportation to and from downtown Ketchikan, usually from the cruise-ship dock close to the tour center (see Visitor Information & Services, page 20).

Crab lovers won't balk at the hefty price tag for the **Wilderness Exploration and Crab Feed** (4 hours; $129/adult, $82/under 13; multiple daily tours), offered by **Experience Alaska Tours**, because it includes a rare all-you-can-eat Dungeness crab feast. Buses depart outside the tour center and drive south to the George Inlet Lodge, an old cannery dorm that was moved here and refurbished. There are seventy-nine steps down to (and up from) the lodge and dock (van service is available, if needed). Passengers are outfitted in raingear and ferried in open boats (dress warmly) across the Tongass Narrows to investigate crab pots. Underwater cameras and video monitors allow you to see what the crabs and any other passing wildlife are up to in the murky depths; then crab pots are hauled up and tour guides pass around live crabs to touch (carefully). Counting and measuring crustaceans comprise genuine research for which the operators have a research license; it's all strictly catch and release. Then visitors are returned to the lodge for a sumptuous lunch featuring crab in the starring role. (Don't feel as if you're eating a friend—the crabs served come from Petersburg, not the crab pots you've just been investigating.) While you eat, you're treated to a hair-raising video of crab fishers at work in the storm-wracked Bering Sea. There's a gift shop to explore before you're bused back to town. Book the tour through the tour center or as a cruise shore excursion.

ONE OF A KIND

As roars of applause coming from the grounds three times a day attest, the homegrown **Great Alaskan Lumberjack Show** hits the mark with many visitors. Shows feature log rolling and climbing, ax throwing, and crosscut-saw antics, interspersed with occasional cries of "timber!" The show (1.5 hours; 420 Spruce Mill Wy; 907/225-9050, 888/320-9049; *www.lumberjackshows.com*; multiple daily shows; $30.60/adult, $15.30/5–12, free/under 4) is one of the most popular attractions in Southeast Alaska. Ironically, the pulp mills, which were mostly foreign owned, have all closed in Southeast Alaska. (Prince of Wales Island has a big sawmill, but there aren't many of those left, either.) What remains is an homage to a vanished way of life that shaped the region for many decades.

ROAD TRIPS

It's worth braving Ketchikan's congested roads to reach Revilla Island's beautiful parks and trails. A small vehicle is best for finding a parking space (at a premium downtown) and navigating narrow city streets. Ketchikan's one highway, Tongass Avenue, stretches 18.4 miles north from downtown and almost 13 miles south, for a grand total of 31.3 miles. For the full round-trip drive alone, allow 2.5 hours, with added time for stops at Ward Lake, Totem Bight State Historical Park, and Settlers Cove north of town and Saxman Native Village, Rotary Beach Park, and scenic waterfalls to the south. All but the last 4.5 miles of Tongass Avenue South are paved.

North Tongass Hwy *(37 miles/1.5 hours)*

Head north from downtown Ketchikan on Front Street opposite the Tour Center, past **Eagle Park** and through the tunnel, an object lesson in what lies just below Revilla's rain-forest exterior. Expect heavy traffic for the next 3 miles.

On the north side of the tunnel, you pass **Harborview Park** on your left. Perched above the road to the right are some of Ketchikan's loveliest homes and tall trees, often dotted with eagles. At mile 2.0 is the **Misty Fjords National Monument ranger station**. Just 0.3 mile north is the **ferry terminal** for AMHS ferries and the Inter-Island Ferry Authority; 0.5 mile north of that is the **airport ferry** to Gravina Island.

Traffic usually thins out at mile 6, where you pass Ward Cove with the cannery to the west and, at mile 6.7, Revilla Road. This is the turnoff to **Ward Lake Recreation Area** (1.3 miles along Revilla Road).

At mile 8.7 you pass **Refuge Cove State Recreation Site**, with fourteen picnic sites and toilets. Then, at mile 9.9 is the turnoff to **Totem Bight State Historical Park**.

Near the end of the road at mile 18.2 is **Settlers Cove State Recreation Site**, well worth a visit. Along with a small campground, picnic sites, and a gravel beach to the falls is the lovely **Lower Lunch Falls Loop Trail** (0.25 mile). The short boardwalk trail through lush rain forest is easy, but there are stairs. The road ends 0.25 mile north of the park.

South Tongass Hwy *(26 miles/1 hour)*

Starting again from Front Street, in front of the tour center, head south past the Coast Guard Station. At mile 2.5 is **Saxman Native Village** to your left. Look up to see long rows of totem poles marching east. At mile 3.5 is **Rotary Beach Park**, with picnic shelters and toilets. The road curves back to the northeast.

Just before Herring Cove Bridge, at mile 8.2, is the turnoff for the **Rainforest Sanctuary**. The pavement ends at mile 8.5. At mile 10.2 and mile 10.9, you pass two scenic waterfalls on the left. The road ends at mile 12.9. Beyond is the now-closed **George Inlet Cannery**, which can be toured. A 2-mile walk up a gravel road takes you to the **Silvis Lake picnic area**, which has several trails to follow.

For contact information for outfitters and tour operators listed in this chapter, see sidebar on pages 46–47.

CANOEING & KAYAKING

Ketchikan makes for an interesting urban sea kayaking experience. Colorful waterfront buildings with equally colorful histories can be investigated from underneath, and nearby islands close to town are fascinating to explore.

Southeast Sea Kayaks offers a short kayak trip (2.5 hours; $76/adult, $56/ages 3–12; up to 12 in a group; June–Aug on the hour beginning at 7am) from its downtown Ketchikan location on the north side of the tunnel, a 15-minute walk from the visitors bureau. No experience is required. Start by learning kayak ABCs near the dock, then paddle past cruise ships to the islands across Tongass Narrows. This is a good choice for families; kids as young as six who weigh at least 40 pounds can participate. Triple kayaks allow small fry to participate comfortably. Listen to mammal sounds under the water with hydrophones. Raingear is provided.

The aptly named Whiskey Cove was a popular destination during Prohibition. Today, **Alaska Travel Adventures** takes small groups kayaking in two-person kayaks (2.5 hours; $69/adult, $46/under 13) with two departures daily (8am and 1pm). Instruction is included.

If your heart is set on canoeing, rather than kayaking, you can try this mountain lake canoe trip (3.5 hours; $79/adult, $53/under 13; May–Sept) offered by **Alaska Travel Adventures**. Billed as a "Rainforest Canoe Adventure," it includes a bus tour and paddle on Lake Harriet Hunt. A snack is provided, along with raingear and transportation.

Suitable for paddlers ages 12 to adult, a tour (4 hours; $139) offered by **Southeast Sea Kayaks** includes 45 minutes' transportation from downtown to remote **Orca's Cove**, where you take to the water and explore rain-forested islands and waters teeming with wildlife—whales, sea lions, seals, seabirds and nesting bald eagles, and tide pools with sea stars, sun stars, sea cucumbers, and shellfish. A smoked salmon and soft drink snack is served. Free transportation is provided from cruise ships. Booking 30 days in advance is recommended in July and August.

CYCLING

Ketchikan's hilly streets, frequently connected by steep staircases, make it difficult or impossible to tour residential Ketchikan by bike. The pleasantest ride is to follow the **bike path to Saxman Native Village**, not quite 3 miles south of town. Those with nerves of steel might try biking north 10 miles to **Totem Bight State Historical Park**. Past the ferry terminal, the road gets quieter. Otherwise, the less-traveled **South Tongass Highway** may be a better choice, although the road is rougher. If time allows, consider cycling on Prince of Wales Island. Alaska Kustom Kayaking (6488 Klawock-Hollis Hwy; 907/755-2800; *www.alaskakustomkayaking.com*) rents bikes for $20/day, or $30/overnight.

On Revilla island, **bikes can be rented** from two places, only one of which is in town; surprisingly, it's the **Great Alaskan Lumberjack Show** (420 Spruce Mill Wy; 907/225-9050, 888/320-9049; *www.lumberjackshows. com*), which rents bikes for $8 an hour. You can also rent a bike from **Southeast Exposure Sea Kayak**, located 14 miles north of Ketchikan. Rentals start at $22 per day and include hybrid, cruiser, and mountain bikes. Their tours are for cruise-ship passengers only and can be booked as shore excursions.

FISHING

Ketchikan has too many fishing options to list in full: Check with the tour center for more choices.

Most charter fishing trips start at 4 hours; for visitors who long to fish but don't have that much time, **Family Air Tours** has an unusual fishing charter (2 hours; $250/adult, $200/under 13 accompanied by 2 adults, 2-person minimum, 4-person maximum) that includes everything, even the fishing license. There is an hour of flight time and an hour for lake or river fishing—salmon, grayling, or trout. Transportation to and from their dock, which they provide, adds about 10 extra minutes total.

Also from Family Air Tours is a guided fly-fishing trip (4 hours; $375/adult, $325/under 13 accompanied by 2 adults; 2-person minimum, 4-person maximum) that includes license and instruction. Transportation time to and from their dock is extra. See listings under One Day, page 48, for more fly-fishing options.

Alaskan Fishing Adventures creates customized **kayak fishing** trips (up to 4 hours; $175/adult, $100/under 13) around your schedule. Gear, snacks, and transportation are included in the price; fishing licenses are available at extra cost. Processing ($1.25/pound plus shipping) is also available. Destinations vary, and times can be adapted to your schedule.

Ketchikan Charter Boats has customizable guided ocean fishing charters (4 hours). Gear and snacks are provided; licenses, processing, and shipping are available but extra. **Ketchikan Fishing Reservations** can help you put together a fishing or fishing-and-lodging package (4-hour trips start at $150). They'll work with groups of up to eighteen. Licenses, processing, and shipping are extra; all else is included.

HIKING

Just getting around Ketchikan on foot amounts to a strenuous hike. The city's steep hills and staircases can challenge most fitness levels. Still, the panting urban explorer is rewarded not only with superb views but also with quaint and quirky neighborhoods, rushing streams, and even wildlife, all within blocks of the cruise-ship dock.

From Downtown

The city's shortest historical hike, the **Married Man's Trail** (10 minutes downhill), starts from Cape Fox Lodge at the top of the funicular. This recently refurbished trail follows the low-profile route taken by Ketchikan's married men in days of yore when visiting Dolly Arthur and the town's other prostitutes. Outside the front of the lodge, turn left and follow signs to the Married Man's Trail and down the steeply wooded hillside to Creek Street. For a more strenuous hike, retrace your steps up the hill. The round trip is less than a mile.

With a Car

Ward Lake Recreation Area, north of downtown, has several terrific hikes to suit all levels of fitness, including one wheelchair-accessible trail. Seven miles along the North Tongass Highway, take Revilla Road to reach this lovely recreation area with picnic grounds, two idyllic campgrounds (Signal Creek and Last Chance), and easy to moderate trails. Allow 45 minutes round trip for transportation to the recreation area.

Ward Lake Trail (30 minutes), a popular family hike, circles pretty Ward Lake with no appreciable elevation gain. From Revilla Road, turn onto Ward Lake Road and follow signs. The wide, springy 1.3-mile trail meanders through spruce, hemlock, and cedar rain forest with interpretive signs on area geology, flora, and fauna. In July and August, there are berries to pick. Several streams feed into the lake, which attracts birds and waterfowl. In late summer, be on the alert for bears; a half-eaten salmon on the trail is a giveaway that furry fish eaters are in the vicinity. Near the large day-use parking lot are covered picnic shelters, pit toilets, and secluded picnic sites along the lake, with fireplaces and tables.

Access **Ward Creek Trail** (2 hours) from the Ward Lake Trail, or follow signs from Revilla Road to a new parking lot with wheelchair trail access. This 2.5-mile trail with several spurs and a 100-foot elevation gain connects campgrounds and day-use areas as it follows beautiful Ward Creek to fishing platforms, viewing decks, and Last Chance Campground. There are accessible restrooms and rest stops along the way, making this a good choice for mobility-impaired hikers.

Rebuilt in the late 1990s, the **Connell Lake Trail** (3 hours) runs nearly to Talbot Lake. From Revilla Road, take the Connell Lake Road past Last Chance Campground to the parking area. The trail is 2.3 miles one way, with a 100-foot elevation gain. Starting from across the dam, built in 1953, the trail meanders through rain forest thick with salmonberries and huckleberries. At the lake there is fishing and a tent platform. Plans are afoot to extend and improve the trail.

It must say something about Alaska that there are more than a few Perseverance Trails scattered across the state, but this **Perseverance Trail** (3 hours) requires less perseverance than some, with a 450-foot elevation gain. Start from the Ward Lake parking lot. The trail is boggy in places, with boardwalk and some stairs, which can be slippery when wet, through the muskeg. There are tent platforms at the lake, along with fishing and berry-picking opportunities.

For contact information for outfitters and tour operators listed in this chapter, see sidebar on pages 46–47.

ONE DAY

NATURE

As Misty Fjords National Monument becomes increasingly popular, tour providers have proliferated to meet the demand. Check at the tour center for more cruise opportunities.

Alaska Cruises, owned by Goldbelt, Juneau's native corporation, offers a combined flightseeing trip and cruise through **Misty Fjords National Monument** (5–6.5 hours; $150/adult, $125/child; May–Sept daily). Passengers cruise the waters one way and return by air, or vice versa. By boat, the route runs south past Saxman Native Village to Point Alava, the southern tip of Revilla Island, then east and north into Behm Canal and Rudyerd Bay, heart of the national monument, to a large float in one of the smaller inlets, where the boat and floatplanes tie up and exchange passengers.

After switching at the float to plane or boat, you make the return trip. If weather conditions prevent flying, the entire trip is made by boat. (**Note**: this will add another 90 minutes to your trip, so plan accordingly.) The comfortable boat is heated, with restroom facilities. A meal served onboard is included.

Passengers receive a map describing cruise highlights, and an onboard naturalist points out the area's geology, flora, and fauna. Highlights include the New Eddystone Rock, named by eighteenth-century explorer Captain George Vancouver for England's

Eddystone Lighthouse. The New World version is a tall, handsome, mostly basalt islet covered with trees. Several spots offer terrific birding; humpback whales and harbor seals are almost certain to be encountered. Amateur geologists can check out beautiful marble outcroppings, glacial scars, and honeycombed cliffs of limestone, eaten away at the waterline into caves. Especially interesting are the signs of intense volcanic action; two tectonic plates meet here. Rudyerd Bay's 3,000-foot cliffs tower over the water with dozens of waterfalls.

The MV *Stimson* (907/225-3661; *mvstimson.com*), a refurbished 57-foot tugboat, takes passengers out on customized fishing and/or sightseeing trips for a full day or longer to **Misty Fjords** (8–10 hours; $250), nearby islands, and more. Fish for crab and shrimp, along with the usual tour amenities.

Bear Watching

Southeast Aviation has a **Misty Fjords trip** (5.5 hours; $575; 4-person minimum) that includes bear watching at Hyder's Fish Creek Wildlife Observation Deck.

For trips to the Anan Wildlife Observatory, see Four Hours or Less, page 36.

Flightseeing

Alaska Seaplane Tours recently introduced a **Paddle 'n' Fly Tour** (5.5 hours; $469), combining a wilderness kayak trip and seaplane bear-watching tour to Prince of Wales Island; a picnic lunch is included.

Wildlife Tours

Island Wings Air Service offers a **whale-watching trip** (6 hours; $600, $450 per person for party of 3–8) that includes a stop for lunch in Petersburg, with flights over Grindall Island's sea lion colony and the opportunity to get a bird's-eye view of the local humpback whale population. You'll fly over LeConte Glacier and the Stikine River Valley.

ONE OF A KIND

Alaska Deep Six Dive Center (4705 N Tongass Hwy; 907/225-4667, 866/333-7749; *www.alaskadeepsix.com*) offers a rare opportunity to investigate Southeast Alaska under water on **snorkeling and diving tours** (3–5 hours). Snorkeling is open to anyone able to swim (participants under age 16 must be accompanied by an

Ketchikan Outfitters & Tour Operators

Alaska Amphibious Tours 907/225-9899, 866/341-3825; www.akduck.com

Alaska Cruises 29 Main St, Ste 205; 907/225-8636, 800/228-1905; www.mistyfjord.net

Alaska Hummer Adventures 907/866-253-8257; www.akhummer.com

Alaskan Fishing Adventures 907/225-1272, 888/315-2925; www.yakfishalaska.com

Alaska Seaplane Tours 420 Front St; 907/225-1974, 866/858-2327; www.alaskaseaplanetours.com

Alaska Travel Adventures 907/247-5295, 800/791-2673; www.alaskaadventures.com

Alaska Wilderness Outfitting 857 Fairview; 907/225-2343; www.latitude56.com/camping/outfit.html

Cape Fox Tours 907/225-4846; www.capefoxtours.com

Carlin Air 907/225-3036, 888/594-3036; www.carlinair.com

Classic Tours 3820 Baranof Ave; 907/225-3091; www.classictours.com

Experience Alaska Tours 907/225-9050, 888/320-9049; www.catchcrabs.com

Family Air Tours 907/247-1305, 800/380-1305; www.familyairtours.com

Island Wings Air Service 907/225-2444, 888/854-2444; www.islandwings.com

Ketchikan Charter Boats 907/225-7291, 800/272-7291; www.ketchikancharterboats.com

adult); divers must have diving experience. Wet suits, gear, snacks, and transportation are included. Water temperatures may be much colder than you're used to: even in summer they can be in the 40s. Tours can be customized. Most dives are from the shore, usually a rocky shore, and thus involve carrying heavy equipment into the water yourself.

Ketchikan Fishing Reservations 907/247-7117, 800/928-3308; www.ketchikanfishing.com

Lighthouseexcursion.com 907/225-6919; www.lighthouseexcursion.com

Misty Fjords Air & Outfitting 1716 S Tongass Hwy; 907/225-4656, 877/228-4656; www.mistyfjordsair.com

Pacific Airways 907/225-3500, 877/360-3500; www.flypacificairways.com

Panhandle Motorcycle Adventures 907/247-2031, 907/723-5578 cell; www.panhandlemoto.com

Promech Air 1515 Tongass Ave; 907/225-3845, 800/860-3845; www.promechair.com

Seahorse Ventures Horse-Drawn Trolley Tours 2878 S Tongass Ave; 907/225-3672; www.horsetrolley tours.com

SeaWind Aviation 1249 Tongass Ave; 907/225-1206, 877/225-1203; www.seawindaviation.com

Southeast Aviation 1249 Tongass Ave; 907/225-2900, 907/723-3102 cell, 907/723-7045 cell, 888/359-6478; www.southeastaviation.com

Southeast Exposure Sea Kayak Outdoor Activity Center, 37 Potter Rd, Knudson Cove; 907/225-8829; www.southeastexposure.com

Southeast Sea Kayaks 1430 Millar St; 907/225-1258, 800/287-1607; www.kayakketchikan.com

MV *Stimson* 907/225-3661; mvstimson.com

Tailor Made Tours 907/254-7286, 907/254-7287

Taquan Air 1007 Water St; 907/225-8800, 800/770-8800; www.taquanair.com

FISHING

Several carriers offer longer fly-fishing charter trips by air (4–8 hours) to nearby lakes and rivers. **Carlin Air** offers half- and full-day fly-fishing and spin-casting fishing charters; all gear plus lunch are provided (4 hours, $400; 8 hours, $700). **Island Wings Air Service** offers tours including all gear, licenses, food, and beverages (4 hours, $400; 8 hours, $800). **Misty Fjords Air & Outfitting** puts together fly-fishing charters (average 6 hours; starting at $390/flight hour and $240/standby hour). Gear and lunch are included; however, you're responsible for getting your own fishing license.

Southeast Aviation offers a Seaplane & Salmon Rendezvous (4.5 hours; $295; minimum age 16) that includes a Ketchikan flyover, flight to Knudson Cove, and boat ride to the salmon. For kings, you'll need to come in May; silvers and pinks run in June off and on until September. Fishing licenses are extra and can be purchased on the boat. Ground transportation back to Ketchikan (30 minutes) is included. Snacks and beverages are available on the boat.

Alaskan Fishing Adventures' Ketchikan Kayak Fishing takes you fishing from a kayak (7–8 hours; $225/adult; $150/under 13); license, food, gear, and transportation are provided. Destinations are flexible, as are times. Guides are CPR trained; there is one guide per four clients, and groups are kept small. Processing and shipping are available for your catch.

Knudson Cove Marina (407 Knudson Cove Rd N; 907/247-8500, 800/528-2486; *www.knudsoncove marina.com*), located 15 miles north of Ketchikan, rents charter fishing boats (starting at $85 per day). Various specials are offered during the fishing season. Guided trips are also available; salmon and halibut charters start at $125 per person.

HIKING

From Downtown

The popular **Deer Mountain** hike (5 hours) starts from downtown. It's a moderately difficult outing, 5 miles round trip, with a 3,000-foot elevation gain. Follow

Deermount Avenue away from the water, then turn onto Ketchikan Lakes Road for 0.5 mile to the trailhead. The trail ascends through cedar, hemlock, and spruce forest; beyond the tree line vegetation is alpine. Early on you'll walk on gravel, then boardwalk and some stairs; toward the summit, it gets steeper. Wildlife includes mountain goats, black bears, Sitka black-tailed deer, ptarmigan, red squirrels, and all kinds of birds. Summit views are excellent in good weather. There's a USFS A-frame shelter near the top.

By Plane

Island Wings Air Service will fly you into Tongass National Forest for a self-guided wilderness hike (4–10 hours; $250/person, 2-person minimum). You'll need to bring your own food and supplies.

KAYAKING

Southeast Exposure Sea Kayak offers most of its tours exclusively to cruise-ship passengers. This **"Guides Choice" Kayak Trip** (6 hours; $125/person, 2-person minimum) is an exception, open to independent travelers with kayak experience. As the name says, the destination is up to the guide but usually involves a trip of 7 to 10 miles. Trips start and end at their Knudson Cove location 14.5 miles north of town. You'll need to arrange your own transportation there.

The **Misty Fjords day trip** (10 hours; $369) offered by **Southeast Sea Kayaks** includes transportation, lunch, 4 hours to and from the fjords by boat, kayaking, and a hike at Rudyerd Bay.

If you're an experienced kayaker and want to rent a kayak for a day or longer, see Two Days or More, pages 50–51.

TWO DAYS OR MORE

GENERAL OUTFITTING SERVICES

Alaska Wilderness Outfitting rents camping equipment, skiffs and inflatable boats, motors, fuel, and more, available on request. **Misty Fjords Air & Outfitting** flies campers to USFS cabins and other destinations, as well as outfitting trips with boats, outboard motors, and fishing and camping gear.

AIR TAXIS AND CHARTER FLIGHTS

Air carriers offer air taxi service to USFS cabins inside the Tongass in the Ketchikan area. **Alaska Seaplane Tours** takes two passengers with gear for a week of camping (about $379/hour). **Carlin Air** flies to USFS cabins and can handle three to five passengers with up to 1,200 pounds of gear. **Family Air Tours, Island Wings Air Service, Pacific Airways, SeaWind Aviation, Southeast Aviation,** and **Taquan Air** offer similar services.

KAYAKING

Southeast Exposure Sea Kayak rents kayaks to experienced kayakers (single plastic kayak $30/day for 1–5 days, $25/day for 6 or more days; single fiberglass kayak $45/day for 1–5 days, $40/day for 6 or more days; double fiberglass kayak $55/day for 1–5 days, $50/day for 6 or more days; 2-day minimum). Bear in mind that they are located in Knudson Cove, 14.5 miles north of Ketchikan on Potter Road, which is north of the marina. They also offer kayaking instruction ($50/hour).

　　Southeast Sea Kayaks rents to experienced kayakers (single plastic kayak $40/day for 1–3 days, $35/day for 4 or more days; single fiberglass kayak $45/day for 1–3 days, $40/day for 4 or more days; double fiberglass kayak $65/day for 1–3 days, $60/day for 4 or more days). They rent bearproof food boxes and rubber boots ($2/day each). Their downtown location is a 10-minute walk north of the tour center; they also have kayaks for rent out at George Inlet Lodge, 12 miles south of town, a better location for those headed to Misty Fjords. They offer kayaking instruction (3-hour class; $55).

HYDER/STEWART

East of Ketchikan at the end of Portland Canal—the long, narrow fjord that separates the United States from Canada—are the twin "cities" of **Hyder**, Alaska

Self-Guided Kayaking

Experienced kayakers can pick up a Tongass National Forest *Ketchikan Area Kayaking Guide* at the Southeast Alaska Discovery Center; it has comprehensive information on nearby destinations, launch points, scenic highlights, and weather. The booklet includes rough maps, but kayakers are advised not to rely on these. Charts and detailed area maps are sold at the Discovery Center.

If you aren't a well-seasoned kayaker, stick with a guided tour. This region is subject to extreme tidal currents. What's more, Tongass Narrows and Clover Passage are among Southeast Alaska's busiest waterways. Floatplanes, ferries, cruise ships large and small, barges, commercial vessels, and sportfishing and sightseeing tour boats ply these waters daily. Kayakers need to be on their toes.

If you've got only a day to work with, **Tongass Narrows** is a great place to investigate. **Betton Island**, across Clover Passage from Knudson Cove (14.5 miles north of downtown on the North Tongass Hwy), can be explored in a day. The island's ½-mile-long **Betton Island Trail** is an easy hike along a boardwalk through the forest. Guided tours visit the island, so you may have to share. You can also launch from **Settler's Cove State Park**, 5 miles north of Knudson Cove. Just west of Betton Island, the tiny **Tatoosh Islands** are popular with kayakers, seals, and seabirds.

(population 100), and **Stewart**, British Columbia (population 700). Both towns are accessible by a spur road off the Cassiar Highway as well as by water and air. **Taquan Air** has **scheduled flights** between Ketchikan and

Hyder twice a week, Mondays and Thursdays. American visitors should bring photo identification and proof of citizenship to cross the international border.

Amenities in Hyder/Stewart include several hotels and B&Bs on both sides of the border. There are two museums in Stewart: **Toastworks** (306 5th Ave; 250/636-2344), a museum devoted to toasters (yes, really), and the **Stewart Historical Museum** (603 Columbia St; 250/636-2568).

Nearby are several top-notch attractions. The **Fish Creek Wildlife Observation Site** operated by the Forest Service offers superb **black and brown bear watching**, July through mid-September when the salmon are running. Permits are required (see Wildlife Viewing Permits, page 12). Airline charter tours are offered from Ketchikan; check with the tour center.

Visitors can rent a car or take a tour to see two magnificent glaciers nearby. **Salmon Glacier**, the fifth largest in North America, can be viewed from the Granduc Road, 25 miles northwest of Stewart. **Bear Glacier**, 20 miles east of Stewart on the spur road Highway 37A, is stunning. For bookings and information, as well as accommodation and dining options, contact the **Stewart & Hyder International Chamber of Commerce** (222 5th Ave/Main St, Stewart, BC; 250/636-9224, 888/366-5999; *www.stewart-hyder.com*).

MISTY FJORDS NATIONAL MONUMENT

In drizzly Ketchikan, it helps to see the glass of rainwater as half full rather than half empty. The wet stuff is what keeps the area lush and fresh. When weather is wet, the fjords get misty and the effect is at once spectacular and spooky. The subtle beauty of the fjords is even more impressive when you have the time, and are close enough, to enjoy it. First-rate raingear is a must. So is familiarity with bear best practices (see the introduction, page 10). This is brown bear country, especially in July and August when berries and salmon draw sows and cubs.

To appreciate the benefits of rain, kayak out to Misty Fjords, where the number of waterfalls flowing down sheer rock walls seems to grow exponentially in wet weather. Unless you are experienced in multiday wilderness kayaking, your best bet is a guided trip.

Southeast Sea Kayaks leads **multiple-day kayak trips** into Misty Fjords ($999–$1,350 for 4–5 days). Walker Cove, Manzanita, Rudyerd Bay, and Winstanley are popular destinations.

The **MV *Stimson*** has **customized fishing and/or sightseeing trips** for several days or more to Misty Fjords National Monument, nearby islands, hot springs, and Prince of Wales Island.

Tongass National Forest Cabins and Shelters

Within Misty Fjords are fourteen USFS cabins, some accessible by kayakers visiting Rudyerd Bay, and four shelters, accessed by floatplane, boat, and/or trail. Advance planning is necessary to book these popular destinations (see the introduction, page 15). Most cabins and shelters include a skiff and oars; some have mooring buoys.

Rudyerd Bay Trails

The Forest Service maintains eleven trails within the national monument. Of these, two are in Rudyerd Bay. The most popular is the beautiful, steep, but short (just under 1 mile) **Punchbowl Lake Trail**, which starts at Punchbowl Cove where there is a mooring buoy. The trail includes boardwalk and, in places, stairs. A little over halfway is the gorgeous Punchbowl Creek waterfall; the trail follows the stream up to Punchbowl Lake where there is a shelter, with skiff and oars. Within the lake is an island with a smaller lake in it. **Nooya Lake Trail**, a little over a mile, is more difficult. It leads from Rudyerd Bay to Nooya Lake, where there is a shelter with a skiff. Bears are very active at this site. Fresh- and saltwater fishing, including cutthroat, Dolly Varden, grayling, kokanee, and salmon, are good at most sites.

PRINCE OF WALES ISLAND

West of Ketchikan is Prince of Wales Island (PWI), at 2,731 square miles second in size only to Kodiak among Alaska islands and the third-largest island in the United States. The island is blessed with terrific fishing

Reading a Totem Pole

Totem poles are unique, beautiful, and elaborate works of art, products of rich cultures with plenty of leisure. Traditionally poles served multiple purposes that evolved as the societies that produced them—Haida, Tlingit, and Tsimshian—came in contact with other cultures. Unfortunately, the first westerners—often missionaries—who encountered them appropriated or destroyed many poles, wrongly believing them to be idols designed for religious worship.

Some totem poles were family emblems, like a coat of arms. Some commemorated important events. Others told stories, which themselves are a form of intellectual property in Native coastal cultures. Some poles shamed or ridiculed individuals who failed to pay debts. Mortuary poles were simple and somber, with a hollow space to contain the deceased's ashes and little adornment apart from a crest on top. After contact with western societies, cremation fell out of favor and mortuary poles served as traditional grave markers.

Poles might be erected alone or in front of a clan house. Some were part of the house itself—pillars or house posts. Paints were made from salmon eggs, copper pebbles, seashells, lichens, and other natural substances. Carved

and several hundred miles of paved road, more than any other destination along the Inside Passage south of Haines and Skagway; along the roads are trails, cabins, fishing, picnic sites, and campgrounds.

The mountainous island makes an excellent getaway from the hustle and bustle of Ketchikan. The downside is that PWI has been heavily logged, although a moratorium on logging in the Tongass National Forest in recent years has helped to minimize the impact.

Much of the native population is Haida, whose ancestors pushed north into Tlingit territory from

from red cedar, poles were often raised at potlatches and then allowed to follow the natural forest cycle, weathering and eventually rotting in place.

Poles have their own language. Learning to recognize the stylized ovoid forms used by the artist helps in interpreting a pole. Raven, eagle, octopus, grizzly bear, killer whale, beaver, frog, and thunderbird are commonly portrayed, along with human beings. A tall hat signifies the watchman. Potlatch rings—bands around the pole—often positioned on a figure's hat, indicate wealth. The phrase "top man on the totem pole," referring to someone in authority, indicates a misunderstanding of pole design. The bottom of the totem pole is the more honored position.

The art of carving totem poles nearly died out in the early twentieth century, but projects of the federal Civilian Conservation Corps (CCC) helped regenerate interest, along with the movement to revive indigenous arts across the United States decades later. Today, great Native carvers work throughout Southeast Alaska; their work is often displayed beside the work of their ancestors.

Many museums in communities throughout the Inside Passage have free publications describing local totem poles.

the Queen Charlotte Islands in British Columbia, to settle PWI in the 1770s. The island's three historic Native Alaskan communities each feature extraordinary totem poles. The charming town of Craig offers all amenities and services. Smaller towns and several fishing resorts, from rustic to sumptuous, offer lodging and dining. For information, contact the **Prince of Wales Chamber of Commerce** (PO Box 490 Klawock, AK, 99925-0490; 907/755-2626).

Year-round daily ferry service, provided by the **Inter-Island Ferry Authority** (907/826-4848; 866/308-4848;

www.interislandferry.com; $60/car, $30/adult), links Ketchikan and PWI. Ketchikan air charters fly to Hollis, Craig, and Thorne Bay (see Ketchikan Outfitters & Tour Operators sidebar, pages 46–47). **Alaska Car Rental** allows vehicles (SUVs only) to be taken to PWI. For a detailed map with roads, trails, picnic sites, and campsites, pick up the USFS publication Prince of Wales Island Road Guide ($5) in Ketchikan. The USFS also maintains two ranger stations on PWI: Craig (900 9th St; 907/826-3271) and Thorne Bay (off Sandy Beach Rd; 907/828-3304). There are nineteen USFS cabins and a shelter on PWI.

ACCOMMODATIONS

Ketchikan has a wide choice of comfortable accommodations.

Best Western Landing Hotel ($–$$; 3434 Tongass Ave; 907/225-5166, 800/428-8304; www.landinghotel. com; ⌖), directly across Tongass Avenue from the ferry terminal, is a large hotel with big rooms that come with microwave oven and refrigerator. Amenities include a coffee shop and restaurant, ample free parking, and complimentary van service.

At the **Gilmore Hotel** ($; 326 Front St; 907/225-9423, 800/275-9423; www.gilmorehotel.com), you'll have to schlep your suitcase upstairs, but when you do you'll be rewarded with comfortable, classic Alaska ambience. This 1927 hotel is a popular choice for Alaskans. A free continental breakfast is served. **Annabelle's**, the hotel's fine-dining restaurant ($$$; Sun–Thurs 7 am–9:30pm, Fri–Sat 7am–10:30pm), provides room service. Parking is a challenge; the downtown location is ideal for carless visitors.

Ketchikan Youth Hostel ($; in First United Methodist Church, Grant and Main St, PO Box 8515, Ketchikan, AK 99901; 907/225-3319) gets good marks for cleanliness, but it's on the Spartan side and lockout rules apply. Nonetheless, given Ketchikan's dearth of cheap accommodations, it fills up quickly; reservations are advised. There's a four-night maximum stay.

The Narrows Inn ($$–$$$; 4871 N Tongass Ave; 907/247-5900; www.narrowsinn.com; ⌖), a 15-minute drive from downtown, is an attractive waterfront hotel and marina that offers good views, comfortable rooms with refrigerator and microwave oven, and a fine seafood-oriented restaurant with moderate prices. Kids under 12 stay free.

WestCoast Cape Fox Lodge ($$$; 800 Venetia Wy; 907/225-8001, 866/225-8001; *www.westcoasthotels. com;* &), owned by the Saxman Native Corporation, is one of Alaska's premier hotels, with spacious, comfortable rooms, glorious views, and excellent service. The **Heen Kahidi Restaurant** serves up the views along with fine dining.

DINING

Ketchikan has a fairly meager selection of good restaurants. This won't pose much problem for cruise-ship visitors, but for independent travelers, finding a place to eat can be challenging. Ask a local, and you are likely to be directed to Bar Harbor or Burger Queen.

When Ketchikaners celebrate, they head to the charming **Bar Harbor** ($–$$; 2813 Tongass Ave; 907/225-2813; summer Sun–Thurs 7am–9pm, Fri–Sat 7am–10pm; winter Tues–Sat 11am–8pm), in a waterfront cottage a mile north of downtown. In fine weather, dine outside overlooking the boats. Indoors, the decor is year-round Christmas lights with quirky pictures and a homey feel. Prices are moderate. The crab chowder is a standout.

From the outside, **Burger Queen** ($; 518 Water St; 907/225-6060; spring, summer Tues–Sat 11am–7pm; &) resembles a fast-food chain restaurant down on its luck; inside, it's a terrific burger joint serving Solidarity Polish Sausage, halibut and chips, entrée salads, and fountain drinks (try the wild huckleberry shake). Portions are huge.

Hotel New York Café ($; 207 Stedman St; 907/225-0246; Tues–Sat 7am–2pm; longer hours in summer), a cheery, historic 1904 café south of Creek Street on Stedman, makes an excellent stop for breakfast or lunch. Nosh on a blackened halibut burger or fish-and-chips as you watch the bustling town go by. After a long hiatus the hotel café, now in the hands of Bar Harbor's capable owners, has begun to offer dinner again (call for hours); the accent is on fresh seafood.

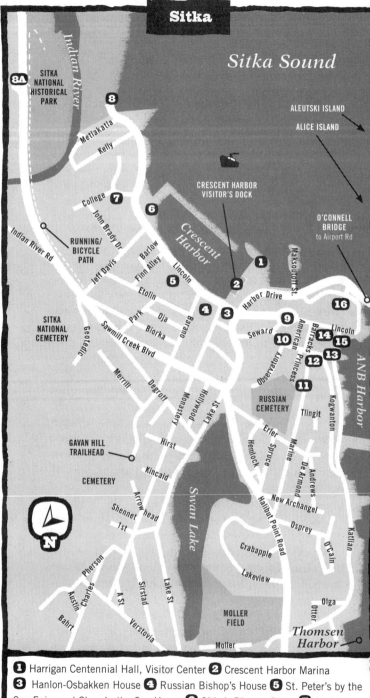

Sitka

Sitka Sound

ALEUTSKI ISLAND
ALICE ISLAND

O'CONNELL BRIDGE
to Airport Rd

Indian River

SITKA NATIONAL HISTORICAL PARK

Metlakatla
Kelly
College
John Brady Dr
RUNNING/BICYCLE PATH
Indian River Rd
Jeff Davis
Barlow
Finn Alley
Etolin
Park
Oja
Biorka
Sawmill Creek Blvd
Geodetic
Merrill
Degroff
Monastery
Lake St
Hollywood
Barano
Lincoln

CRESCENT HARBOR VISITOR'S DOCK

Crescent Harbor

Harbor Drive

Maksoutoff St.

SITKA NATIONAL CEMETERY

GAVAN HILL TRAILHEAD

CEMETERY

Hirst
Kincaid
Arrowhead
Shennet
1st

Swan Lake

Seward
American
Observatory
Princess
Barracks
Lincoln
Kogwanton

RUSSIAN CEMETERY

Tlingit
Erler
Spruce
Hemlock
Marine
De Armond
Andrews
New Archangel
Osprey
Halibut Point Road
Crabapple
Lakeview

ANB Harbor

Pherson
Charles
Austin
Bahrt
A St.
Sirstad
Lake St.
Verstovia

MOLLER FIELD
Moller

O'Cain
Katlian
Olga
Otter

Thomsen Harbor

N

---

1 Harrigan Centennial Hall, Visitor Center **2** Crescent Harbor Marina **3** Hanlon-Osbakken House **4** Russian Bishop's House **5** St. Peter's by the Sea Episcopal Church; the See House **6** Sitka's Blarney Stone **7** Sheldon Jackson College **8** Sitka National Historical Park **8A** Side trip to Alaska Raptor Center **9** St. Michael's Cathedral **10** Rose Hill Place **11** Grave of Princess Maksoutoff **12** Russian Blockhouse **13** Sitka Tribe Community House **14** Alaska Pioneer's Home **15** Totem Square **16** Castle Hill

Chapter 2

SITKA

Sitka is the only Inside Passage city fronting the Pacific Ocean. A graceful exception to the typically lackluster Alaskan cityscape, it's dotted with cultural and historic architectural gems. The natural setting, on the west coast of Baranof Island, is equally stunning, with the pristine Sitka Sound, snowcapped peaks, and myriad islands and islets to explore by boat or floatplane—all providing some of the best whale-watching, kayaking, and tide-pooling in Southeast Alaska.

Sitka has a remarkably high quality of life for a small, isolated community. It is home to two colleges—the University of Alaska Southeast at Sitka and Sheldon Jackson College, founded in 1878—and to the Island Institute, sponsor of a major literary event, the annual Sitka Symposium. Strike up a conversation with a Sitkan, and you're likely to find a cosmopolitan individual with informed opinions. Downtown Sitka is richly saturated in history, from the landmark Russian Orthodox cathedral to the totem trail that winds through the lush rain forest of Sitka National Historical Park.

Owing to its location, getting to Sitka poses more of a challenge than reaching other Southeast destinations. Stormy weather and rough conditions in aptly named Peril Strait can delay or prevent cruise ships from reaching Sitka. The lack of a deep-water dock requires that passengers on large cruise ships be ferried by tender into town. But Sitka's unique attractions ensure that it continues to attract cruise ships and independent travelers. With the advent of the high-speed car ferry in 2004, connecting Sitka and Juneau three times a week in a four-hour crossing, Sitka is more accessible than ever before.

HISTORY

Sitka—a contraction of the town's Tlingit name, *Shee Atika*—had been home to the Kiksadi Tlingit clan for 9,000 years when the Russians, already settled in the

Deconstructing Salmon

Each of Alaska's five salmon species has at least two names, and chances are good you'll be given plenty of rules of thumb for remembering them—some harder to remember than the names themselves. Here's a primer:

King salmon (a.k.a. chinook, spring), as the name implies, is the biggest and, for many diners, the best-tasting salmon. Alaska's state fish, kings live up to seven years, longer than any other Pacific salmon. Colors range from white to bright pink. Kings are usually the earliest salmon runs; thus in British Columbia, kings are called spring salmon. Kings average 30 pounds, although they can be much bigger; the biggest king on record, caught in 1949 near Petersburg, was 126 pounds.

Sockeye salmon (a.k.a. red) may or may not be the best tasting (some diners swear by it), but it's definitely the prettiest, with flesh of a rich red color. The fish itself turns rosy red when it's time to spawn. Much smaller than kings, sockeyes average 6–10 pounds.

Aleutian Islands, arrived in 1799, led by Alexander Baranof, chief manager of the newly chartered Russian-American Company. Baranof's objective was to set up a new outpost from which to hunt sea otters. After nearly a half century of Russian exploration and exploitation in northwestern Alaska, sea otters there had been hunted almost to extinction. The Russians built a fort north of Sitka called *Mikhailovsk* (now Old Sitka). Their first stay was brief. In 1802 the Tlingit attacked and burned down the fort, massacring most of the residents.

The Russians left, only to return in 1804 with a larger force. For six days they laid siege to the Kiksadi fort at the mouth of the Indian River, in what is now Sitka National Historical Park. During the final night of the siege, the Tlingit slipped away for an exile that would last nearly two decades. The Russians built a

Coho salmon (a.k.a. silver), slightly bigger than sockeye, weigh 8–12 pounds and make excellent eating. They are lovely fish and, from the fisher's perspective, perhaps the most fun, known for fighting vigorously and acrobatically.

Pink salmon (a.k.a. humpback or humpy), the baby of Pacific salmon, generally 3–4 pounds, are mainstays of commercial canneries. During the mid-twentieth century, they suffered serious overfishing; good management has gone a long way toward bringing them back. You have only to see a pink at spawning season to understand the name: the males develop a large, fascinatingly grotesque hump.

Chum salmon (a.k.a. dog), usually between 7 and 18 pounds, can grow up to 30 pounds. The name refers to the low opinion Alaska Natives have of this somewhat bland-tasting fish, traditionally used to feed sled dogs. However, the abundant chum is an important food source for humans, too, although the least prized by sportfishers.

stockaded community called *Novo-Arkhangel'sk* ("New Archangel") in what is now downtown Sitka.

The Russians moved their American capital to New Archangel in 1808, to take advantage of its wealth in sea-otter pelts, a natural harbor, and proximity to trade routes. Baranof governed the company and colony until 1818, and the city prospered in succeeding decades. An elegant residence was built for Baranof on Castle Hill, where aristocratic Russians attempted to create a sophisticated European cultural milieu; for a time Sitka was known as "the Paris of the Pacific."

The ruinous Crimean War strained Russia's resources and turned its attention away from Alaska. By the mid-1800s, sea otters were mostly hunted out here, too. As a Russian business venture, Alaska had become more expensive than rewarding. Russia persuaded U.S. Secretary of State William Seward to lobby his government to authorize the purchase of

Alaska for $7.2 million. On October 18, 1867, in a ceremony on Castle Hill, Russia transferred ownership of Alaska—which some called "Seward's Folly"—to the United States.

Sitka's population remained less than 1,500 for the rest of the nineteenth century, with fishing and canneries its economic mainstays. In the 1880s, Sheldon Jackson founded three schools in Sitka, as well as the museum that bears his name. Sitka was Alaska's territorial capital for just thirty-three years. In 1900 Juneau, in the midst of a gold boom, was designated the new capital.

World War II brought about a new period of growth. After Pearl Harbor was attacked in 1941, the Naval Air Station on Japonski Island adjacent to downtown Sitka, the only one on the North Pacific, assumed an important role in defense. Sitka's population swelled to 37,000 military and civilian residents, but at the war's end, the population quickly dropped. In 1959, when the first pulp mill opened, Sitka had a population of 6,000. The U.S. Coast Guard now operates the island's air station. Sitka has weathered the same economic squalls that hit other Southeast communities at the end of the twentieth century. The last pulp mill pulled out in 1993, taking hundreds of jobs with it.

SITKA TODAY

Employment is more diversified today, with tourism playing an ever-increasing role in supporting Sitka; primary employers are commercial fishing, tourism, and government. The community, now population 9,200 (City and Borough of Sitka), is also home to some of Southeast's most dedicated environmentalists. Two issues have recently engaged and, on occasion, polarized the community. The state transportation plan—whose agenda includes building a highway across Baranof Island between Sitka and the east coast, so that ferries can avoid the extra time and hazards involved in navigating Peril Strait—has garnered support and opposition. The second issue is the proposed building of a deep-water dock, a joint venture by Sheldon Jackson College and the local Native corporation, which would allow up to two cruise ships to dock close to Sitka National Historical

Park instead of being forced, as now, to anchor out and ferry passengers in and out of Sitka via small tenders. Amid the passionate debates, one thing is clear: Sitkans love their community and take an avid and proactive part in determining its future.

GEOGRAPHY

Sitka is located on the west coast of Baranof Island. With an area of 1,636 square miles, Baranof is separated from Chicagof Island to the north by Peril Strait and from Kruzof Island to the northwest by Sitka Sound. Sitka is 185 miles northwest of Ketchikan, 95 miles southwest of Juneau, and 862 miles north of Seattle, Washington.

CLIMATE

Sitka's average annual precipitation is 95 inches. Average highs in the peak summer months hover close to 60°F (June, 57.7°F; July, 60.8°F; August, 62°F).

Average Temperatures (°F)

	May–Oct	Nov–Apr
High	57.0	41.5
Low	46.2	32.6

Average Precipitation (inches)

Jan	Feb	March	April	May	June
7.24	6.33	6.04	4.78	4.67	3.39

July	Aug	Sept	Oct	Nov	Dec
4.23	6.78	10.94	13.26	9.52	8.58

Average Hours of Daylight

Jan	Feb	Mar	Apr	May	June
6.5	8.5	10.5	13	15.5	17.5

July	Aug	Sept	Oct	Nov	Dec
18	16	14	11.5	9	7

ACCESS

Daily Alaska Airlines flights connect Sitka to Juneau; other Alaskan cities; and Seattle, Washington. Alaska ferries stop at Sitka year-round (see the introduction, page 5). The high-speed *Fairweather* makes three round trips per week (Mon, Wed, Fri) between Juneau and Sitka; sailings are 4.5 hours one way. All major cruise lines except Norwegian Cruise Lines visit Sitka on one-way cruises. Round-trip cruises rarely visit Sitka.

VISITOR INFORMATION & SERVICES

Sitka Convention and Visitors Bureau (Alice Harrigan Centennial Hall, 330 Harbor Dr; 907/747-5940; *www. sitka.org*).

Tongass National Forest, Sitka Ranger District (204 Signaka Wy; 907/747-6671; *www.fs.fed.us/r10/tongass/*).

Post Office: Pioneer Postal Station (338 Lincoln St; 907/747-8491; Mon–Sat 8:30am–5:30pm).

Alaska Public Radio Network: Raven Radio Foundation, KCAW 104.7 FM.

Internet Access: It's free at **Kettleson Memorial Library** (320 Harbor Dr; 907/747-8708; sign up in advance; some rules apply) and the **Devil's Club Café** (Sheldon Jackson College's Rasmuson Student Center; 907/747-5239). Pay access is available at **Highliner Coffee** (327 Seward St, Seward Square Mall, behind Subway; 907/747-4924), **Alaska Computer Center** (205 Harbor Dr; 907/747-0600), and the post office. Fees start at $5 for 30 minutes. A new **Seaport Cyber** outlet and Wi-Fi hot spot has been opened in the **Bayview Trading Company Mall** (407 Lincoln St; *www.seaportel.com*).

WHEELS & KEELS

Alaskan-owned **North Star Rent-a-Car** (Sitka Airport Terminal; 907/966-2552, 800/722-6927) rents cars at the airport, with courtesy pickup and drop-off. Taxi service from **Alaska Classic Taxi & Tours** (907/752-7020) is available 24 hours daily. **Hank's Taxi Service** (907/747-8888) operates 4am–midnight; its cabs are smoke free.

The **Airport Shuttle** (907/747-8443; May–Sept; $5/one way, $7/round trip) makes pickups and drop-offs downtown. At the same price, they operate the **Ferry Transit Bus**. Year-round, the bus meets the ferry and provides bus transport downtown or elsewhere. The **Transit Shuttle** (907/747-7290; May–Sept Mon–Fri 12:30–4:30pm; $7/day pass) provides transport around town. When cruise ships are in port, they run additional hours. During a 30-minute run, the shuttle stops at Crescent Harbor Shelter, Sheldon Jackson Museum, Sitka National Historical Park, the Raptor Center, the Tribal Community House, and O'Connell Bridge. People with disabilities can take advantage of **Community Ride** (907/747-7103; Mon–Fri 6:30am–6:30pm), which offers these plus additional stops.

For water-taxi service, try **Esther G Sea Taxi** (215 Shotgun Alley; 907/747-6481, 907/738-6481 cell; *www. home.gci.net/~egseataxi/*). They take campers, kayakers, and cyclists to Forest Service cabins and other nearby locations ($100/hour for up to 6 passengers and gear). **EZC Transfer Company** (500 Lincoln St; 907/747-5044; $65/hour for up to 6 passengers and gear) goes to similar destinations.

EVENTS

Sitka Summer Music Festival (907/277-4852, in June 907/747-6774; *www.sitkamusicfestival.org*): Since its founding in 1972 by violinist Paul Rosenthal, this annual chamber music festival has attracted large, appreciative audiences that bigger cities in the Lower 48 would envy. Three weeks of evening concerts, held at Harrigan Centennial Hall, feature local and guest musicians from around the world. Some concerts are free. Tickets (around $15/festival seating) are usually available on the day of the concert, but it's best to purchase them early, as concerts often sell out.

Sitka Symposium (Island Institute, Box 2420, Sitka, AK 99835; 907/747-3794; *litsite.alaska.edu/uaa/akwrites/sitka.html*): For more than 20 years, this symposium, held each June for a week over the summer solstice, has explored topics broadly related to the writer's role in the world. Events are open to the public and include faculty talks, readings, a banquet, and a solstice cruise.

Sitka Three-Hour Must-See Itinerary

- Sitka National Historical Park (60 minutes)
- Sheldon Jackson Museum (30 minutes)
- Shopping on Lincoln Street (30 minutes)
- Saint Michael's Russian Orthodox Cathedral (15 minutes)
- Transit time (45 minutes)
- Refueling stops: **Highliner Coffee** (327 Seward St), **Backdoor Café** (104 Barracks St)

Sitka Whalefest (907/747-7964; *www.sitkawhalefest.org*): If you're in town in early November, check out this three-day cetacean symposium, with marine-animal-related scientific and cultural events, including whale-watching tours, art classes, and concerts. Advance registration is required.

FOUR HOURS OR LESS

More than any other Inside Passage destination, Sitka demands to be explored on foot. Walking allows you to appreciate the scope of Sitka's extraordinary and colorful history. The city is so compact that you can stroll to most of its attractions without transportation. For visitors with accessibility issues or tight schedules, taking a van tour is recommended.

WALKING TOURS

Sitka Walking Tour *(2.5 hours)*

This walking tour encompasses downtown Sitka's principal attractions, with an optional side trip to the Alaska Raptor Center. For walking tour map, see page 58.

❶ Start your exploration at the **visitor center** in **Harrigan Centennial Hall**. The hall hosts a variety of cultural and civic events throughout the year and is home to the **New Archangel Dancers**. The **Isabel Miller Museum** is housed here, too. In a large room down the hall, the **Baranof Arts and Crafts Association Gallery** sells works by local artists in summer including paintings, sculpture, jewelry, and handicrafts.

❷ From the hall, walk out the main entrance to the park, past the statue of Alexander Baranof (1747–1819), and turn right on Harbor Drive, following it as it bears right. On your right is the **Crescent Harbor Marina**, where most water-based excursions depart.

❸ Cross Lake Street, turn right on Lincoln Street and head east. The two-story **Bayview Trading Company** building has a variety of shops as well as the perennially popular **Bayview Restaurant**. Pass the **Hanlon-Osbakken House** (419 Lincoln), an exquisite late Victorian–style residence built in 1895. Today it's home to the **Sitka Rose Gallery** and **Wintersong Soap Company**.

❹ Crossing Monastery Street on Lincoln, you pass the **Russian Bishop's House**. Note the flower and vegetable garden featuring the types of plants grown during the Russian tenure in Sitka.

❺ Continuing on Lincoln past Baranof Street, you pass more historic buildings. The **Emmons House** (1895) was built by a naval officer who went on to become a distinguished Alaskan anthropologist. On the same block are **Saint Peter's by the Sea Episcopal Church** and the **See House**. The church was built in 1899, when Sitka was still capital of territorial Alaska, and the building was consecrated as Cathedral of Alaska in 1900. The See (the Bishop's residence) dates to 1905. Both church buildings are in use today.

❻ Retrace your steps to the crosswalk and cross to the harbor side of Lincoln Street to take a look at a large boulder, Sitka's so-called **Blarney Stone**. (The name is likely the brainchild of an enterprising early Sitka promoter.) According to Tlingit legend, the rock was actually used by an early chief as a whetstone to sharpen his knives. Near the stone are public basketball and tennis courts, plus a playground.

7 Return to the other side of Lincoln Street and continue east past **Sheldon Jackson College**, whose attractive buildings line three sides of the broad lawn. Affiliated with the Presbyterian Church, this small college is noted for its environmental sciences program. On campus, the small **Devil's Club Cafe** (Rasmuson Student Center; 907/747-5239; Mon–Fri 8am–4:30pm, Sat 8am–1pm) sells snacks and has free Internet access. The swimming pool in the **Hames P. E. Building** is open to the public (907/747-5231; $4/adult, $2/under 12). At the east end of the campus is the distinctively shaped **Sheldon Jackson Museum**. As you leave the college and continue east on Lincoln, you pass the nondescript Sage Building on your right, housing the college's tiny but excellent **aquarium**.

8 As you reach **Sitka National Historical Park**, passing the parking lot you'll see the visitor center directly ahead.

8A OPTIONAL SIDE TRIP TO THE ALASKA RAPTOR CENTER (90 minutes): Starting from the national park parking lot, take the trail over the bridge out to Sawmill Creek Road. Turn left and follow the bike path a few hundred feet until you see the raptor center sign. Cross the street (with caution; traffic is fast and heavy). Walk up the hill to the **Alaska Raptor Center**. To rejoin the walking tour, return to Sawmill Creek Road and cross to the bike path. Turn right rather than returning to the park. Walk to Biorka Street and follow it to the intersection with Baranof Street. Pass the Market Center; follow Baranof down to Lincoln and turn right.

9 Follow Lincoln Street back toward the center of town. Cross to the harbor side of the street to read the interpretive signs overlooking Crescent Harbor. These describe Sitka's working fishing fleet. Passing Crescent Harbor, continue west on Lincoln. On the right is the **Westmark Sitka Hotel**, formerly the Shee Atika. You pass the post office and Sitka's **main shopping area** and the Shee Atika Office Building on the right. On the ground floor are the new **Tea-Licious Bakery & Gallery** (see Food & Drink, page 78) and the **Little Tokyo Restaurant**, with a top-notch sushi bar. Continue past the art galleries around the back of **Saint Michael's Cathedral**.

As you continue on Lincoln, on the left side of the street is **Building 29**, a National Historic Landmark and one of the few intact examples of secular Russian architecture in North America. Originally a private residence, constructed about 1835, it now houses gift shops. Directly across the street, you'll find **Old Harbor Books** and, inside it, the **Backdoor Café**.

10 Retrace your steps back on Lincoln past the cathedral and turn left onto Cathedral Way, which goes uphill and curves right. Straight ahead is **Rose Hill Place** (315 Seward), a beautiful building dating from 1911, now housing local businesses, and once the home of Miss Loretta Mae Mills, sister of Sitka tycoon W. P. Mills. Miss Mills planted the beautiful balm of gilead tree in the yard. Turn left on Seward. At the corner of Observatory Street, the handsome white building, dating from 1916, is the **Forest Service House**. This was the site of a Russian tea garden until 1867. In 1916, the U.S. Coast and Geodetic Survey built this house as a geomagnetic observatory. Today it houses U.S. Forest Service staff.

11 Turn right on Princess Way to view a melancholy but pretty spot, surrounded by salmonberry bushes: the grave of **Princess Adelaide Maksoutoff**. She was the first wife of Dmitri Maksoutoff, the Russian governor at the time Alaska was transferred to U.S. control.

12 Returning to Seward Street, continue through the 200 block past the apartment building and two cottages, which in the 1920s were barged here from Douglas, where they served as housing for Treadwell Mine workers. Still residences, they are on the National Register of Historic Places. Ahead, in a setting with a panoramic view, is the **Russian blockhouse**, a 1958 reproduction on the site of an original Russian blockhouse, part of the Russian stockade that marked the boundary between Russian and Tlingit territories. The blockhouse is rarely open to the public.

13 Walking around the blockhouse on Kaagwaantaan Street, follow the steps to the right of the **Sitka Tribe Community House** (*Sheet'ka Kwaan Naa Kahidi*: "House for the people of Sitka"), down to Katlian Street. You can take a 20-minute detour to see the **Alaska Native Brotherhood (ANB) Hall**, built in 1914, on the left; this organization was an early champion of Native rights. Across the street from the hall on the right is **Ludvig's Bistro**.

14 From the Sitka Tribe Community House, take the steps up to the grounds of the adjacent **Alaska Pioneer's Home** set higher up. This handsome building erected in 1934 is a major Sitka landmark. It replaced earlier buildings on the site that opened in 1913 to house destitute elderly prospectors who had resided at least five years in Alaska. The home continues to house elderly Alaskans. Along with its colorful flower garden and great view of Totem Square and the ANB harbor beyond, there's a small gift shop inside, run by the residents, which they open for business when the mood strikes them.

15 Follow the steps down to Lincoln Street and turn right. Note the **Sitka Hotel**, dating from 1939, as you continue west to **Totem Square**. Weather permitting, you'll have a good view of Mount Edgecumbe. The square contains a hodgepodge of historical items: a handsome totem pole, Tlingit petroglyphs, a Russian cannon, and three old anchors recovered from the harbor. Small cruise ships dock at the marina. Signs describe the site where the USS *Jamestown* docked in 1879, two years after the U.S. Army had pulled out of Alaska. It was sent to restore order to the near-lawless town and prevent a looming war between Sitka settlers and the Tlingit.

To the left of Totem Square is the attractive **Cable House** (2 Lincoln St), the old WAMCATS building, on the National Register of Historical Places. The Washington-Alaska Military Cable and Telegraph System was an ambitious effort undertaken between 1900 and 1904 to link key Alaskan sites together and to the outside world. Sitka was connected to Juneau, Valdez, and Seattle by separate undersea cables. The historical function of the building as a communications center continues. Today it houses Sitka's public radio station, Raven Radio. **Evergreen Natural Foods** is here, along with an art gallery and café.

16 When you reach the end of Lincoln Street, turn back and head east to **Castle Hill State Historic Site**. You can either walk the 178 steps up to the summit or, for an accessible route, go around the street across from the Cable House to a series of ramps that lead up from the harbor side. From the top, you'll have a good view of O'Connell Bridge to Japonski Island, Sitka Channel, and Sitka Sound. It was here that the formal transference of Alaska from Russia to the United States took place.

Follow the ramp down on the harbor side and take Harbor Drive back to Harrigan Centennial Hall. Along the way, to the right you pass **Kettleson Memorial Library**.

Guided Walks

Exploring the evidence of Sitka's long and complex history with a knowledgeable guide can be rewarding. The **Alaska Walking Tour Company** leads a **comprehensive walking tour** (2 hours; $35), at a slow pace, that covers Alaska history with a tour of Sitka National Historical Park and a visit to the Alaska Raptor Center.

Tribal Tours offers a **Tlingit-accented guided walk** (2 hours; $25/adult, $15/child) from the Community Tribal House along Crescent Harbor to Sitka National Historical Park. The tour focuses on local Tlingit culture and history, as well as edible and medicinal plants. Those who prefer not to make the full round trip on foot are given a free transit pass to ride back.

HISTORY & CULTURE

See Walking Tour, page 66, for other historical sites.

With its green onion dome, the lovely blue-and-white **Saint Michael's Russian Orthodox Cathedral** (15 minutes; Cathedral Wy and Lincoln St; 907/747-8120/3560; summer when cruise ships and ferries in port 9am–4pm, other times check hours posted on door or call; donations welcome) is a Sitka landmark. The cathedral is a reproduction of the original, which was designed by Bishop Innocent and built between 1844 and 1848 out of spruce logs and lined with sailcloth for insulation. That building was destroyed in the devastating fire of 1966 that leveled much of downtown Sitka. During the fire, Sitka residents, at considerable personal risk, saved nearly all the contents of the cathedral. The now-fireproof cathedral retains the original design, in the shape of a cross with three altars and two smaller chapels. The wooden doors, painted gold, are original, as are most of the icons and the chandelier. Many icons date from the early nineteenth century; miracles are attributed to some. Icons and other items are identified and described, and visitors can listen to a recorded narrative of the church's history. Sometimes a priest is on hand to answer questions. This is an active church community, and visitors are welcome at Sunday services.

Tucked inside the cavernous Harrigan Centennial Hall is the charming, homey **Isabel Miller Museum** (30 minutes; 330 Harbor Dr; 907/747-6455; *www.sitka.org/ historicalmuseum/*; May–Sept daily 8am–5pm, Oct–April Tues–Sat 10am–4pm; $3 donation), possibly the only museum in Alaska for which admission includes a deluxe Theobroma chocolate bar. There are other good reasons for visiting, too. The museum, operated by the Sitka Historical Society, contains a colorful cross section of the region's history, from delicate Tlingit basketry to Russian colonial artifacts and a scale model of Sitka, circa 1867, at the time when ownership of Alaska was transferred from Russia to the United States at a ceremony held just blocks away. Displays bring to life Sitka's colorful and unusual history, including its role in the development of long-distance flight and in World War II.

A perennially popular Sitka attraction is the **New Archangel Dancers**, a troupe of women, all local volunteers, who perform Russian, Moldavian, and Ukrainian folk dances in colorful, authentic costumes. Performances (30 minutes; 907/747-5516; $7/adult, $4/child) usually take place in Harrigan Centennial Hall on days when cruise ships and/or ferries are in port, but other locations are sometimes used. Call the hotline for locations or check at the visitor center, where upcoming performance schedules are posted.

The long, mustard-yellow **Russian Bishop's House** (30 minutes; 501 Lincoln St; 907/747-0110; *www.nps. gov/sitk/pphtml/facilities/*; May–Sept 9am–5pm, rest of year by appointment; $3/adult, free/under 12) dates from the 1840s. The bishop's house offers a fascinating glimpse into the lives of Russian Alaskans. It was designed for Bishop Innocent, who also designed the cathedral. The Sitka National Historical Park acquired the house in 1972; restoration is still ongoing. The house has been restored to its appearance as a boy's school in the 1850s. Upstairs are the bishop's austere private quarters, where he slept, dined, and greeted visitors.

(Spartan is the *mot juste*.) In the large chapel, up to 100 boys crowded in for services. Downstairs, exhibits demonstrate how Russian expats built their houses in the early 1830s. A scale model of New Archangel displays the downtown layout, including buildings on Castle Hill. (**Note**: although part of the national park, the Russian Bishop's House is not included in general park admission.)

Sitka Tribe Community House (200 Katlian St; 907/747-7290, 888/270-8687; *www.sitkatribe.org*) serves as a community and cultural center for the Sitka Tribe and showcases the tribe's culture and history with the **Sheet'ka Kwaan Naa Kahidi Dancers** (30 minutes; schedule varies, call for performance times). The building, adjacent to the Pioneer Home, is fronted by two large carved wooden panels representing the Eagle and Raven moieties. The design of the building follows that of a classic Tlingit clan house. Inside is a theater in which dance performances are given. Dancers in Tlingit regalia perform a story and three traditional songs in Tlingit, interpreted by a narrator and accompanied by traditional drumming.

Not only is **Sheldon Jackson Museum** (1 hour; 104 College Dr; 907/747-8981; mid-May–mid-Sept daily 9am–5pm, rest of year Tues–Sat 10am–4pm; $4/adult summer, $3/adult winter, free/under 19) Alaska's oldest museum, dating from the 1890s, it's one of the best. The small octagonal building is crammed with fascinating Native Alaskan history. It was founded by Presbyterian missionary Sheldon Jackson, who played an important role in conserving Native Alaskan history and culture for future generations. As education agent for Alaska, Dr. Jackson made many trips across the territory, collecting the artifacts on view here. He showed superb judgment, choosing items that demonstrated the range, quality, and distinctive identities of Native cultures. The collection was first displayed in a smaller building, which it soon outgrew; the current building was designed and completed in 1897 expressly to house this collection. In summer, Native artists demonstrate traditional arts and crafts in the museum and are happy to answer questions.

Sitka National Historical Park, the 107 acres of forest at the mouth of the Indian River at the south end of Lincoln Street, is the oldest federally designated park in Alaska, created in 1910 to commemorate the 1804 battle of Sitka. Trails, including the famous **Totem Trail**, crisscross the park. Also on site are a visitor center, a theater, a large bookstore with gifts as well as books, and displays of Tlingit and Russian artifacts. (1 hour; 106 Metlakatla St; 907/747-0110; *www.nps.gov/sitk/*; May–Sept daily 8am–5pm, rest of year Mon–Fri 8am–5pm; $3/adult, free/under 13).

The **Southeast Alaska Indian Cultural Center** (907/747-8061) is also housed in the building. Here visitors can observe Tlingit craftspeople at work carving totem poles and masks and engraving silver jewelry. Classes are offered in these and other traditional skills. The park includes the Russian Bishop's House on Lincoln Street. Throughout the summer, park rangers lead free guided walks through the park and Russian Bishop's House, and conduct naturalist programs on the flora and fauna of Sitka. Talks on the Battle of Sitka and on the park's totem poles are given regularly. Check the park visitor center for details.

Guided Tours

Sitka has so much to see that when time is limited, taking a vehicle-based cultural tour makes sense. You'll see more and get less tired doing so. The **Ferry Stopover Tour** operated by Sitka Tours (about 3 hours, depending on the ferry schedule; $12/adult, $6/child) picks up passengers whose ferry is stopping over for a few hours at the ferry terminal, brings them into town, and touches some of the high spots, including the Sitka National Historical Park and Saint Michael's Cathedral. There's time for a bit of shopping, then buses return to the terminal. Passengers who want to simply explore Sitka for a few hours on their own can take the bus in and back and opt out of the tour.

Tribal Tours has several tours. The **Comprehensive Cultural Tour** (2.5–3 hours; $42/adult, $32/child) includes 45 minutes of narrated coach tour, with 45 minutes at Sitka National Historical Park, 30 minutes at the Sheldon Jackson Museum, and a 30-minute performance by the Sheet'ka Kwaan Naa Kahidi Dancers. Another tour (3.5 hours; $55/adult, $45/child) adds a visit to the Alaska Raptor Center to the historical tour.

SHOPPING

Sitka's reputation as the fine arts capital of Southeast Alaska is well deserved, and its excellent arts and crafts galleries showcase the work of local artists. Most are clustered along Lincoln Street. Reflecting Sitka's Russian heritage, several galleries specialize in the work of Russian artists, including Siberian Native peoples, some of whom share a history and culture with Alaska Natives.

Art

ALASKA NATIVE AND REGIONAL ART: Before shopping for Native Alaskan art, you might want to investigate the **Southeast Alaska Indian Cultural Center** (in Sitka National Historic Park Visitor Center; 907/747-6281; daily 8am–5pm), where local Tlingit artists practice traditional crafts and are happy to talk with visitors. Some, like silversmith Dave Galanin at **Dave Galanin Silverworks** (907/747-3795), sell their art to the public.

Among the top locally owned Sitka galleries selling the work of Alaska Natives is **Artist Cove Gallery** (241 Lincoln St; 907/747-6990). Works range from traditional to highly innovative in media such as fabric, basketry, and glass. Works include elegant jewelry and unusual wall hangings by non-Native local and Alaskan artists. **Sitka Rose Gallery** (419 Lincoln St; 907/747-3030, 888/236-1536) occupies several ground-floor rooms in the historic Hanlon-Osbakken House. Alaska and Russian Native artists are well represented; there's a wide selection of sculptures and spirit masks. Local artists and jewelers also have work here.

For an excellent selection of prints and paintings, along with various other media and an intriguing selection of used Alaskana (such as old *Mileposts*), try the **Fishermen's Eye** (239 Lincoln St; 907/747-6080), formerly known as the Impressions Gallery. Just down the street is **Fairweather Prints** (209 Lincoln St; 907/747-8677), which offers silkscreened and handpainted clothing, moderately priced jewelry by local artists, art, and ceramics. Imports include the work of producers' cooperatives in developing countries. This is a good place to shop for the teenage girl on your list.

The **Sheldon Jackson Museum Gift Shop** carries a superb selection of Native Alaskan art, art cards, and Alaskana, although prices are steep. The **Isabel Miller Museum** has a small gift shop; along with typical museum gift shop offerings, it features quirky items made by museum volunteers.

Alaska Borealis Artworks, in a small gallery in the WAMCATS building (2A Lincoln St; 907/747-6707), carries watercolors, carvings, ceramics, glass, and jewelry by local artists. Prices are lower than at some galleries in town. If you find yourself empty-handed at the airport, don't panic. The **Airport Gift Shop** (Sitka Airport Terminal; 907/966-2553), usually open when planes are in, has an excellent and representative assortment of local gifts at reasonable prices.

Sharing space with the Sitka Rose Gallery, the **WinterSong Soap Company** (419 Lincoln St; 907/747-8949, 888/819-8949) sells herbal soaps, salves, lotions, cosmetics, and bath items. You can buy these products throughout Alaska, but this is where they are made.

RUSSIAN AMERICAN ART: The biggest selection of Russian American art in Sitka is carried by the **Russian American Company** (407 Lincoln St, Ste A; 907/747-6228, 800/742-6228). It occupies much of the second floor of the Bayview Trading Company mall. Nesting dolls, lacquerware, Fabergé eggs, amber jewelry, porcelain tea sets, and Christmas ornaments are among the items for sale. Smaller, but with an excellent assortment of Russian gifts, both religious and secular, at moderate prices is **Archangel Michael Icons, Books & Gift Shop** (223 Lincoln St; 907/747-8101). All proceeds from this shop go to the upkeep of the cathedral.

Books

Old Harbor Books (201 Lincoln St; 907/747-8808) is not only one of the state's best bookstores, it has the **Backdoor**, a top-notch café attached to it (food is made at what used to be Mojo's next door); a blackberry bar goes down well with a latte and the chance to peruse your latest bookstore find. Books include a huge selection of Alaskana, travel and outdoor, and general-interest titles; the staff is knowledgeable and courteous. At the **Sitka National Historical Park Visitor Center** a large bookstore sells many works on native Alaskan culture. The **Sheldon Jackson**

Good Buys

Perhaps the most entertaining place to shop in Sitka requires wheels to get to: **Theobroma Chocolate Company** (Sawmill Creek Rd; 907/966-2345, 888/985-2345; *theobroma chocolate.com*), started by a former Department of Fisheries biologist in the 1990s. Tour the factory (notice the antique wrapping machine) and explore the gift shop, where you can buy chocolate Chilkat blankets and salmon. *Theobroma* means "food of the gods" in Latin, and the company does its best to live up to the name. The factory and store, located 5 miles south of town at the industrial park, are open to visitors. Nibble free samples while you watch a video on the history of Theobroma, and be glad the wrapping machine is prone to breaking down; miswrapped chocolate bars are sold as seconds at deeply discounted prices. A popular bike tour stops here (see Four Hours or Less, page 85).

Museum has a smaller but excellent assortment of the books, as well. The **Isabel Miller Museum** has works on local history.

Clothing & Sundries

Although Sitka—unlike Ketchikan and Juneau—has successfully barred big chain stores from coming in, it has paid a price for this, literally: there is no inexpensive place to buy clothes in Sitka. Many locals order online or shop when they visit Juneau or Seattle. For clothes other than souvenir gifts, your best choice is probably **Rain Country** (201 Katlian, Ste 104; 907/747-6422, 800/770-6422).

Sitka Work & Rugged Gear (407 Lincoln St, Ste F; 907/747-6238) carries the big names in moderately priced and upscale outdoor attire, from boots to raingear, with an ample selection. **Orion Sporting Goods** (Lakeside Plaza, 705 Halibut Pt Rd; 907/747-3541) sells a broad assortment of sporting goods, with an emphasis on hunting and fishing; **Mac's Sporting Goods** (213 Harbor Dr; 907/747-6970) has a similar selection, plus fishing and hunting licenses; the same company owns the men's sporting goods store **Russell's** (208 Lincoln St; 907/747-3395), which sells sportswear and shoes.

If your camera needs TLC or you want help downloading pictures from a digital camera, **Southeast Camera Inc.** (303 Lincoln St, Ste 3; 907/747-3999) can help.

Food & Drink

If you have the impression that Sitka caters to foodies, you're right: restaurant and retail food businesses offer the quality and variety usually encountered only in a much larger town. So when cruise-ship cuisine begins to pall, it may be time to hit a few Sitka high spots.

A welcome addition to downtown Sitka in 2003, the **Tea-Licious Bakery & Gallery** (315 Lincoln St, Stes 110 and 114; 907/747-4535) offers light lunches, high teas, and delectable snacks; in keeping with Southeast Alaska's love affair with the bean, espresso drinks are served. Half of the shop sells dozens of teas, teapots, and gifts.

Sitka has two large grocery stores within walking distance of downtown: **Lakeside Grocery** (Lakeside Plaza, 705 Halibut Pt Rd; 907/747-3317), with a large assortment of whole and organic produce and meat, plus ethnic foods, and **Market Center** (210 Baranof St; 907/747-6686). **Sea Mart** (1867 Halibut Pt Rd; 907/747-6266) is too far to reach on foot from downtown; it's a top choice with thrifty residents, and its gigantic revolving door, the size of a small merry-go-round, has to be seen to be believed. The **House of Liquor** (Lakeside Plaza, 705 Halibut Pt Rd; 907/747-5075) has a large selection of wine.

NATURE

Hidden in a grim building off Lincoln Street is **Sheldon Jackson Aquarium** (15 minutes; Sage Bldg, Sheldon Jackson College; 907/747-5244; mid-May–Aug Mon–Fri 9am–3pm; $3/adult, free/under 13), a real gem. Don't be fooled by the dingy surroundings: you can spend longer than you might think at this tiny but excellent aquarium. Along with a large tank, six smaller tanks contain unusual residents of local waters, such as the Irish lord, which looks like a grumpy, gout-ridden old reprobate, and bizarre calcareous worms that look like ashy snake fireworks with red tips. Best of all are three enormous touch tanks containing sea stars, sun stars, chitons, nudibranches, and sea cucumbers that visitors are encouraged to handle.

A short walk from the national park, the popular nonprofit **Alaska Raptor Center** (1 hour; 1000 Raptor Wy; 907/747-8662; *www.alaskaraptor.org*; May–Sept daily 8am–4pm; $12/adult, $6/under 12; memberships available)—formerly known as the Raptor Rehabilitation Center and first opened in 1980—nurses raptors, mostly bald eagles and owls, back to health while educating the public. The center treats about 200 wild birds each year, most of which are returned to the wild. On the 17 scenic, wooded acres are a bald eagle flight training center with displays, a theater and large gift shop, and nature trails. The birds, housed in spacious mews, have names and decided personalities along with the grim stories behind their arrival at the center—from close encounters with cars to ingesting poisons at a dump or having their nests felled in logging operations. Tours introduce visitors to each resident and the work of the center.

Flightseeing

Harris Aircraft does not offer flightseeing tours per se but will happily take passengers along on **scheduled flights** to Baranof Warm Springs, Kake, and Port Alexander.

Wildlife Tours

Fascinating marine life can be glimpsed below the surface, too. The **Glass-Bottom Boat Tour** (2 hours; $79) takes visitors on a boat with underwater windows disclosing a fascinating world just feet from shore. Explore Sitka's rich undersea and intertidal environment from the comfortable interior of a heated boat. Life observed through the glass windows includes sea stars, crabs, sea cucumbers, sea slugs, sea urchins, anemones, moon jellies, and forests of gently waving sea grasses. Scuba divers with video cameras and

Tide-pooling in Sitka

Some of the best tide-pooling in Southeast Alaska is to be found in and around Sitka. Exploring an intertidal zone at low tide can be enchanting, when rare and wonderful creatures, normally hidden, are revealed in profusion. Small, clear pools are home to tiny hermit crabs, barnacles, mussels, and sea anemones. Clinging to rocks are sea stars in brilliant colors, from hot orange-pinks to sky blues and purples. Rocks are carpeted with seaweeds resembling delicate grasses or gigantic rubbery ropes. Live sand dollars and a rich variety of shells—some occupied by critters, some empty—wait to be discovered. For information on tides, check at the Sitka National Historical Park Visitor Center or pick up a tide table in a sporting goods store. Below are some of Sitka's best tide-pooling bets:

- Halibut Point State Recreation Site (Halibut Point Road), see page 83

- John Brown's Beach (Japonski Island), see page 87

- Totem Beach (Sitka National Historical Park), see page 86

underwater microphones feed fish and demonstrate what's out there. The oddly shaped vessel is restroom-equipped but not wheelchair accessible; it has a viewing area above the water, too. Offered by **Sea Life Discovery Tours**, tours include unusual snacks such as kelp marmalade cookies and kelp pickles. Independent travelers are welcome; cruise-ship passengers need to book through their cruise ship.

Also providing water-taxi service, **Esther G Sea Tours Taxi** will put together a **marine wildlife–viewing tour** (2 hours, $85; 3 hours, $110; 4 hours, $140). They'll also help put together longer tours, including booking a floatplane. Tours can be customized to focus on bird-watching, whale-watching, or a combination of elements.

A highly experienced major player among Southeast Alaska tour operators, **Allen Marine** operates a popular **shore excursion** (3 hours; $99/adult; $79/ages 3–12) exclusively for cruise-ship passengers, as well as two tours for independent travelers: an **Evening Wildlife Quest** (2 hours; Tues, Thurs 6–8pm; $59/adult, $30/child 3–12) and a **Morning Wildlife Quest** (3 hours; $79/adult, $40/ages 3–12; Sat, Sun 8:30–11:30am). Depending on weather conditions and where the marine life is hanging out, destinations vary. The focus is on ensuring that passengers see the wildlife. For a pleasant change, advance reservations are not required for independent travelers. Tours board 15 minutes before departure from Crescent Harbor next to Harrigan Centennial Hall. Note that schedules may be incompatible with cruise-ship itineraries.

Sitka's Secrets specializes in tours (3.5 hours; $100) to **Saint Lazaria National Wildlife Refuge**, a birder's paradise. The island consists of 65 acres of marine-bird habitat, about 15 miles west of Sitka, just south of Kruzof Island (home to the pleasingly shaped Mount Edgecumbe). Tour boats circumnavigate the island. Among the birds on view are auklets, cormorants, gulls, murrelets, murres, oystercatchers, and puffins. Custom charters are available.

Some Allen Marine and Esther G tours also visit Saint Lazaria National Wildlife Refuge.

ONE OF A KIND

The **Find Your Alaska Muse** tour (4 hours; $50) offered by **Sitka Bike & Hike** aims to combine an adventure in the natural environment of Tongass National Forest with a creative endeavor—visual art, photography, or writing. To that end, the company provides guides with backgrounds in the arts to lead tour groups into the wild and help them find a way to express what they experience. Advance booking is required. The tour comes with snack, water bottle, rain poncho, notepad, and a Theobroma chocolate bar to inspire you.

ROAD TRIPS

Sitka has about 15 miles of paved highway, fewer than any other destination covered in this book. Nonetheless, many of Sitka's best views, parks, hikes, and wildlife viewing opportunities are found along its scenic roads.

Halibut Point Road (15 miles/45 minutes)

Begin this road trip from downtown Sitka at Harbor Drive and Lake Street. If you're coming from the airport, follow Airport Road over the O'Connell Bridge where Airport Road turns into Harbor Drive. Lake Street begins where you cross Lincoln Street.

At Sitka's one and only stoplight, turn onto Halibut Point Road. You pass **Swan Lake** on the right, crammed with water lilies and stocked with rainbow trout, not swans. **Moller Park** offers picnic facilities and fishing access. On the left, off Katlian Street, is a mall containing Lakeside Grocery, one of Sitka's three supermarkets, plus a liquor store and Orion Sporting Goods. Also here is Blatchley Middle School, housing one of Sitka's two **public swimming pools** (907/747-8670).

On the other side of Katlian is **Thomsen Harbor**. Just north of here, bald eagles congregate in search of fish or other goodies, just like other scavengers but far more impressive to look at. **Seamart** (1867 Halibut Pt Rd) is Sitka's other big supermarket, and its ample deli section makes an inexpensive alternative to the town's mostly high-priced dining options.

The road hugs the coastline, moving first west, then north. At mile 1.7, beyond Sitka's 'burbs, **Pioneer Park** has attractive views, a picnic shelter, and beach access. About 0.5 mile on is **Sandy Beach**, at mile 2.2, with swimming and good views of Mount Edgecumbe. Spot humpback whales here in fall and early winter. At low tide, live sand dollars can be found; be sure to leave them on the beach to bask in the sun another day.

Beyond Sandy Beach 1.5 miles, look for **Harbor Mountain Road** to the right. Beautifully paved for about a mile, it morphs into a corkscrewing gravel road ending 2,000 feet up and 4 miles on. Here you'll find a scenic view and picnic sites amid subalpine vegetation and the **Harbor Mountain Ridge Trail**. It's a rough drive, so investigate road conditions first and think carefully before bringing your rental car. Trailers and RVs won't be able to handle the hairpin curves. Allow about 1 hour for the round-trip drive, with extra time to marvel at the view.

Continuing on Halibut Point Road, at mile 4.3 is **Halibut Point State Recreation Site**. Several short, easy trails lead to the beach. Parking and sheltered picnic facilities with fireplaces and toilets are here.

At mile 6.6 is the **Alaska Marine Highway Terminal** at Starrigavan Bay for all Alaska ferries, including the high-speed ferry to and from Juneau. Farther on 0.5 mile is the start of **Starrigavan Recreation Area**, highly recommended, with camping, picnicking, hiking, and abundant wildlife.

At mile 7, **Old Sitka State Historic Site** has signage describing the history of the first Russian settlement of Fort Archangel Michael, built here in 1799 and burned down in 1802 by the Tlingit. There are views, picnic shelters, a boat launch, and trails.

Opposite Old Sitka, across the highway, is **Starrigavan Creek and estuary**. Watch for birders who, in their ecstasy, may not be watching for you. To the right of the creek, the gravel Nelson Logging Road winds along its banks to a shooting range. If time doesn't allow a visit to Saint Lazaria Island, get your feather fix at the bird-viewing platform.

At the end of Halibut Point Road is the lovely **Starrigavan Campground**, recently renovated and expanded. Stop to fill your water bottle at the artesian well. Even if time does not allow you to take one of Sitka's longer hikes, you can get a feel for them by following one of the trails here. **Note:** Baranof Island's brown bear population also enjoys the recreation area; occasionally their presence has caused the campground to be closed to human visitors. Brush up on your bear etiquette and be prepared to share the view with furry residents (see the introduction, page 10).

Sawmill Creek Road *(15 miles/45 minutes)*

Start back at the junction of Harbor Drive and Lincoln Street. Take Lake Street up to the stoplight and turn right onto Sawmill Creek Road. In 0.5 mile, you pass **Sitka National Cemetery**, one of the country's smallest, open to the public daily 8am–5pm. On the right is a popular bike path and the northern boundary of **Sitka National Historic Park**. Past the cemetery to your left, Indian River Road leads to Sitka's popular **Indian River Trail**. Watch carefully for pedestrians crossing the busy road on their way to the **Alaska Raptor Center** on your left. At mile 1.7, look for the sign indicating the **Mount Verstovia trailhead**, one of Sitka's loveliest and most challenging climbs.

The increasingly scenic road runs past Jamestown Bay and Thimbleberry Bay, with beautiful homes perched on the cliffs above sheltered coves and snow-studded peaks in the background. On the left at mile 3.7 is the trail to **Thimbleberry Lake** and **Heart Lake**.

Just over 4 miles along is popular **Whale Park**, with parking and restrooms. The park perches on steep cliffs above the point separating Thimbleberry and Silver bays. Even if you don't visit during prime whale-viewing time (fall and winter), you can sometimes spot an errant cetacean or two. Signage and viewing stations with telescopes are located at different levels on the cliff, connected by stairs down to the water. A hydrophone at the parking lot level allows you to listen in on any whale gossip going around. You can also listen to recordings of whale songs. Upper levels of the park are wheelchair accessible.

Continue on Sawmill Creek Road to Blue Lake Road (which leads to the lovely **Sawmill Creek Campground**). The 2-mile gravel road winds up the side of the narrow, steep Sawmill Creek canyon and offers beautiful views, as well as access to the 1-mile **Beaver Creek Trail**.

Back on the highway, just beyond the Blue Lake Road turnoff, is **Sawmill Cove Industrial Park**, site of the closed pulp mill and the open **Theobroma Chocolate Company**, whose factory can be toured; there's a store onsite (see Good Buys sidebar, page 77).

Beyond the industrial park, the road turns to gravel. It's worth negotiating the next 2 miles to Herring Cove; the drive offers more spectacular water and mountain views.

CYCLING

Seeing spread-out Sitka by bicycle makes sense, because it allows you to cover more ground in less time. You can also explore Sitka's paved road system by bicycle in fairly short order, but there's plenty to stop and see along the way.

On the **Downtown Sitka Bike Tour** (3 hours; $40/adult, $12/ages 10–12), you'll take a look at residential neighborhoods, visit Sitka National Historical Park and the Alaska Raptor Center, and finish up at Theobroma for some well-deserved chocolate. These tours by **Sitka Bike & Hike** go ahead rain or shine. Kids must be at least 4 feet 10 inches, age 10 or over, and accompanied by a parent or guardian. Advance booking is required.

Yellow Jersey Cycle Shop rents bikes, including mountain bikes ($20/half day, 10am–2pm or 2–6pm; $25/day, 10am–6pm; $30/24 hours; $100/week; $300 deposit required).

FISHING

Sitka affords superb fishing opportunities, often together with whale and sea otter sightings. Plenty of boats can be chartered for a half day or longer and, because Sitka's harbors are downtown, transportation, which is usually complimentary, doesn't add much time to the trip. **Sitka's Secrets** (500 Lincoln St #641; 907/747-5089; *www.sitkasecret.com;* $100) offers short fishing trips (about 4 hours). If you want to go out on your own, **Sitka Sound Ocean Adventures** rents three sizes of skiffs ($40/half day).

For other choices, pick up the long list of charter operators at the visitor center, or see One Day, page 91.

HIKING

Sitka's enchanting trails range from very short and easy to more than challenging. A good resource is the booklet *Sitka Trails*, put out by the Alaska Natural History Association and sold around town.

From Downtown

Combine your visit to the **Sitka National Historical Park Visitor Center** with an easy 0.75-mile hike (1–2 hours) through tall cedar, spruce, and hemlock along which are interspersed eleven cedar totem poles. Although not original (most are reproductions of poles collected by Governor John Brady for an exposition in 1904 and

No, Not that John Brown

Sitka visitors are often puzzled by a neat one-headstone graveyard on the trail from the Coast Guard Station to John Brown's Beach. So are Sitka residents. The generic name "John Brown" on the grave marker has not made identification easy. Intrigued by the mystery, local historian Robert DeArmond investigated ship logs, employment and burial records, and newspaper archives for clues, all to no avail. Karen Meizner of the Sitka Historical Society speculates that a Native is buried here, some-one given a "western" name for employment purposes. Another theory holds that the grave-stone is a ruse, a prospector—or pirate's—way of marking the site where treasure was hidden while ensuring that no one else dug it up. The mystery may never be solved, but the melancholy grave adds a haunting touch to the beau-tiful surroundings.

later carved by members of the CCC in the 1930s), the poles blend beautifully with their surroundings. When the tide is out, rocky **Totem Beach** makes for good tide-pooling and eagle watching. An additional 0.75-mile hike winds through the forest along and across the Indian River to the site of the original Kiksadi clan Tlingit fort. In summer, park rangers give free talks and lead daily walks through the park. Check at the park visitor center for times and topics. A trip to the Raptor Center and back adds 1 mile and 1 hour to the trip. Allow 50 minutes for the round-trip walk from Harrigan Centennial Hall to the national park visitor center. Taking the **Community Ride** shuttle (Mon–Fri 6:30am–6:30pm; $2/adult, $1/child, senior, disabled) from Crescent Harbor to the park's parking lot, a 15-minute ride, will save time.

For a spot of easy urban hiking, visit **Japonski Island** and **John Brown's Beach** (1–2 hours). Follow Harbor Drive to Japonski Island over the O'Connell Bridge past the airport and continue on to the Coast Guard Station. Along the way you'll have a panoramic view of Sitka Sound and, if you're lucky, Mount Edgecumbe. At the far end of the parking lot, a short (0.15-mile) trail leads to John Brown's Beach, a spot popular with families. A tiny, sandy beach is surrounded by rocky tide pools; at low tide expect to encounter a rainbow of sea stars, chitons, sea urchins, and anemones. A small grave marks the final resting place of Mr. Brown (see sidebar, opposite). To shorten the 5-mile round trip from Centennial Hall, take the **Airport Shuttle** (907/747-8443; $5 one way, $7 round trip); call for downtown pickup points and schedule.

Sitka Cross Trail (2 hours), an easy urban trail with a 100-foot elevation gain, parallels downtown Sitka and can be combined with longer hikes (such as the Gavan Hill and Indian River trails) or a trip to the Alaska Raptor Center. Access the trail from just beyond the Indian River trailhead up the Indian River Road (which runs east off Sawmill Creek Road). Although close to town, it feels wild and makes a good introduction to local flora and, sometimes, fauna. Terrain includes old-growth and new forest and peat bogs. It ends at the top of Charteris Street, northwest of town.

With a Car

Sitka's campground at Sawmill Creek has attractive wooded sites but is less-visited than better-known Starrigavan. Yet it has a lot to offer, including the moderately easy **Beaver Lake Trail** (1.5 hours, plus 40 minutes for transportation), 2 miles round trip, with 250 feet of elevation gain. The well-marked trailhead is at the campground, which is at the end of the rough, gravel-surfaced Blue Lake Road (access from Sawmill Creek Road; see Road Trips, page 83). After crossing a bridge over the creek, the trail continues uphill steeply for the first 0.25 mile, then levels off with boardwalk through muskeg and forest. The trail extends around a pretty lake framed by mountains and stocked with arctic grayling. There are several fishing platforms along the trail. This is one of the most scenic short hikes in Sitka.

Starrigavan Recreation Area

This lovely area at the north end of Halibut Point Road has several delightful, short, easy hikes. Allow 45 minutes round trip for transportation. Bears are fond of the area, which features top ursine culinary choices: salmon and berries. In 2004, a bear that had come too close to humans had to be killed. Always dispose of food and garbage in bearproof containers.

The easy 0.5-mile **Starrigavan Estuary Life Interpretive Trail** (20 minutes), with no elevation gain, is fully accessible. It starts from the Starrigavan Campground. Walk to the bird-viewing deck and the fish-viewing deck across Starrigavan Creek. In addition to self-guided trail brochures, interpretive signs are provided. Birds (great blue herons, kingfishers, sandpipers, and mergansers) congregate at the estuary, and it's a great place to watch spawning salmon in late summer.

The enchanting **Mosquito Cove Loop** (1 hour), 1.5 miles, with 100 feet of elevation gain, starts off from the Bayside Loop of the Starrigavan Campground at the end of Halibut Point Road. It winds through hemlock, spruce, and cedar forest, then emerges at Mosquito Cove and follows the shoreline east to Starrigavan Bay and the campground. It's a good choice for birders and beachcombers.

Starting from the Old Sitka boat launch site 7 miles out of town on Halibut Point Road, the 2-mile round-trip **Starrigavan Forest and Muskeg Interpretive Trail** (1 hour) is an easy walk with an elevation gain of 150 feet. It's considered accessible, but wheelchair users should be in good condition to try it. Self-guided trail brochures are usually available at the trailhead. The trail, some of which is boardwalk, winds through forest and muskeg and has good views of the Upper Starrigavan Valley and Sitka Sound. The trail ends at the fish-viewing deck on Starrigavan Creek, where it joins up with the Estuary Life trail.

The Thimbleberry Lake Trail and **Heart Lake Trail**, though connected, are quite different (2 hours, plus 30 minutes for transportation). The round trip to Thimbleberry Lake is an easy, wheelchair-accessible 0.25-mile hike with a 100-foot elevation gain to a pretty lake (30 minutes). The second trail, 1.5 additional miles round trip (not suitable for wheelchairs),

Ferry Break

Hiking the easy, scenic trails in the Starrigavan Recreation Area makes a good break for Alaska ferry passengers who want to stretch their legs. From the ferry terminal, a pedestrian walkway runs north past Old Sitka and the boat launch, then across the Starrigavan Creek estuary to lovely Starrigavan Campground. Bring your water bottle and fill it at the campground's fine artesian well. Allow 45 minutes to an hour for the round-trip walk from the terminal to the campground (about 1.4 miles). Check campground postings for information on recent bear sightings and brush up on bear-encounter rules.

with 350 feet of elevation gain, on to Heart Lake has not been maintained, can be hard to find, and is often muddy and mushy, especially around the lakeshore. You can fish for brook trout, stocked in 1928, in both lakes; bears are often encountered. From Heart Lake, the trail continues on to Blue Lake Road not far from the turnoff from Sawmill Creek Road. Reconstruction of the Heart Lake Trail is planned for 2006, which should make this a more enjoyable outing.

Guided Hikes

Tribal Tours, a **hiking and coach tour** (2.5 hours; $50), combines a drive out Halibut Point Road to the site of Old Sitka with a hike through the **Starrigavan Recreation Area**. The emphasis is on natural history, along with Tlingit history and culture. A snack, rain poncho, and transportation to and from the airport, ferry terminal, harbor, or other Sitka destination are included in the price.

Solo travelers not anxious to meet a brown bear can join free **ranger-led hikes** (times vary) on popular **Tongass National Forest Sitka trails**. Destinations include the Beaver Lake Trail, Mosquito Cove Trail, and Indian

Sitka Outfitters & Tour Operators

Alaska Classic Taxi & Tours 907/752-7020

Alaska Walking Tour Company 1302 Sawmill Creek Rd, Ste 32; 907/747-4897; jxmarie@yahoo.com

Allen Marine 907/747-8100, 888/747-8101; www.allenmarinetours.com

Baranof Wilderness Lodge 800/613-6551; www.flyfishalaska.com

Esther G Sea Taxi 215 Shotgun Alley; 907/747-6481, 907/738-6481 cell; www.home.gci.net/~egseataxi/

Fly Away Fly Shop 101 Lake St, Ste B; 907/747-7301, 877/747-7301; www.flyawayfishshop.com

Harris Aircraft 400 Airport Rd; 907/966-3050; www.harrisaircraft.com

Murray Pacific Supply 475 Katlian Ave; 907/747-3171, 800/478-3171

Sea Life Discovery Tours 221 Harbor Dr; 907/966-2301, 877/966-2301; www.sealifediscovery tours.com

Sitka Bike & Hike 877/292-5325; www.sitkaadventures.com

Sitka Charter Brokers 315 Lincoln St, Ste 210; 907/747-0616, 888/409-0616; www.sitkacharters. com

Sitka Sound Ocean Adventures 907/747-6375, 907/738-6375 cell; www.ssoceanadventures.com

Sitka's Secrets 500 Lincoln St, Ste 641; 907/747-5089; www.sitkasecret.com

Tribal Tours 429 Katlian St; 907/747-7290, 888/270-8687; www.sitkatribe.org

Yellow Jersey Cycle Shop 329 Harbor Dr, Ste 101; 907/747-6317; www.yellowjerseycycles.com

River Trail. Along the way, rangers discuss geology, flora, and fauna. Call the **Sitka Ranger District** (907/747-4225, 907/747-6671) for details.

KAYAKING

The sudden, recent closing of Baidarka Boats, a result of the owner's tragic death, has left a sad void in the Southeast Alaska kayaking community, but a couple companies are helping to fill it. **Allen Marine** has started to rent kayaks (single kayak: $50/day, $45/2–4 days, $40/more than 4 days; double kayak: $60/day, $50/2–4 days, $45/more than 4 days) through its retail operation (not its tour division); the company may offer more services, such as tours, in future. **Sitka Sound Ocean Adventures** continues to offer kayak rentals (single kayak: $30/half day; double kayak: $40/half day), and offers kayak trips (2 hours: $65/person for 1, $55/person for 2; 4 hours: $100/person for 1, $85/person for 2; group and family rates available).

ONE DAY

CYCLING

For daily bike rentals, see listing under Four Hours or Less, page 84.

FISHING

It can seem there's a fishing charter for every man, woman, and child in Sitka. Many operators offer one-day trips as well as multiday charters for salmon and halibut fishing. To sort out the choices, pick up a list at the visitor center or try **Sitka Charter Brokers**, which specializes in half- to full-day fishing charters. Expect to pay upward of $100–175 per person for 4 hours, including fishing gear, snacks, and transportation. A full day of fishing (8–10 hours) can run up to $300 with a two- or three-person minimum.

Fishing licenses can be purchased on board charter trips, and cleaning is often included. Also offered, but costing extra, are processing, packing, and shipping. **The Fresh Fish Company** (475 Katlian St; 907/747-5565) can process and ship your catch. **Fly Away Fly Shop**, tucked under the Westmark Sitka Hotel, has a broad selection of fly-fishing gear. They rent poles ($60/

day) along with rods, reels, waders, and boots, and claim to have the biggest selection of flies in Southeast Alaska.

HIKING

From Downtown

Indian River Trail (8.5 hours) is a long hike—11 miles round trip, with 700 feet of elevation gain—but it's not a difficult one; although it's a fair climb, the rise is gradual. Access is from the pumphouse and dam at the end of Indian River Road, which runs north from Sawmill Creek Road. The trail follows Indian River (fishing prohibited) and goes through rain forest and muskeg and on to attractive Indian River Falls. The last mile is the hardest. If the weather is wet, be prepared for muddy sections. If the weather is fair, there are gorgeous views, especially of the Sisters. There are also plenty of good spots for picnicking, but look out for bears—and for berries—in mid- to late summer.

Gavan Hill–Harbor Mountain Trails (8–10 hours) qualify as an in-town hike only if you are prepared to start from the end of Baranof Street and hike up stairs—a lot of stairs—which, while they replaced what was often a steep mud slide of a trail in wet weather, do involve a fair bit of exertion and a 2,500-foot elevation gain. (If you feel like chickening out, the trail meets up with the **Sitka Cross Trail** less than a mile along; take the Cross Trail west or east to get back to town.) The Gavan Hill Trail eventually links up with the Harbor Mountain Ridge Trail. The trail along Harbor Mountain Ridge runs 2 miles (2 hours one way) to Harbor Mountain Road, which—if you have a vehicle waiting—you can drive down. It's easier to hike this trail as locals do: starting from the end of partially paved Harbor Mountain Road, east off Halibut Point Road, 4 miles out of town (see Road Trips, page 82). Despite the challenges, this is a very popular trail. The views from Harbor Mountain can be worth the pain and suffering. At the road summit, a short (0.10-mile) walk brings you to the Harbor Mountain Shelter, with five attractive picnic sites set in a subalpine environment.

A woman canoes along Ketchikan's colorful Creek Street.

A clan house and pole in Totem Bight State Historical Park, Ketchikan.

Flyfishing on the shores of Sitka Sound, near Harbor Point.

Passengers admire the scenery from the deck of the MV *Taku* from Juneau to Sitka (above); St. Michael's Cathedral in Sitka (right).

Sightseers get a front-row seat to a diving humpback whale in Glacier Bay National Park & Preserve, north of Juneau.

Hikers on a ridge in Tongass National Forest overlooking Juneau (above); and flightseeing over the Juneau icefield (right).

Fort Seward in Haines, dwarfed by the dramatic Chilkat Mountains (left); kayaking near the Mendenhall Glacier, near Juneau (above).

Rafting on the Taiya River at Dyea, near Skagway (above); a train rounds a bend in the Sawtooth Mountains near Skagway (next page).

Moiety System

The Tsimshian, Haida, and Tlingit evolved matri-
lineal social structures in which their lineage
determined who raised them and whom they
could marry. Each person belonged to one of
two moieties: Eagle or Raven. A child's moiety
was always the same as the mother's. Marriage
was always to a person of the opposite moiety.
Thus, a young boy whose mother was a Raven
would have a father who was an Eagle. The boy
would be raised by the mother and her siblings
as a Raven; the males of the Raven moiety, usually the mother's brothers, would take a major
hand in raising the boy. In adulthood, the boy
would marry a woman from the Eagle moiety.
Each moiety was subdivided into clans, such as
Beaver or Killer Whale; within each clan were
houses, smaller units. The ingenious moiety
system thus avoided inbreeding and promoted
alliances between different clans.

With a Car

Mount Verstovia Trail (6 hours, plus 20 minutes for transportation) is the most difficult of popular Sitka hikes,
2.5 miles one way, with a 3,300-foot elevation gain.
Access is from Sawmill Creek Road (see Road Trips,
page 83). The trail ascends steeply through an area
that was logged by the Russians a century and a half
ago; look for their charcoal pits left over (signs posted)
about 0.25 mile along the trail. The trail switches back
and forth across the southwest flank of Mount Verstovia, and the vegetation, which starts with alder and
salmonberry thickets, changes to mountain hemlock,
then subalpine meadow, and finally to rocky alpine
vegetation. The official trail ends at the 2,550-foot level,
but the true summit (also called Arrowhead) is 800 feet
farther up. The last mile of informal trail can be quite
tricky and is not a good choice for children. Before you

attempt it, get a Sitkan to describe it to you, including the aches and soreness suffered the day after. If you're lucky enough to have a rare, blue-sky day, the view can be your reward. If not, a sense of accomplishment will have to do.

Guided Hikes

Mount Edgecumbe, a gorgeous mountain on Kruzof Island that looms across Sitka Sound like a graceful if slightly lopsided miniature Mount Fuji, can be climbed in a single day (8 hours). **Sitka Bike & Hike** leads day trips up the mountain. Hikers are taken by water taxi to Kruzof Island and guided up Mount Edgecumbe, 14 miles round trip, with 2,000 feet of elevation gain. The hike is strenuous, so a high degree of fitness is required. The trail begins through muskeg and forest. About halfway up, the path gets quite steep. The last portion of the climb includes a slog through volcanic ash above the timberline.

KAYAKING

Sitka Sound Ocean Adventures offers a **full day of guided kayaking** ($160/person for 1, $125/person for 2; group and family rates available); they also rent kayaks.

For contact information for outfitters and tour operators listed in this chapter, see sidebar on page 90.

TWO DAYS OR MORE

GENERAL OUTFITTING SERVICES

Murray Pacific Supply bills itself as "the most complete fishing and marine supply store in Southeast Alaska," and that could be right. Regardless, it's fun to wander the overflowing aisles loaded with sturdy outdoor wear and fishing and boating gear (both commercial and recreational). They provide navigational charts, fishing licenses, and more. This is a good bet for stocking up on outdoor recreation supplies of all kinds.

FISHING

For charter options, see listings under Four Hours or Less, page 85, and One Day, pages 91–92.

FLIGHTSEEING

Harris Aircraft outfits multiday charter wilderness trips.

KAYAKING

Sitka Ocean Sound Adventures designs multiday guided kayaking excursions ($180/person per day for 1 person, $150/person per day for 2, $130/person per day for 3).

For kayak rentals, see Four Hours or Less, page 91, and One Day, page 94.

HOT SPRINGS ADVENTURES

Thanks to the region's volcanic past, numerous hot springs are scattered along the Inside Passage. Baranof Island has two hot springs—Goddard Hot Springs and Baranof Warm Springs—both of which are popular destinations from Sitka. **Sitka Sound Ocean Adventures** outfits and guides trips. Not far from the hot springs are several USFS public-use cabins (see the introduction, page 15).

Seventeen miles south of town, **Goddard Hot Springs** is maintained by the city of Sitka. Long used by Alaska Natives and discovered by Russians shortly after they arrived in Sitka, the springs were used by all to cure ailments from arthritis to syphilis and were named for a Doctor Goddard who built a health resort here. The resort was purchased by the territory in 1939 and served as an adjunct to the Sitka Pioneer's Home until 1946. After thirty years of disuse, the springs were refurbished by the city of Sitka, which built cedar buildings, outhouses, and boardwalks over the squishy terrain. Two shelters each contain a "hot tub" of sorts, able to fit two to four bathers. Cold water is added to the hot water to keep temperatures fit for humans. One spring, accessed from a trail off the boardwalk, is open to the elements. Its shallow and somewhat muddy bottom makes it less popular than the others. The springs keep the ground in the vicinity on the damp side, so— along with insects in midsummer—camping here can be a challenge.

There are two Forest Service cabins in the vicinity of the springs. **Kanga Bay Cabin**, 12 miles south of Sitka (40 minutes by boat), and 8 miles north of the springs (20 minutes by boat), has water and mountain views and sleeps six. **Sevenfathom Bay Cabin** is 22 miles south of Sitka (90 minutes by boat) and 8 miles south of Goddard Hot Springs (20 minutes by boat). It sleeps up to eight and is 5 minutes by boat from the **South Baranof Island Wilderness**, which has wildlife viewing, fishing, and more recreation cabins.

Twenty miles east of Sitka across Baranof Island is the tiny village of Baranof Lake. A picturesque waterfall rushes down from the lake to Warm Springs Bay, which fronts the east side of the island. At **Baranof Warm Springs**, a public bathhouse has three rooms containing bathtubs that can be filled with hot-springs water like something out of an old western movie. More fun, but more work, are the privately owned hot-springs pools, open to the public and situated a 15-minute hike up a boardwalk and trail, with signage, from the village. Despite the lukewarm-sounding name, the springs are plenty hot—at least 104°F.

Nearby **Baranof Wilderness Lodge** (800/613-6551; *www.flyfishalaska.com*) provides board, lodging, and guided fishing packages, including transportation by air to and from Sitka. A much less-expensive option is to book the USFS **Baranof Lake Cabin**, which sleeps up to six and comes with a skiff and oars for use on the lake. However, it is *not* accessible on foot from the village; access is by boat (if you don't bring a folding kayak, a small motor for the skiff is recommended). Access is by floatplane, a 25-minute ride from Sitka.

KRUZOF ISLAND

Just a 30-minute water-taxi ride from Sitka, this island is home not only to **Mount Edgecumbe** but also four popular USFS recreation cabins. Evidence of the mountain's explosive origins are found in volcanic rock formations and beaches strewn with pumice, making for fascinating exploration. Be prepared for brown-bear encounters. Sitka black-tailed deer also reside on the island. If you plan to climb Mount Edgecumbe (see Hiking, page 94), bring maps, compass, and appropriate gear. Views from atop Edgecumbe are among the most spectacular in Southeast Alaska.

In addition to water-taxi and charter-air service, visitors can reach the island by kayak. However, surf can be treacherous here, especially at low slack tide. Only experienced or guided boaters should attempt it.

Two of the cabins are on the east side of the island. The popular **Fred's Creek Cabin**, which sleeps up to eight, is located close to the Mount Edgecumbe trailhead. Northwest of Sitka is **Brent's Beach Cabin**, with room for up to six people, a rare white-sand beach and, nearby, interesting volcanic rocks and saltwater fishing. Two cabins on the west side, **North Beach Cabin** and **Shelikof Cabin**, are a little harder to reach. Access is by air or a boat ride and 7.5-mile cross-island hike. Shelikof Cabin is especially popular, with gorgeous beaches and ocean views. See the introduction, page 15, for information on booking Forest Service cabins.

ACCOMMODATIONS

Sitka has a smattering of good lodging choices.

Built in 1939, the centrally located, remodeled **Sitka Hotel** ($; 118 Lincoln St; 907/747-3288; *www.sitkahotel. com*) has several spacious apartment suites accommodating large parties. Rooms without bath are inexpensive. Rooms in back have views of Castle Hill and the harbor. **Victoria's Restaurant** serves all meals.

Sitka Youth Hostel ($; 303 Kimshan St; 907/747-8661 June–Aug) is a fair hike from downtown, located inside a Methodist church in a residential neighborhood. Check in by 6pm. Lockout rules apply and gear can't be stored. There's a 3-day limit.

Westmark Sitka ($$$; 330 Seward St; 907/747-6241, 800/544-0970; *www.westmarkhotels.com*; &), Sitka's most luxurious hotel, has good views of Crescent Harbor and Sitka Sound. Formerly known as the Shee Atika, the hotel was recently sold but is still managed by Westmark. There are free local calls and free parking. The lounge offers casual dining; the **Raven** dining room serves upscale fare.

DINING

When it comes to dining, Sitka leads the culinary pack among Inside Passage destinations. Excellent Asian, hearty Russian, and southern Mediterranean cuisine, plus fabulous bakeries—it's all available in this compact but cosmopolitan city.

The popular Mojo's, once next door to Old Harbor Books, has evolved into a strictly behind-the-scenes kitchen for the **Backdoor Café** ($; 104 Barracks St, behind Old Harbor Books; 907/747-8856; Mon–Sat 6:30am–5pm, Sun 9am–3pm). On weekend mornings, you'll find a cross section of Sitka here, chatting over a latte and cinnamon rolls. They do a brisk lunch business, too.

Bayview Restaurant ($; 407 Lincoln St; 907/747-5440; Mon–Sat 5am–8:30pm, Sun 5am–3pm; shorter hours in winter; &), a bustling, Russian-accented restaurant, is accustomed to feeding tourists in a hurry, along with a steady stream of dedicated locals who come for the borscht and salad specials, and hearty breakfasts. Try to get a table with a view over the harbor.

Highliner Coffee Company ($; 327 Seward St; 907/747-4924; *www.highlinercoffee.com*; Mon–Sat 5:30am–5pm, Sun 7:30am–4pm), a Sitka institution (the entrance is at the back of 327 Seward), roasts its own coffee beans. Order your brew from the drive-through window or go inside for drinks, a phenomenally good bakery, computers with Internet access, and cordless phones for rent.

Little Tokyo ($$–$$$; 315 Lincoln St; 907/747-5699; Mon–Fri 11am–9pm, Sat–Sun noon–9pm) has a top-notch sushi bar as well as bento-box lunches, teriyaki and yakitori dishes, burgers, sandwiches, bagels, and pizza. The owner also operates **Kenny's Wok & Teriyaki** ($; 210 Katlian St; 907/747-5676), with lower-priced Chinese and Japanese food and the same hours.

Since 2002, proprietors Colette Nelson and Lisa Bower have offered fine Mediterranean fare in tiny **Ludvig's Bistro** ($$$; 256 Katlian Ave; 907/966-3663; Tues–Sat lunch noon–3pm, tapas 3–5pm, dinner 5–9pm); reservations are a must. A small menu is supplemented with specials. Seafood gets top billing; paella is a standout. Lavender baklava makes a good finish. Selections on the excellent wine list are barged up from the Lower 48.

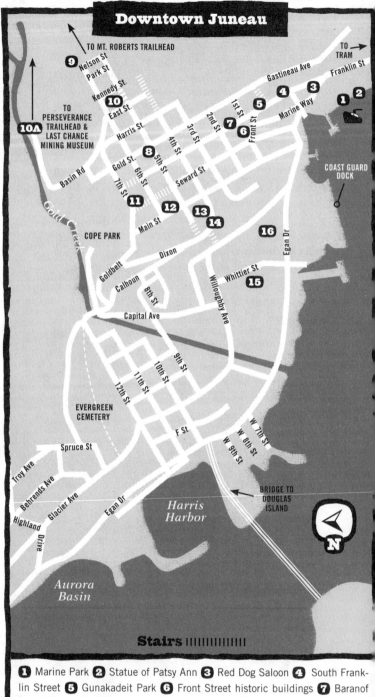

Downtown Juneau

Stairs ||||||||||||||||||

1 Marine Park **2** Statue of Patsy Ann **3** Red Dog Saloon **4** South Franklin Street **5** Gunakadeit Park **6** Front Street historic buildings **7** Baranof Hotel **8** St. Nicholas Russian Orthodox Church **9** Mount Roberts Trailhead **10** Chicken Yard Park, Kennedy Street Mineworkers Houses **10A** Side trip up Basin Road to Last Chance Mining Museum **11** House of Wickersham **12** State Capitol Building **13** Juneau–Douglas City Museum **14** State Office Building (SOB) **15** Alaska State Museum **16** Centennial Hall

Chapter 3

JUNEAU

In a perennial tie with Fairbanks as Alaska's second-largest metropolis, Juneau is the largest city in Southeast Alaska. With 60-odd miles of paved highway, suburbs, even a superstore or two, the city's frontier origins are not immediately obvious—but they're here and worth exploring. Looming 3 miles north of town is the city's biggest attraction: Mendenhall Glacier. Unlike the tidewater glaciers of Glacier Bay, Mendenhall is a valley glacier, calving into a pristine lake. Hiking and boating excursions bring visitors face to face with this fast-moving river of ice.

Juneau is the principal jumping-off point for trips to Glacier Bay National Park and Preserve, which is also reachable from Skagway and Haines. The popularity of Glacier Bay, combined with restricted access to it, has put pressure on the tourism industry to come up with additional wonders for visitors to marvel at. There's no shortage: Icy Strait is coming into its own as prime whale-watching country. Some cruise ships stop at the Tlingit town of Hoonah on Chichagof Island, while others cruise Yakutat Bay to get a glimpse of Alaska's longest tidewater glacier: Hubbard Glacier.

But first and foremost, Juneau is a government town. However counterintuitive it seems to have a state capital located so inaccessibly, Juneau works. Many attempts to move the capital have been made over the years, and all have failed. Every year, lobbyists and legislators return for a round of deal making, like the humpback whales returning to Lynn Canal.

HISTORY

Juneau's human history is a short one. The Tlingit did not settle here, although they maintained winter camps nearby at Auk Village and on Douglas Island. It took a gold strike to bring significant settlement to Juneau, nearly 20 years before the Klondike gold rush.

Guided by Chief Kowee, an Auk Tlingit from Admiralty Island, Richard Harris and Joe Juneau struck gold near the mouth of Gold Creek in 1880. Kowee helped them find bits of ore "as large as peas and beans," Harris reported. In 1882, gold was discovered on Douglas Island. Soon the Treadwell Mine and, on the mainland, the Alaska–Juneau Gold Mining Company (known as AJ) were founded. In the ensuing population boom, as the towns of Juneau and Treadwell grew, nearby Tlingit communities were displaced.

Dreams of placer gold that could be scooped up in pans by solo prospectors soon evaporated. Although modest placer strikes kept the towns humming for awhile, by the end of the decade they were played out. There was plenty of gold, but it was deep underground and thinly dispersed.

The need to get at the less-than-accessible gold spawned new techniques in mine engineering that required enormous capital investment and development. The AJ Mine excavated a tunnel 6,500 feet through solid rock to get to the ore from Last Chance Basin. Miners flooded in from across the world; at the height of the high-tech mining boom, Douglas's four Treadwell Mines employed more than 1,000. Businesses sprang up to supply the mines and miners. In 1900, a decision was made to move the territorial capital from Sitka to Juneau.

Years of extractions weakened the Treadwell Mines and the buildings that served them. In 1917 the mines experienced a catastrophic collapse, and three closed for good; the then-unemployed miners left the area. World War I and the Great Depression created economic hardship. With rising inflation and production costs, by World War II gold mining was finished in Juneau.

Territorial government, then statehood in 1959, was the new foundation of employment. By 1966 more than half of Juneau's workers labored in the government sector. The Alaska Marine Highway System, which connected Inside Passage towns in 1963, and the discovery of oil on the North Slope in 1968, revitalized the region and the state.

JUNEAU TODAY

The population of the City and Borough of Juneau today is 31,187. Primary employers are government, tourism, mining, fishing, and fish processing. Not surprisingly, in a town where government is the major employer, its citizens pay attention to politics and aren't shy about expressing their views. If you're stuck for a conversational topic in Juneau, ask residents what they think about The Road. The proposal to connect Juneau to Skagway by road has replaced the old debate about whether to move the capital from Juneau to the interior as the hot political topic. Signs and bumper stickers stake out positions pro and con, and feelings run high on both sides.

In recent years, Juneau has expanded its cruise facilities. On a single day, the city can handle five huge cruise ships plus smaller boats. Juneau strives to strike a balance between maintaining the environment that draws visitors and keeping the tourists from loving it to death. Although residents are more than grateful for the economic benefits that cruise ships and tours bring, the noise of helicopter and floatplane flightseeing tours, from dawn till dusk in summer, and up to 10,000 tourists dispersing through downtown on a busy day, take a toll. The paradox of tourism's impact on the toured is encountered across the globe. As much as anywhere in Alaska, Juneau's citizens are conscious of the need to preserve their surroundings.

GEOGRAPHY

Juneau is located on the mainland, separated from Douglas Island to the west by Gastineau Channel. Farther west, across Stephens Passage, are Admiralty, Baranof, and Chichagof islands (known locally as the "A, B, C" islands). North on the mainland, across Icy Strait from Chichagof Island, lies Glacier Bay National Park and Preserve, with the town of Gustavus southeast of the bay's entrance. Juneau is 224 miles north of Ketchikan, 93 miles south of Skagway, 90 miles southeast of Haines, and 909 miles north of Seattle.

CLIMATE

Annual precipitation is 56.47 inches—and 98.4 inches of snowfall. In the peak season, Juneau experiences average high temperatures in the low 60s (June, 61.6°F; July, 64°F; August, 62.7°F).

Average Temperatures (°F)

	May–Oct	Nov–Apr
High	57	36
Low	43	28

Average Precipitation (inches)

Jan	Feb	Mar	Apr	May	June
4.3	3.9	3.5	2.9	3.5	3.1
July	Aug	Sept	Oct	Nov	Dec
4.3	5.3	7.2	7.9	5.4	5.1

Average Hours of Daylight

Jan	Feb	Mar	Apr	May	June
6.5	8.25	10.5	13.25	15.45	17.45
July	Aug	Sept	Oct	Nov	Dec
18.25	16.5	14	11.5	9	7

ACCESS

Alaska Airlines has frequent daily flights between Juneau and Anchorage, other Alaskan cities, and mainland U.S. cities. Alaska ferries connect Juneau to other Inside Passage towns year-round (see the introduction, page 5). All major cruise lines and most small ones include Juneau on their itineraries.

VISITOR INFORMATION & SERVICES

Juneau Convention & Visitors Bureau/Tongass National Forest information, Centennial Hall Visitor Center (101 Egan Dr; 907/586-2201, 888/581-2201; *www.travel juneau.com*) has a kiosk on the cruise dock in summer, when cruise ships are in port.

Ferry Break

Ferry stopovers in Juneau can run a couple of hours—long enough to make it worthwhile to get off the boat. But because you're well north of downtown, where can you go? Get two or three companions together and rent a taxi (legions of taxis meet incoming ferries) for a jaunt to Mendenhall Glacier, where you'll have time to hike a few trails and check out the visitor center. Leave 20 minutes at the end to stop off at the Auke Bay Marina for a take-out halibut burger and blackberry shake from the Hot Bite (see Dining, page 149).

Post Office: 709 W 9th St; substation 127 S Franklin St; Mon–Fri 8am–4:30pm, Sat 8am–2pm.

Alaska Public Radio Network: Capital Community Broadcasting, KTOO 104.3 FM.

Internet Access: **Juneau Public Library** (292 Marine Wy; 907/586-5249) has free Internet access. Sign up at the front desk; time limits apply. Printouts are fifteen cents a page. They offer free wireless access to users with laptops and Internet cards. Fee access is available at **Seaport Cyber** (175 S Franklin St, upstairs in Senate Mall; Wi-Fi hot spot at AMHS terminal; 907/463-9875; *www.seaportel.com*; $5/hour). Printouts are free.

WHEELS & KEELS

Rent-a-Wreck (907/789-4111, 888/843-4111; *www.juneau alaska.com/rent-a-wreck/*) has vehicles ranging from compact cars ($34.95/day) to seven-passenger vans ($70/day) and 15-passenger vans ($100/day), with courtesy pickup and drop-off 8am–5pm daily. Although they're not auto-showroom specimens, the vehicles are sound, more than able to manage the 60 miles of road you'll be driving. **Budget Rent-a-Car** (907/790-1086, 800/796-1086) also has a Juneau outlet.

Juneau Three-Hour Must-See Itinerary

- Mendenhall Glacier (1 hour)
- Alaska State Museum (30 minutes)
- Mount Roberts Tramway (30 minutes)
- Shopping on South Franklin Street and transportation (1 hour)
- Refueling stops: **Valentine's Coffee House** (111 Seward St), **Paradise Lunch & Bakery** (245 Marine Wy)

Juneau's public transportation, **Capital Transit** (907/789-6901; daily, express service Mon–Fri; $1.50/adult, $1/under 19, free/under 6), serves downtown Juneau, Douglas Island, Mendenhall Valley, Lemon Creek, and Auke Bay. Pick up a schedule at the Centennial Hall Visitor Center. Taxi service is provided by **Capital Cab** (907/586-2772) and **Juneau Taxi** (907/790-4511). Expect to pay $30 or more, one way, from the airport to downtown, about $35 from the ferry terminal to downtown. To keep expenses down, do as locals do: share a cab. **Trans-Port Shuttle** (907/209-7433) takes passengers to and from the ferry terminal, airport, and downtown hotels for $10 one way. Call 24 hours ahead to schedule a pickup.

At present, Juneau does not have a water-taxi service. Alaska ferries serve nearby communities on Admiralty and Chichagof islands.

EVENTS

Juneau Jazz & Classics (907/463-3378; *www.jazzand classics.org*): In this annual series, musical events are held around town for 9 days at the end of May, including free brown-bag lunchtime concerts. As the name suggests, offerings span the full music spectrum from soul music to string quartets.

Celebration (Sealaska Heritage Institute; 907/463-4844; *www.sealaska.com*): Southeast nations—Tlingit, Haida, and Tsimshian—gather for 3 days in early June, in even-numbered years, to celebrate their culture with dance, parades, sports competitions, juried art shows, and sales of Native arts.

FOUR HOURS OR LESS

Juneau has an abundance of attractions within easy reach of downtown or a 20-minute ride from the ferry dock or airport. Both easy and challenging hikes start from the city center. Floatplanes take off from Gastineau Channel, just yards from the cruise-ship docks; wildlife cruises embark from Auke Bay marina a short drive from town.

WALKING TOUR

Juneau Walking Tour *(2 hours)*

This walking tour includes stairs and several steep hills. If accessibility is an issue, check out one of the guided tours (see History & Culture, page 114) by bus, trolley, or van. Interpretive signs in downtown Juneau identify historical sites and places of interest. Note that numbers on those signs do not correspond to walking-tour numbers in this guidebook. For walking tour map, see page 100.

❶ Start at the **Marine Park visitor information kiosk** open seasonally near the main cruise-ship dock. The **Juneau City Hall** is across the street, with Bill Ray's vivid mural depicting a Tlingit creation myth. In Marine Park is a statue of the *Hard Rock Miner* and a pavilion where free concerts are given.

❷ Stroll down the cruise-ship dock to the statue of the bull terrier **Patsy Ann**, brought to Juneau from Portland, Oregon, in 1929. She became known as Juneau's "official greeter" of ships; although deaf, she had an uncanny ability to sense when a boat was about to dock. During her 15 minutes of fame until her timely death in 1942, her image appeared on postcards throughout the United States. Fifty years later, a statue was commissioned and placed here. A plaque tells her quirky story.

❸ Return to Marine Park, then cross Admiral Way to a city landmark: the **Red Dog Saloon**. Touristy as they come, it's still got a lot of character, with swinging doors, sawdust on the floor, and an assortment of stuffed animals (real ones) that stare down sternly on patrons. Along with the pub grub, there is a souvenir shop.

❹ From the Red Dog Saloon, turn left and proceed up **South Franklin Street**, the heart of historic downtown Juneau. Today it's packed with art galleries and shops. As you walk up the street, note the **Lucky Lady Irish pub** on your left, once owned by Mary Joyce, a famous local character in the 1930s. Continuing up South Franklin, on your right you pass the **Senate Mall**, home to **Juneau Flyfishing** (see Juneau Outfitters & Tour Operators, pages 130–31), **Juneau Artists Gallery**, and **Seaport Cyber**. Across the street is the distinctive **Alaska Steam Laundry Building**, dating from 1901, which now houses the Emporium Mall. The **Alaskan Hotel & Bar** has a checkered past. Built in 1913 as an upscale hotel for nobs from the south to bunk at, over the years it slid downhill to brotheldom, nearly coming to an end when the building was condemned in the 1970s. It was bought and saved by a local family that set to work restoring it. Stop for a look around the ornate lobby. The bar, popular with locals and visitors, features live music, primarily blues and folk.

❺ Continue past **Mount Juneau Trading Post** and **Hearthside Books** to tiny **Gunakadeit Park** on the right, at the intersection of Front and Franklin streets. Note the painted wooden dance apron depicting the *gunakadeit*, a sea monster figuring in Tlingit legend—sightings of it are considered good luck. The *Old Witch* totem pole in the State Office Building tells the vivid story of this monster's human origins. Just past the park is the post office.

❻ Take a detour left onto **Front Street** for a look at some of Juneau's oldest historic buildings. The **Imperial Bar** started out life as the Louvre Saloon in 1891 and retains the old pressed-tin ceiling. At Front and Seward streets is the **Valentine Building**, built in 1913, whose ornate golden ceiling is intact and can be viewed in the Juneau Drug Company, which occupies the building today.

7 Returning to Franklin, continue on to the **Westmark Baranof Hotel**. Built in the late 1930s, the Baranof was intended to be an elegant showplace for the territorial capital. Despite the Depression economy, the design and decor were lavish, showcasing works by leading Alaska artists Sydney Laurence and Eustace Paul Ziegler. In 1984 arson destroyed much of the hotel, including priceless paintings. The hotel is now fully restored; visitors can view works by Laurence and Ziegler that were rescued from the fire. During the restoration, a skylight that had been plastered over during the blackouts of World War II was rediscovered, with glass etched in an art deco design. Leaving the Baranof, note the staircases up the hill to the right. Some houses in Juneau are accessible only by such stairs. At the corner of Second and Franklin is the **Observatory** bookstore.

8 Continue up Franklin to Third Street and turn right. Then go up one block to Gold Street and take a left turn up the hill. (There's a public bench at the corner of Gold and Third streets, if you need a rest.) This is a residential neighborhood of quaint homes, lovely gardens, and very narrow streets. Continue up to Fifth Street and turn left. On the right side is **Saint Nicholas Russian Orthodox Church** (326 5th St; 907/586-1023; Mon–Sat 8:30am–5pm; $2 donation). It's a small octagonal building, each side of which represents a day of the week (the eighth side is a "day for God"). With its Russian architecture, unusual shape, and gold onion dome, the 1894 cathedral is one of Southeast Alaska's most distinctive buildings. It houses antique religious icons; there is a gift shop and bookstore. Visitors are welcome at Sunday services. In keeping with tradition, worshippers stand during the service.

9 Retrace your steps along Fifth back to Gold and continue up to Sixth. Turn right. On the left, at the intersection of Sixth and Harris is the attractive **Juneau International Hostel**. Turn right on Sixth. This is the **Starr Hill** residential neighborhood of Juneau, with panoramic views. Three blocks along Sixth, past East, Kennedy, and Park streets, you'll find the well-marked **Mount Roberts trailhead** (6th and Nelson Sts). A long staircase starts the trail. Even if you aren't hiking the trail, climb the stairs and turn around for a panoramic view of downtown Juneau, water, and islands.

10 Returning on Sixth, on the left, at the corner of Kennedy and Sixth, is **Chicken Yard Park**, perched on the hillside, with a playground. A convent's chicken yard once occupied this space, as depicted by the sculpture of a nun feeding a chicken. If you have the energy, turn down Kennedy for a quick look at the historic **Kennedy Street Mineworkers houses**, built in 1913, still private residences; then return to Sixth Street and continue along Sixth to Gold Street.

10A For an optional side trip, if you continue on Gold past Seventh Street, you'll get to Basin Road, along which is the **Perseverance trailhead** and the **Last Chance Mining Museum**.

11 For the rest of this tour, go up Gold to Seventh Street and turn left. On Seventh, between Franklin and Seward, is the **House of Wickersham**. (**Note:** If time is short or if you've had your fill of hills and staircases, you can skip the rest of this tour and get downtown in minutes by taking the Franklin steps down to Franklin Street.) Across the street from the House of Wickersham, stairs descend from Seventh Street down to **Cope Park**, bordering Gold Creek, site of the city's public tennis courts, sports fields, and picnic areas.

12 Continue west on Seventh to Main Street and turn left. Follow Main down to Fourth to see the **State Capitol Building**.

13 Turn right on Fourth to take a look at the **Juneau–Douglas City Museum**, with two historic totem poles outside.

14 Walk back up Main Street to Fifth, turn left, and take the footbridge and stairs down to Willoughby Avenue. Or save yourself a bit of walking and do as locals do: go through the **State Office Building** (known affectionately—and otherwise—as the SOB), taking the elevators at the far end down to the ground floor and out onto Willoughby.

15 On Willoughby, bear right and proceed to Whittier Street. At the intersection of Willoughby and Whittier is the **Driftwood Lodge**, where you can rent bikes, and the **Fiddlehead/Di Sopra Restaurants**. Turn left on Whittier and walk to the **Alaska State Museum** grounds.

16 Continue south on Whittier and turn left onto Egan Drive. As you walk back toward the cruise dock, notice **Centennial Hall** on your left, home to the **Juneau Convention & Visitors Bureau**, with information on the area and the Tongass National Forest. Continue on Egan past Centennial Hall until you return to your starting point at the Marine Park kiosk.

HISTORY & CULTURE

Sealaska Heritage Institute (1 Sealaska Plaza; 907/463-4844; *www.sealaskaheritage.org*) is the headquarters of the Sealaska Corporation, one of Southeast Alaska's thirteen regional Native corporations, and the building is a Juneau landmark. The institute is charged with the task of preserving and celebrating the rich cultural heritage and history of the region's tribes—Haida, Tsimshian, and Tlingit. During the biennial Celebration, winning entries in the juried Native art competition are exhibited in the lobby. It's worth dropping by for 10 minutes to see what's on display. The institute also houses archives of historic films, recordings of stories and songs, and rare photographs; plans are afoot to make these available to the public.

On the eighth floor of the **State Office Building, a.k.a. SOB** (20 minutes; 333 Willoughby Ave; 907/465-2921; Mon–Fri 9am–5pm), the **Alaska State Library** is worth a look, even by those whose eyes glaze over at the word "archives." Inspect the historical photos on display, including 100-year-old photographs of Tlingit elders in full regalia. If the weather has prevented you from investigating totem poles outside, here's a chance to explore one—the weathered but beautiful **Old Witch Pole**—while you stay dry indoors. Pick up a flyer in the library that recounts the intricate Tlingit myth behind the pole. In the atrium is the impressive **Kimball Theatre Pipe Organ** (a type of organ designed to be played as an accompaniment to silent films), brought to Juneau in 1928, restored, and returned to use in 1977. When someone can be found to play it, free brown-bag noon concerts are offered on Fridays. The atrium is also the site of Juneau Jazz & Classics concerts when they're forced indoors by the weather. On sunny days, locals bring their lunch to the enormous terrace that overlooks downtown, Gastineau Channel, and cruise ships.

Above—directly above—downtown, at the top of the staircase that runs up from Fifth and Seward streets, the lovely old **House of Wickersham** (20 minutes; 213 7th St; 907/586-9001; *www.dnr.state.ak.us/parks/units/wickrshm*; admission by donation), a mansion with a view to die for, was the residence of the first judge to preside in Alaska's interior. Judge James Wickersham was elected Alaska's delegate to Congress in 1908 and served through Alaska's establishment as a territory. Bills he introduced included the one that established McKinley National Park and the first attempt at statehood in 1916. After retiring to Juneau in 1928, he put his stamp on his home, as he did on the entire state. The building contains his first-rate collections of ivory, basketry, silver spoons and tea cups, and historic documents. The house has been undergoing renovation; currently only the downstairs is open to the public. Plans are afoot to open the upper two floors. If you're lucky, you'll be offered Russian tea (in which Tang is, perplexingly, an ingredient) and cookies.

The state's Legislature meets in the fairly nondescript but official-looking **State Capitol Building** (4th and Main Sts; 907/465-3800) that dates back to 1931. Work of Alaskan artists is incorporated into the decor; the marble in the lobby comes from Prince of Wales Island, near Ketchikan. Guided tours (30 minutes; call for reservations) are offered June through August, or you can pick up a self-guided-tour brochure and check it out on your own.

Kitty-corner from the SOB is the small, charming **Juneau–Douglas City Museum** (45 minutes; 155 Seward St; 907/586-3572; *www.Juneau.org/parksrec/museum*; $3), surrounded by flowers and two impressive totem poles: **Harnessing of the Atom,** carved by Amos Wallace in 1967, and **Four Story Totem,** carved by John Wallace in 1940; inside, you can pick up flyers describing the totem poles. Your entry fee allows you a vivid look at Juneau's contribution to gold-mine engineering. The amounts of gold were vast but scattered so thinly that extracting it became a matter of high technology. A 26-minute video gives a sense of just how much creative work went into this effort.

The fine **Alaska State Museum** (1 hour; 395 Whittier St; 907/465-2901; *www.museums.state.ak.us*; mid-May–mid-Sept daily 8:30am–5:30pm, mid-Sept–mid-May Tues–Sat 10am–4pm; $5/adult, $3/adult in winter, free/under 19) first opened in 1900. Gardeners may want to start their exploration in the arboretum outside, where plantings of native flowers, shrubs, and trees are identified and their historical uses explained. Indoors, a permanent gallery features Alaska's human history, with emphasis on the state's indigenous peoples. Upstairs, a Russian American gallery highlights that exotic era of exploration and fur-hunting. Alaska's successive gold rushes and the role of gold mining are also covered. Temporary galleries feature traveling exhibits. A large display of Alaskan wildlife occupies the center of the ramp that connects the museum's two floors. The store sells Alaskana, especially books on native cultures, native arts and crafts, and children's gifts. Free guided tours are given in summer.

Plenty of tours include a visit to the **Last Chance Mining Museum** (1 hour; 1001 Basin Rd; 907/586-5338; mid-May–mid-Sept daily 9:30am–12:30pm, 3:30–6:30pm; $4), but it's easily reached on foot, too, via Basin Road. Bypass the gold panning (an unauthentic touch, considering Juneau was never a major source of placer gold). Instead, cross the metal footbridge over Gold Creek and head up the steep path to the museum. Formerly the Compress building of the Alaska Juneau Gold Mining Company, the museum is a work in progress and labor of love. As funds and time allow, the Gastineau Channel Historical Society continues to develop the museum. Inside is some of the machinery that once extracted the ore from the dirt. Train enthusiasts will enjoy the many cars assembled on the hill above the museum; the locomotives and cars that got the miners in and out of the mines are displayed in rusty majesty.

You can complement a visit to the Last Chance Mining Museum with the underground **Juneau Gold Mine Tour** (3 hours; $59/adult, $35/under 13), offered by **AJ Mine/Gastineau Mill Enterprises** (907/463-5017; *jharmon@gci.net*). The tour gives you a firsthand look at this fascinating world, including demonstrations of equipment. Hard hats are provided.

Founded in 1979, the excellent **Perseverance Theatre** (914 3rd St, Douglas; 907/364-2421; *www.perseverance theatre.org*), based in Douglas, has premiered more than fifty theatrical plays, including Pulitzer Prize winners, and produced innovative pieces such as an all-Native staging of *Macbeth*, set in Tlingit culture. Ticket prices are kept low (about $25), with some performances designated "pay as you can" to encourage attendance.

Shrine of Saint Therese (see Road Trips, page 123).

GUIDED TOURS

Juneau is big and sprawling enough to require wheels to reach some of its best attractions. If you don't have a vehicle, there are several easy ways to create your own customized road trip.

Juneau Trolley Car Company has red trolleys that shuttle around Juneau in a narrated loop tour (30 minutes; $14/adult, $10.50/under 12). A ticket buys you a 1-day pass, good for unlimited rides, and can be purchased from the conductor. Stops include the cruiseship docks, two of which—the Franklin and floating docks—are a fair hike from downtown, the shopping district, both museums, Saint Nicholas Church, and the Mount Roberts tramway.

If your primary goal is to see heaving ice, the distinctive sky-blue buses of **Mendenhall Glacier Transport** can get you there; they run to and from Mendenhall Glacier daily in summer 9am–6:30pm ($5 one way). Buses start at the cruise dock. MGT also offers a combination tour of Juneau (2.5 hours; $26) that includes a 45-minute visit to the glacier and a 40-minute stop at the Macauley Salmon Hatchery. **Last Frontier Tours** offers tours (2.5 hours; $30) of Juneau with stops at Mendenhall Glacier, as well as buses direct to the glacier ($5 each way).

Juneau Taxi & Tours has seven-passenger vans that can be booked by groups (up to 4 hours; $55/hour). With a full complement of passengers, each pays less than $8 an hour, beating any commercial alternative. **Capital Cab** (907/586-2772) has a similar deal. You can either leave the destination up to your knowledgeable driver or pick and choose where you want to go. Ferry passengers often band together and make full use of their 2- or 3-hour stopover this way (see Ferry Break sidebar, page 105).

SHOPPING

Art

ALASKA NATIVE ARTISTS: Most of Juneau's excellent locally owned galleries are in the downtown historic district, but the superb **Raven's Journey Gallery** (435 S Franklin St; 907/463-4686) is a notable exception. Hidden among the generic emporiums at the south end of town, this gallery has a comprehensive assortment of Native Alaskan work, from mammoth-ivory carvings and Yupik spirit masks to jewelry, basketry, and handmade felt dolls in Tlingit dancing regalia. Downtown, the **Mount Juneau Trading Post** (151 S Franklin St; 907/586-3426) is a gold mine of coastal Native art and carvings—including argillite, a black stone related to soapstone available only from the Queen Charlotte Islands. Upstairs, the **Gallery of the North** (147 S Franklin St; 907/586-9700) sells fine art in a variety of media, sculpture, jewelry, rugs, and more, mostly from Alaskan and northern Canadian artists. Prices range from moderate to staggering.

JUNEAU ARTISTS: The **Decker Gallery** (233 S Franklin St; 907/463-5536) is the principal downtown outlet for the work of popular Juneau artist Rie Muñoz. Fans of her work may want to visit the **Rie Muñoz Gallery** (2101 Jordan Ave; 907/789-7411) near the airport. The **Juneau Artists Gallery** (175 S Franklin St; 907/586-9891) is an artists' cooperative whose members staff the shop and produce the art, including traditional crafts, such as Russian egg painting, and beaded jewelry, handweaving, etchings, ceramics, and art glass. Across the street and upstairs, **Wm Spear Design** (174 S Franklin St, Ste 201; 907/586-2209) sells quirky enameled pins and zipper pulls made by Juneau's Bill Spear. Here's where to buy a tiny enameled kidney or pancreas, broccoli spear, octopus, squid, and just about every breed of dog and sportfish. On Front Street, just off Franklin, **Annie Kaill's** (244 Front St; 907/586-2880) is a craft gallery with a good representation of Alaskan artists.

Books

Hearthside Books (Front & Franklin Sts; 907/586-1726) is stuffed with Alaskana, maps, and travel resources. Its Nugget Mall location (907/789-2750) is bigger, with a large selection of fiction and children's books. For pre-owned titles, check out **Rainy Day Books** (113 Seward St; 907/463-2665), which stocks new titles, too. By far the most fun for browsers is the **Observatory** (200 N Franklin St; 907/586-9676), where you can easily spend an hour or more in conversation with its fascinating owner, Dee Longenbaugh, whose passion is maps and Alaskan history. For those on a budget, **Friends of the Juneau Public Libraries** (downtown library; and Airport Shopping Center, Glacier Hwy and Shell Simmons Dr) has eclectic offerings starting at twenty-five cents. Find books on local flora and fauna at the **Alaska Native History Association Bookstore** at Mendenhall Glacier Visitor Center and the **Gastineau Guiding Nature Center** on Mount Roberts, and books on Alaskan history at the **Alaska State Museum**.

Clothing & Sundries

Antique hunters can get their fix at **Déjà Vu** (2 Marine Wy, Ste 1022; 907/463-6700). The **Foggy Mountain Shop** (134 S Franklin St; 907/586-6780) is downtown Juneau's purveyor of outdoor wear and gear, sleeping bags, backpacks, and boots, and has friendly, knowledgeable staff. It's open year-round. The suburban malls are your best bet for nonsouvenir clothing. Try the **Mendenhall Center**, accessed from the Mendenhall Loop Road off Egan Drive, and the **Airport Shopping Center** and **Nugget Mall**, both near the airport and accessed from the Old Glacier Highway. At the Nugget Mall is **Nugget Alaskan Outfitter** (8745 Glacier Hwy; 907/789-0956, 800/478-6848), a large store in which outdoor sports are well represented, including big and small names in outdoor retail.

Fred Meyer (8181 Old Glacier Hwy; 907/789-6500) and **Costco** (5225 Commercial Blvd; 907/780-6740), while lacking in local color, carry everyday and outdoor wear, as well as camping and outdoor gear.

Good Buys

Making beer is an old Alaska tradition; in 1903, four breweries were operating in the Juneau vicinity, but the tradition died out until the **Alaskan Brewing Company** (5429 Shaune Dr; 907/780-5866; *www.alaskanbeer.com)* opened in 1986. Today one of many thriving Alaska microbreweries, it offers seven brews from light to dark, including ales, stouts, and a smoked porter. Their beers have collected awards, including two at the 2004 Great American Beer Festival for Alaskan ESB and Alaskan Smoked Porter. You can sample these and other beers on a brewery tour (30 minutes; May–Sept daily 11am, 4:30pm, winter daily Thurs–Fri; free) that offers the usual primer on brewing and a chance to sample the finished product. Beer is not the most portable of purchases, but the brewery will gladly put you in touch with distributors that can help you order it. There's also a gift shop.

Food & Drink

Taku Smokeries (550 S Franklin St; 800/582-5122; *www. takustore.com*) sells and ships smoked and dried salmon, halibut, and salmon caviar. In addition to fudge, the **Alaskan Fudge Company** (195 S Franklin St; 907/586-1478, 800/323-8343) sells chocolate bears, salmon, and sea otters, as well as ice cream for which long lines form on hot days. For a more mundane grocery experience, head to **Alaskan & Proud Market**, a.k.a. the A&P (in Foodland Shopping Center, 615 W Willoughby Ave; 907/586-3101), which covers all the bases. The shopping center has a pharmacy, a liquor store, and other services. For organic and whole foods, try **Rainbow Foods** (224 4th St; 907/586-6476). Fred Meyer and Costco also sell groceries (see Clothing & Sundries, page 116).

NATURE

Juneau has no zoo, but it does have a dynamite small **aquarium** at the **Macaulay Salmon Hatchery** (45 minutes; 2697 Channel Dr; 907/463-4810, 877/4632486; *www.dipac.net*; summer Mon–Fri 10am–6pm, Sat–Sun 10am–5pm; $3), and it's well worth a visit. Its select denizens include adorable Pacific spiny lumpsuckers, looking like extras from *Finding Nemo*, and the decorated warbonnet, a fish with a face that only a mother could love. The brisk hatchery tour introduces visitors to the salmon's five- to seven-year cycle (depending on salmon species); describes the mercy killing of the dying salmon that return to the hatchery to spawn; and demonstrates how milt and eggs are blended in 5-gallon drums to create the next generation of salmon fry that are then released into the water. Some tours include the hatchery and aquarium, or you can take Capital Transit, drive, or bike here.

Get a comfortable introduction to the region's temperate rain forest flora while you ride in one of the golf carts that navigate the steep trails of the 51-acre mountainside **Glacier Gardens** (1 hour; 7600 Glacier Hwy; 907/790-3377; *www.glaciergardens.com*; May–Sept daily 9am–6pm; $17.95/adult, $12.95/child). The gardens are landscaped with rhododendrons, azaleas, Japanese maples, and shrubs, set among ponds, waterfalls, lagoons, and lush evergreens. Planters fashioned from giant upturned spruce roots are stuffed with colorful annuals. Admission includes the tour by golf cart, but some prefer to hike the steep trails up Thunder Mountain where, if the weather cooperates, there's a terrific view of Gastineau Channel and Douglas and Admiralty islands. Tour guides are knowledgeable about the flora, wild and domestic. Some locals treat the gardens like a health club and jog the trails. A popular spot for weddings, the gardens have a gift shop and café, with plenty of seating and parking.

The only road-accessible glacier in Southeast Alaska, the handsome blue **Mendenhall Glacier** (1.5 hours) feeds into Mendenhall Lake, surrounded by lush forest, a salmon-bearing river, and plenty of wildlife. The glacier is moving fast and melting faster. Trails with interpretive signage and visitor center displays point out the rapid changes this area is undergoing, where land once covered by ice is rebounding and supporting plant and animal life. Many tours spend as little as an hour here, but you could just as easily spend all day exploring the trails and **visitor center** (8465 Old Dairy Rd; 907/789-6640; *www.fs.fed.us/r10/tongass/districts/mendenhall*; daily May–Sept 8am–6:30pm, Oct–April Thurs–Fri 10am–4pm, Sat–Sun 9am–4pm; $3). Take Glacier Highway north to Mendenhall Loop Road; turn right and continue to the visitor center. You can reach the park from downtown on the blue MGT bus ($10 round trip); or if you have time, take a Capital Transit bus ($1.50 one way) to Glacier Spur Road and walk the final mile up the road to the visitor center.

The visitor center gets crowded, but there are plenty of restrooms and hardworking Tongass National Forest staff to direct traffic. In inclement weather you can still enjoy the glacier while staying comfortably warm and dry inside; floor-to-ceiling picture windows showcase the main event. In the exhibit hall, interactive displays with videos add up to a mini science center. A theater shows a 15-minute film on the glacier. The large bookstore sells books, videos, DVDs, and recordings of all things Mendenhall and Southeast, including an excellent assortment of educational materials for kids. To leave the hordes behind, just head out on one of the less-traveled trails (see Hiking, page 126). If your visit is short, take the half-mile, easy **Photo Point Trail** (20 minutes) to get a good look at the glacier across the lake. It's wheelchair accessible and paved, with benches.

Flightseeing

When time is at a premium, the most compact flightseeing option is a **flyover of the Juneau icefield** (up to 1 hour, plus up to 1 hour for transportation). Alaska Seaplanes and Wings of Alaska offer flyover tours; expect to pay from $100 to $150 per person.

The helicopter version of an **icefield tour** usually includes one or more landings and a thrilling opportunity to hike on the ice (1–2 hours, plus up to 2 hours for transportation), available from Coastal Helicopters, Era Helicopters, North Star Trekking, and TEMSCO Helicopters. Prices range from $185 to $300. Coastal and Era also offer **icefield dogsled tours** with professional mushers. Prices start at $389.

Wings of Alaska offers a trip to **Taku Wilderness Lodge** (3.5 hours; multiple daily departures in summer; $145/adult, $115/under 12) that combines an icefield flyover with a landing at this historic lodge in Taku Inlet and an outstanding salmon bake. While you eat, you'll be regaled with tales of the lodge's interesting history. It was once owned by entrepreneur, musher, and sled-dog raiser Mary Joyce (whose photo is posted in Juneau's Lucky Lady pub, which she once owned). Today the lodge is owned by Ken Ward, the founder of a local airline, Ward Air. When you're stuffed, stroll the grounds and explore two short trails. In early summer, mosquitoes are abundant; cover up and bring bug juice. The short return flight is via Taku Inlet, a meandering fjord with beautiful scenery.

In addition to flightseeing, floatplane companies arrange charters for sightseeing or fishing fly-ins. **Wings of Alaska** and **Alaska Seaplane Service** offer regular and charter service to nearby communities, including Tenakee Springs, Angoon, Gustavus, Hoonah, Pelican, Elfin Cove, Haines, and Skagway.

Wildlife Tours

Lynn Canal and the waters around Juneau teem with marine mammals. All summer, humpback whales, which have made the long swim north from Baja, California and Hawaii, feed here. Seeing these enormous mammals breach and watching their graceful backs arcing through the waters is a truly awesome experience. They aren't as showy as killer whales; their dorsal fins are smaller and their brownish-gray color doesn't stand out like the brilliant black and white of the orcas, but there is something majestic about the whale's slow movements and elegant flukes that show above the water as it prepares to dive. Along with humpbacks are occasional orca pods, as well as Steller sea lions and harbor seals. Dall's porpoises, like miniature orcas, sometimes surf on boats' bow waves. Bald eagles are a common sight, lining trees along the shore and in the air.

According to experienced tour operators, whales come to know them personally and are able to pick out their boats and pay a visit. In any event, whale watching today is almost a science. Operators know where the animals are and share that information with other operators, working to ensure that everyone sees the wildlife. Boats may stay out on the water a little longer if there is something to be seen. If a pod of orcas decides to show off, you might return later than planned. If you're on a tight schedule, it's wise to allow up to 30 minutes leeway. Many fishing-charter operators also set up customized whale-watching and nature cruises for as many passengers as their boats will accommodate (see fishing listings under One Day, page 137).

You won't find **Orca Enterprises** in any shore excursion brochures, but they offer popular **whale-watching excursions** (3.5 hours; 9:30am, noon, 3:30pm, 6pm; $105/adult, $79/ages 6–12, $49/under 6) that include transportation from your cruise ship or hotel. Four trips a day are offered, which include snacks and beverages; one of their boats accommodates wheelchair users.

Equipped with five jet boats each carrying eighteen to thirty-five passengers, **Dolphin Tours** does a good job of bringing you to the whales (3 hours; $99.75/adult, $78.75/ages 2–12, free/under 2). They guarantee at least 2 hours on the water. Round-trip motorcoach transportation from anywhere in Juneau is included.

ONE OF A KIND

You can't miss the two red tram cars that run all day between the waterfront and up 2,000 feet to **Mount Roberts**. Although the price may seem as steep as the 6-minute ride, it buys unlimited trips all day, and there are attractions and trails to explore at the top (1–2 hours). Unless the weather is truly awful, summit views are extraordinary; behemoth-sized cruise ships look like bath toys. The tramway complex houses a full-service restaurant, a large gift shop, and a theater, which shows a free film on Native culture. Like the tram, it's owned by the Native Goldbelt Corporation (490 S Franklin St; 907/463-3412, 888/461-8726; *www. alaska.net/~junotram/*; May–Sept daily 9am–9pm; $21.95/adult, $12.60/ages 6–12).

In a building nearby, Gastineau Guiding Company operates a **nature center** with an excellent gift and book shop and a smaller theater showing nature films. They also offer guided walks along the network of trails that explore the alpine meadows, which are often snow covered well into June. Wildlife include ptarmigan, eagles, ravens, hoary marmots, mountain goats, and Sitka black-tailed deer. The **Juneau Raptor Center** usually has a bald eagle or two on display. If you hike up the Mount Roberts Trail, you can take the tram down ($5).

Juneau's indoor climbing gym, just south of downtown and open year-round, the **Rock Dump** (2 hours; 1310 Eastaugh Wy; 907/586-4982; *www.rockdump.com*; day pass $10/adult, $8/under 14) has a variety of features to climb. They offer classes and rent climbing gear for all ages, although to belay you must be 14 or older.

ROAD TRIPS

Glacier Hwy/Juneau Veterans Memorial Hwy
(80 miles/2.5 hours)

This scenic drive has many turnouts offering views of Mendenhall Glacier, Shelter Island, Lynn Canal, and the Chilkat Mountains. The road crosses rivers and trailheads. Expect to travel at between 30 and 40 mph.

As you head north from downtown, the name of the road you're on will change several times: South Franklin becomes Marine Way, which becomes Egan Drive for 9 miles, then Glacier Highway, and finally Juneau Veterans Memorial Highway. Collectively, they are known as Highway 7.

As you head northwest, Gastineau Channel, to your left, becomes increasingly shallow. At mile 3.8 is the **Macaulay Salmon Hatchery** (see Nature, page 118). North and east is the suburb of Lemon Creek, where you'll find Costco, accessed from the Old Glacier Highway that runs roughly parallel to the main highway.

Two miles north of the hatchery is the **Mendenhall Wetlands State Game Refuge**. At mile 6 there is a wildlife observation platform on the west (left) side of the highway. Look for birds, including bald eagles. Two miles farther north, past Fred Meyer at mile 8.5, is the junction with Old Glacier Highway, which leads west to the **Nugget Mall** and airport, as well as the **Rie Muñoz Gallery** and the **Guesthouse Inn**, all within a few blocks.

From mile 9.3 of Highway 7, the Mendenhall Loop Road leads, via the Glacier Spur Highway, to **Mendenhall Glacier Visitor Center**, 3.4 miles from Highway 7. If you stay on the Loop Road you'll rejoin Highway 7 at mile 12.1. Access to **Mendenhall Lake Campground** and the **Skaters Cabin Picnic Area** is from the loop road.

On Highway 7 at mile 10 is a **Mendenhall Glacier viewpoint** with parking and the trailhead for the **Kaxdigoowu Heen Dei/Mendenhall River Trail**. At mile 11.4 is **Auke Lake**, definitely worth a stop, with a parking area. Salmon spawn here in mid- to late summer. Just beyond it is the campus of the University of Alaska Southeast.

At mile 12.4 is the village of **Auke Bay**. A number of boat tours, as well as the **Gustavus ferry**, depart from here. This is also home to the popular fish-and-chips hangout the **Hot Bite**. At mile 13.8 is the **Alaska ferry terminal**.

Past Auke Bay, traffic and human habitations thin out and the landscape becomes wilder. At mile 14.7 is the turnoff for the 2-mile loop road that runs along the **Auke Village Recreation Area**. At mile 18.8, **Inspiration Point** has some of the highway's best views. There are several turnouts.

At mile 22.5 the **Shrine of Saint Therese of Lisieux** (April–Sept daily 8:30am–10pm; free), patron saint of Alaska, is open to the public. There is a large parking area and public restrooms. Follow the trail down to the waterfront past the gift shop and lodge; a causeway leads to a small island with an old stone chapel dating from 1938, still in use and also open to the public. On the mainland is a small reproduction of a medieval European labyrinth laid out in sand and a large and unusual garden, called the "columbarium," containing plants of biblical significance.

At mile 23.5 is the **Peterson Lake trailhead**. Watch for bears fishing for salmon in Peterson Creek. From a turnout at mile 26.5, a gravel road leads to the **Herbert Glacier trailhead**. The river is scenic and makes a good place to stop and stretch. At mile 27.7 is **Eagle Beach State Park**. There is plenty of parking along the highway. If you drive into the park, you'll be subject to day-use fees ($5). The park recently has been expanded and upgraded, and is wheelchair accessible.

Stop at the turnout at mile 32.2 to get a look at the site of one of Alaska's greatest maritime disasters: the sinking of the SS *Princess Sophia*. The ship was carrying 353 passengers—many of them leading citizens of northern communities—and crew from Skagway bound to Vancouver, British Columbia, when it went aground on October 24, 1918. Because weather conditions made a rescue operation dangerous, rescue ships decided to wait out the stormy night to attempt it. By morning, the ship had sunk; there were no survivors.

Along the last 8 miles of the highway, vistas open up, and for the first time you can see for miles, a rare opportunity to experience the sheer size of the wilderness that surrounds Juneau. At mile 38 is the **Point Bridget trailhead** and **Point Bridget State Park**. The road ends at mile 39.5 at **Echo Cove**, where there is a large parking area and boat launch.

North Douglas Hwy *(26 miles/50 minutes)*

This scenic drive features glacier viewpoints and several easy roadside hikes. Head north on Egan Drive and take the Juneau-Douglas Bridge across Gastineau Channel. Turn right onto the North Douglas Highway.

At mile 7, Eaglecrest Road runs 5.2 miles up to the **Eaglecrest Ski Area**. There are several trails along the way; it's a popular, if challenging, route for cyclists. During the summer, kayak, jet ski, and other watersport trips depart from the **boat launch** at mile 9.5.

The scenery becomes increasingly wild as the highway turns north. You'll reach **False Outer Point** at mile 11.4. From the road, a short trail runs down to the rocky beach, along which you can walk a fair way. At miles 12 and 12.3 are the **Rainforest Trail** and **Outer Point Trail**, respectively. The road ends abruptly at mile 13.

South Douglas Hwy *(4.6 miles/30 minutes)*

Not really a highway at all, this road is reached by heading north on Egan Drive and taking the Juneau-Douglas Bridge across Gastineau Channel, then turning left instead of right after crossing the bridge. You'll run through the attractive suburb of Douglas (2,000 residents). At the south end, downtown Douglas, is the **Perseverance Theatre** and **Savikko Beach Park**, with access to the **Treadwell Mine Historic Trail**.

Thane Road *(11 miles/30 minutes)*

If you've rented a car and want to get your money's worth by driving all of Juneau's highways, you might as well check out the road south of town. Take Highway 7 south (the name changes to Thane Road) past the cruise docks and Rock Dump climbing gym on to mostly residential neighborhoods. Four miles along the road is the **Sheep Creek trailhead**. At 4400 Thane Road is the **Thane Ore House Salmon Bake** (907/586-3442; *home.gci. net/~tohalaska/*; May–Sept daily 11:30am–4pm, 4–9pm). They serve lunch and dinner, with a dinner revue June through August (7pm). The road ends at Bishop Point.

For contact information for outfitters and tour operators listed in this chapter, see sidebar on pages 130–31.

CANOEING, KAYAKING & RAFTING

You can gaze at Mendenhall Glacier from the waters of beautiful Mendenhall Lake just as aboriginal peoples first did, in a traditional 12-seater Tlingit canoe. **Mendenhall Lake canoe trips** (3.5–4 hours; $95) offered by **Auk Ta Shaa Discovery** include native storytelling, gear, and a hearty snack.

Alaska Travel Adventures offers **sea kayaking tours** (3.5 hours; $79/adult, $53/under 13). Paddle the waters off Douglas Island in two-person kayaks and point your camera back at the mainland. Spot sea mammals, herons, and eagles. Transportation and instruction are included in the price.

Mendenhall River Raft trips (3.5–4 hours) start on placid Mendenhall Lake, with close-up views of the glacier, then head down the Mendenhall River, with some modest rapids (Class II and III). Transportation, gear, and snacks are provided. Participants must weigh more than 40 pounds. Native-owned **Auk Nu Tours** offers this river float trip (4 hours; $99.75/adult, $66.49/under 13; May–Sept daily, departures 8am, 11:30am, 3pm). **Alaska Travel Adventures** has a similar float trip (3.5 hours; $99/adult, $66/under 13).

For kayak rentals, see listing under Two Days or More, page 141.

CYCLING

Juneau has an active cycling community but as vehicular traffic has grown, cyclists have been getting squeezed. Bikes are forbidden on Egan Drive, so you'll need to take the Old Glacier Highway to reach **Mendenhall Glacier** and points north. The road south of town is less traveled, with wider shoulders. Douglas Island is also a popular destination (the Douglas bridge has wide shoulders for cyclists); head north on the **North Douglas Highway** for 13 miles of great views and beach access. Or try the **Eaglecrest Hill Climb**: turn onto the Eaglecrest Road; it's a 5-mile uphill climb to the resort, closed in summer. See below for bike rentals.

Cycle Alaska, located in Lemon Creek, offers a 10-mile bike tour (3.5 hours; $45) along the beach from the **Mendenhall Wetlands to Outer Point**. The trip includes a snack, time for beachcombing, and, if you're lucky, the sight of spawning salmon. Mendenhall Glacier is even more impressive from a distance.

Cycle Alaska also rents bikes ($15/half day; $30/full day). In addition to their tours (see above and listing under One Day, page 137), they arrange custom outings and provide trailhead drop-offs. In downtown Juneau, the **Driftwood Lodge** (435 Willoughby Ave; 907/586-2280, 800/544-2239; *www.driftwoodalaska.com*) rents bikes ($15/half day; $25/full day).

FISHING

Compared with other Inside Passage destinations, Juneau is not a fishing mecca. Nonetheless, it has an abundance of charter fishing choices. Charter operators are well aware of time pressures facing visitors on tight schedules, and many have half-day tours. **Juneau Sportfishing and Sightseeing** and **Orca Enterprises**, both based in Auke Bay, offer **fishing charters** (4 hours).

For fly-fishing and ocean charters, see listing under One Day, page 137.

HIKING

Juneau offers abundant scenic trails for all fitness levels. Many are within easy walking distance of downtown and lead to breathtaking views of channels and islands. Two resources are especially helpful to hikers: Mary Lou King's excellent guide, *90 Short Walks Around Juneau* (Taku Conservation Society/Trail Mix, Inc.), is highly recommended and sold in every Juneau bookstore. The *Juneau Area Trails Guide* (USFS) is a detailed trail map, widely available.

From Downtown

Even if you lack the stamina to climb **Mount Roberts**, you can access several miles of well-marked alpine trails, easy to moderately difficult, from the top of the tramway. Stop by the Gastineau Guiding Nature Center, where you can view a video of local fauna and flora in the Marmot Theatre, hear a naturalist talk, or purchase an audio trail guide. Knowledgeable staff can advise you on trail conditions (trails can be covered in snow well into June). Allow 90 minutes; for information, see One of a Kind, page 121.

With a Car

The tranquil **Kaxdigoowu Heen Dei/Mendenhall River Trail** (45 minutes, plus 45 minutes for transportation; &.) starts from the parking lot at the Mendenhall Glacier viewpoint at mile 10 of Highway 7. The 2.1-mile, paved trail runs through meadow once used to pasture cows and affords beautiful glacier views. It leads to Montana Creek, for which the trail ("Very Clear Water Trail" in Tlingit) is named.

Attractive **Eagle Beach State Park** (45 minutes, plus 1.5 hours for transportation; 907/465-4563; $5 day-use fee; &.), at mile 28.5 of the Glacier Highway, is a work in progress. In addition to the new campground with sixteen sites (some wheelchair accessible), there are accessible trails and telescopes for viewing the abundant wildlife in the estuary here, into which the Eagle River flows from Eagle Glacier. On a good day, there are spectacular views of the Chilkat Mountains and Lynn Canal and—sometimes—the humpback whales that spend their summers fishing here.

Auke Village Recreation Area

North of town at mile 14.6 of the Glacier Highway is the site of the **Auk Kwan Tlingit winter camp** (1–2 hours, plus 1 hour for transportation), abandoned when an influx of white settlers forced residents to relocate to Douglas Island. All traces of the settlement have disappeared, but the oddly smooth pebble beach is believed to be the work of Tlingit slaves forced to clear it of big boulders (see photographs of the village at the state library). To access the trails and beach, take the 2-mile loop road from the Glacier Highway and park along the side of the road. Notice the impressive, mysterious lone totem pole on the side of the road away from the water. One of the Civilian Conservation Corps projects that restored and re-created totem poles in Southeast Alaska (including those at Totem Bight State Park in Ketchikan), it was carved by Francis St. Clair in 1941.

Trails, several wheelchair accessible, lead through temperate rain forest, with side trails down to covered picnic shelters at the beach. A fairly rough trail leads to **Point Louisa**. If you can, visit at low tide; this is one of the best spots in the Juneau area for tide-pooling. With luck, you can spot sea urchins, snails, anemones, multicolored sea stars, and seaweeds. And keep your eye on the time and tide (we know whom they don't wait for) so that you don't find your way back cut off. This is a popular excursion, and on a fine day, parking is hard to come by. The USFS **Auke Village Campground** has parking, as well as twelve campsites, picnic tables, toilets, and water. There's a pretty picnic area at **Lena Beach**.

Douglas Island

Starting from Sandy Beach in downtown Douglas's Savikko Park, the easy loop **Treadwell Mine Historic Trail** (1 hour, plus 45 minutes for transportation) takes you to the site of the mine cave-in of 1917. The 2-mile trail has a 40-foot elevation gain.

Mountainous Douglas Island has the Inside Passage's only commercial downhill ski runs: **Eaglecrest Ski Area**. Ski area trails (time varies, plus 1 hour for transportation) are open for hiking in summer. Some feature rough terrain, so be sure to check out condi-

The Treadwell Mine Disaster

At the turn of the twentieth century, Douglas Island's four Treadwell gold mines were engineering marvels, using 900 enormous stamps—each weighing close to half a ton—to crush 5,000 tons of rock a day. Gold was extracted using an ingenious system of mercury-covered copper plates that trapped gold particles, which were then washed and screened out from the ore. The mines dug down more than 2,800 feet. At the time of the cave-in, 10 million tons of rock had already been extracted below tidewater. Early signs in 1916 of an impending cave-in were ignored. Then in April 1917, the "natatorium," an enormous indoor swimming pool used for miner R&R, began to crack and, on April 20, suddenly dropped 5 feet. Within hours, three of the mines collapsed and flooded, but the 350 on-site workers escaped unharmed. The mines closed for good, while the one remaining mine struggled on. Periodic attempts were made to resuscitate the mines in later years, but eventually they were abandoned. Gold mining in Juneau, always expensive and technically challenging, was no longer profitable. World War II and rising production costs led to the closure of the last Treadwell Mine in 1944.

tions first, and bring a map along. Plans are afoot to develop some trails.

The **Rainforest Trail** and **Outer Point Trail** (1.25 hours each, plus 1.25 hours for transportation) are close together and run parallel from the North Douglas Highway to the water. The easy Rainforest Trail starts at mile 12 and is 2.5 miles round trip. Maintained by

Juneau Outfitters & Tour Operators

Above & Beyond Alaska 907/364-2333; www.beyondak.com

Adventure Bound Alaska 907/463-2509, 800/228-3875; www.adventureboundalaska.com

Air Excursions LLC 907/697-2375, in Alaska 800/354-2479; www.airexcursions.com

Alaska Boat and Kayak 907/586-8220, 907/789-6886; www.juneaukayak.com

Alaska Discovery 907/780-6226, 800/586-1911; www.akdiscovery.com

Alaska Fly 'n' Fish Charters 907/790-2120; www.alaskabyair.com

Alaska Seaplane Service 907/789-3331, in Alaska 800/478-3360; www.akseaplanes.com

Auk Ta Shaa Discovery 907/790-4990

Auke Bay Sportfishing & Sightseeing 907/789-2562, 800/586-6945; www.experiencealaska.com

Bear Creek Outfitters 907/789-3914; www.flyfishsoutheast.com

Coastal Helicopters 907/789-5600, 800/789-5610; www.coastalhelicopters.com

Cycle Alaska 5454 Jenkins Dr; 907/780-2253

Deep Blue Fishing Charters 907/697-2343, 866/510-2800; www.alaskasportfish.net

Dolphin Tours 800/770-3422; www.dolphintours.com

Driftwood Lodge 435 Willoughby Ave; 907/586-2280, 800/544-2239; www.driftwoodalaska.com

Era Helicopters 907/586-2030, 800/843-1947; www.flightseeingtours.com

Fjord Flying Service 907/697 2377

Four Seasons Marine 907/790-6671, 877/774-8687; www.4seasonsmarine.com

Gastineau Guiding 1330 Eastaugh Wy, Ste 2; 907/586-8231; www.stepintoalaska.com

Glacier Bay Sea Kayaks 907/697-2257

Goldbelt Auk Nu Tours 907/586-8687, 800/820-2628; www.goldbelttours.com

Goldbelt Tours 907/789-4183, 800/478-3610;
www.goldbelttours.com

Juneau Flyfishing Goods 175 S Franklin St;
907/586-3754; www.juneauflyfishinggoods.com

Juneau Sportfishing & Sightseeing 907/586-1887;
www.juneausportfishing.com

Juneau Taxi & Tours 907/790-4511

Juneau Trolley Car Company 245 Marine Wy;
907/586-7433; www.juneautrolley.com

LAB Flying Service 907/766-2222, 800/427-5966;
www.labflying.com

Last Frontier Tours 907/321-8687, 888/396-8687;
lastfrontiertours.com

Mendenhall Glacier Transport 907/789-5460;
www.mightygreattrips.com

North Star Trekking 907/790-4530;
www.glaciertrekking.com

Orca Enterprises 369 Franklin St, Ste 201;
907/789-6801, 888/733-6722;
www.alaskawhalewatching.com

Ripple Cove Charters 907/697-2152, 866/224-
8900; www.gustavus.com/ripplecove

Sea Runner Guide Service 907/586-3754; www.
sea-runner.com

Temsco Helicopters 907/789-9501, 877/789-9501;
www.temscoair.com

Ward Air 907/789-9150; www.wardair.com

Wings of Alaska 2 Marine Wy; 907/586-6275;
www.wingsofalaska.com

Wolf Track Expeditions 907/697-2326;
www.wolftrackexpeditions.com

Juneau Parks & Recreation, it was created to relieve congestion on the Outer Point Trail. The surface of the Rainforest Trail is hard-packed and smooth, raising it above the tree roots—ever present in this shallow-soil region—that can trip unwary hikers. This makes it a good choice for less sure-footed hikers and small kids. The trail descends gradually through lush forest, interspersed with wild blueberries, huckleberries, dwarf dogwood, lupine, and world-record-size skunk cabbage (odoriferous and brilliant yellow in spring). The trail leads to rocky Outer Beach, a protected cove that's a popular fishing spot with seals, bald eagles, and humans. A third of a mile farther along the highway is the Outer Point Trail, similar to the newer Rainforest Trail in terrain. Three miles round trip, it's popular with residents but rougher; there are stairs to the beach. Elevation gain is less than 100 feet.

Mendenhall Glacier

For access information, see Nature, page 118. For longer glacier trails, see One Day, page 140.

The **Trail of Time** (30 minutes), a 0.5-mile loop trail, shows visitors what happens to the landscape after a glacier retreats. Pick up a trail brochure in the visitor center. The easy path (with a 50-foot elevation gain) begins at the top of the stairs behind the visitor center. At Sheep Creek, look for spawning salmon in July and August.

The 1.5-mile **Moraine Ecology Trail** (1 hour), with just a 10-foot elevation gain, is an easy loop that runs south of Mendenhall Lake and includes an especially good spot from which to observe spawning salmon in Sheep Creek, along with the wildlife that feed on them. Of the short trails close to the visitor center, this is your best bet for spotting wildlife, including birds, beavers, and bears.

Beyond the Photo Point Trail is—well, not precisely a trail but, rather, a ceaseless parade of visitors scrambling through and around the lakeside underbrush and gravel flats, and over a few boulders, to reach lovely **Nugget Falls** (1 hour). This is as close to the glacier as most visitors can get and it's well worth the effort. It's about 1 mile each way.

One of the most enchanting trails in the area and highly recommended, the 3.5-mile **East Glacier Loop** (2 hours), moderately easy with a 400-foot elevation gain, branches off from the Trail of Time and winds up through temperate rain forest on the east side of Mendenhall Lake, offering frequent panoramic glacier views amid moss-covered evergreens, alder and willow shrubs, lupines, and bunchberry. Highlights include a close-up look at man-made **A-J Falls**, dating from the gold rush era, and the sight of Nugget Falls thundering into the lake below.

Guided Hikes

If you'd like company on your ramble, join one of the free hikes offered by the **Juneau Parks & Recreation Department** (907/586-0428; *www.juneau.org/parkrec/hike*; Wed open to anyone 18 or older, Sat open to all, but kids under 18 must be accompanied by guardian or parent). The hikes, popular with locals and visitors alike, are a great way to meet residents. Hikes vary in location and duration, depending on weather conditions and the whim of the CPR-trained volunteer leaders. Participants should bring their own snacks, water, raingear, and appropriate footwear. Call the 24-hour hotline for hike locations and meeting times.

Gastineau Guiding leads hikes on the **Rainforest Trail** (3 hours total, 2 hours hiking; $63/adult, $40/child) and **Treadwell Mine Historic Trail** (3 hours total, 1.5 hours hiking; $54/adult, $46/child). Their **Tram & Trek** (2 hours; $49/adult, $32/child) and **Tram & Family Nature Exploration** (2.5 hours; $52/adult, $44/child, free/under 6) include a trip up the Mount Roberts tramway, alpine trails, and visit to the nature center.

ONE DAY

NATURE

In the heart of the Tongass National Forest, within a day trip from Juneau, are some of the most spectacular fjords and islands in Southeast Alaska. Added to the rich beauty of temperate rain forest against a backdrop of glacier-carved inlets is a wealth of wildlife. Mammals, from whales to brown bears, play the starring role.

Although a day trip won't give you time to see much of Gustavus or Glacier Bay, if you have only one day at your disposal, an **Icy Strait day trip** (8 hours) provides an excellent opportunity to experience the range of wildlife and scenery that abounds here. The "tour" is actually a round trip on the **Glacier Bay ferry** that runs between Juneau (Auke Bay Marina) and Gustavus every summer. When Four Seasons Marine took over the ferry in 2004, they added a **whale-watching excursion**

(3 hours; $195/adult, $99/under 12, includes round-trip ferry fare and tour; May–Sept Mon, Wed, Fri, Sat) to the round-trip ferry ride. The entire trip is highly scenic: heading up Lynn Canal to round Point Retreat (the northern tip of Admiralty Island), then south, with the Chilkat Range to the west, and on into Icy Strait and up to Gustavus.

The ferry departs from Auke Bay Marina at 10am, arriving in Gustavus at 1pm. You'll have an hour in Gustavus before the excursion to Point Adolphus departs at 2pm. Returning to Bartlett Cove at 5pm, you'll have half an hour for a quick look around Glacier Bay Lodge or the national park visitor center before the ferry heads back at 5:30pm to Auke Bay Marina, arriving at 8:30pm. There are a few caveats: Although the ferry provides basic food service, it's neither free nor the hearty, sumptuous meal tour operators often provide. There are few dining options for day trippers in Gustavus, so bring hearty snacks. You won't have a trained Park Service naturalist onboard; however, crew members are area residents, including Native Alaskans, and bring a wealth of local knowledge and experience to wildlife viewing. Icy Strait is like a spa for humpback whales in summer, and you're likely to encounter orcas, Steller sea lions, sea otters, harbor seals, and seabirds, as well.

Bear Watching

Admiralty Island has one of the world's highest bear populations per square mile—more than 1,600. The island's Tlingit name, *Kootznahoo*, means "Fortress of the Bears." At the **Stan Price State Wildlife Sanctuary** (1 hour for air transportation) in the Pack Creek estuary, the bears fish for spawning salmon in summer; peak times are July and August. There is an easy 1-mile rain-forest trail to the observation tower. A permit is required to visit (see the introduction, page 12), but it's not necessary to take a tour in order to visit. Park rangers greet arrivals, check permits, and answer questions. Tours vary in length (3–8 hours); the longer you stay, the better your chances of seeing bears. Camping is not permitted on the island.

Alaska Fly 'n' Fish Charters offers bear-watching tours to Pack Creek (5.5 hours; $475). The flight, permit, gear, and guiding are included. They provide a drop-off and pickup service for those who want only transportation to and from the island. Prices for transportation alone start at $175, depending on the size of your party. You are responsible for your own gear and permits. **Alaska Discovery** offers a Pack Creek trip (8–10 hours; $550) that includes transportation (floatplane), sea kayaking, and hiking. Gear and lunch are provided.

Flightseeing

Combine flightseeing and hiking with **North Star Trekking**, which has a glacier hike (4.25 hours; $329; minimum age 12) with 30 minutes by helicopter and 2 hours on the ice. A glacier trek (6.25 hours; $439; minimum age 16) includes 30 minutes in the air and 4 hours on the glacier. Gear, instruction, and snacks are included on both. They also put together custom treks. These trips are best for those with a high level of fitness.

Chartering a plane is a popular way to get to Pack Creek on Admiralty Island. Options include **Alaska Seaplane Service**, **Ward Air**, and **Wings of Alaska**. To put a day trip together during the peak season, you'll need to plan well in advance, because permits are limited. For permit information, contact **Admiralty National Monument** (8461 Old Dairy Rd, Juneau, AK 99801; 907/586-8790).

Tracy Arm–Ford's Terror Wilderness

To the south of Juneau are two spectacular fjords: Tracy Arm and Endicott Arm (Ford's Terror). Yes, there was a Ford, a U.S. Navy crewman, and yes, he was terrified. In 1889, he rowed a dinghy into a narrow opening off Endicott Arm for a quiet fishing trip. There, he was trapped for 6 hours by a suddenly rising wall of water and swirling currents until he could get away and back to his ship. Since Congress established the 653,179-acre Tracy Arm–Ford's Terror Wilderness in 1980, it has become increasingly popular. Sheer rockfaces descend directly to sparkling aqua waters scattered with blue icebergs, calved from tidewater glaciers spawned by the enormous Stikine Icefield. Both fjords make excellent but long day trips from Juneau.

Goldbelt Auk Nu Tours (907/586-8687) started offering this tour into **Endicott Arm/Ford's Terror** (8 hours;

$119; 9am–5pm) in 2004. Getting into the fjord is still difficult; as Ford discovered, currents are ferocious and deadly. The narrow channel can be negotiated only during high slack water; trips are scheduled only on days when this occurs during daylight hours. At the entrance to Ford's Terror, the captain must judge whether it is safe to enter the channel. Time in Ford's Terror is limited by the tide table. Generally you'll have 45 minutes to an hour. The scenery in Ford's Terror is stunning; melting snows from the icefield turn into narrow waterfalls, snaking down near-vertical canyon walls to blue-green, opaque glacial waters thousands of feet below. Sights along the way include gold-mine ruins and the remains of a staggeringly huge landslide that once took out Juneau's power lines. From Ford's Terror, the boat moves on to Dawe's Glacier at the eastern end of Endicott Arm. The huge tidewater glacier with a wildly serrated top and intense blue color often calves in beautiful thick chunks. Look for seals sunning themselves on icebergs and fluffy dots of white— mountain goats high on the mountainside. The barren region suggests what North America might have looked like during the last ice age, of which the Stikine Icefield, the glacier's parent, is one of the few remaining elements. Tours include snacks, hot beverages, and lunch, with sandwiches catered by the excellent Silverbow Bakery in Juneau. Tour dates are determined by tidal conditions; call for details.

Tracy Arm cruises grow more popular every year. Restrictions on boats permitted in Glacier Bay and the time it takes to get there from Juneau have made Tracy Arm an easier destination to visit than the national park. Like Ford's Terror, Tracy Arm takes a few hours to reach, but the extraordinary scenery is a knockout and you don't hear many complaints. From the narrow fjord, its milky green waters full of blue icebergs large and small, rise sheer rock walls, 4,000 feet high, from which waterfalls cascade down among the trees that have managed a foothold there, to the 1,000-foot-deep fjord. Mountain goats, bald eagles, orcas, whales, and seals are often encountered. Tours visit the two tidewater glaciers, North and South Sawyer, that pour from the Stikine Icefield into Tracy Arm. Getting here is less challenging logistically than reaching Ford's Terror, so daily sailings are offered. **Adventure Bound Alaska** has frequent tours to Tracy Arm (9.5 hours; $105/adult, $65/youth; 8:30am–6pm) and can arrange kayak drop-offs. **Goldbelt Tours** offers a similar tour (8.25 hours; $119 adult, $70/child; mid-May–Sept Thurs–Mon 8:45am–5pm). Lunch is served on both tours.

For contact information for outfitters and tour operators listed in this chapter, see sidebar on pages 130–31.

CYCLING

Microbrew fanciers can consume theirs guilt-free following a 2-hour workout on the **Bike and Brew tour** (4.5 hours; $50) offered by **Cycle Alaska**. Cyclists start in the Mendenhall Valley (transportation is provided from downtown); the route includes Auke Bay, Auke Lake, the lovely University of Alaska Southeast campus, and Mendenhall Lake. The 11-mile ride is rated easy to moderate. From the lake, a van transports tired cyclists to the brewery for a 30-minute tour and restorative. Everything, including water bottles and raingear, is provided.

For rentals, see Four Hours or Less, page 126.

FISHING

Alaska Fly 'n' Fish Charters offers **floatplane fishing trips** (4.5 hours, including transportation; $400), including gear, transportation, and instruction in fly-fishing and spin-casting. Fishing licenses are available. Participants must be 12 or older. Fish for trout or salmon, depending on what's running. Tours can be extended for $50 per hour per person. **Bear Creek Outfitters** picks you up, outfits you, and flies you by floatplane for a half or full day of **stream fishing** (half day: 6 hours, $320; full day: 9 hours, $425, 3-person minimum). They'll add you to another party to make up a group, if you're willing. The half-day trip includes 4 hours of fishing; the full-day trip includes 7 hours of fishing; both include 2 hours of transportation. Lunch is included.

Several operators offer **ocean fishing** trips. **Juneau Sportfishing & Sightseeing** has one (8 hours; $215); a fishing license is extra ($10/day, free/under 16). Transportation to and from your hotel or cruise ship, gear, snacks, and lunch are included. Handicapped-accessible boats are available with prior notice. **Auke Bay Sportfishing & Sightseeing** offers three trips (6 hours, $135; 8 hours, $175; 10 hours, $225); food, drinks, and fishing license are not included. (Halibut charters often run a little extra.) They also rent fully equipped skiffs with fishing gear, tackle, and crab pots, (starting at $395/day for up to 4 people) and also put together custom fishing charters, including transportation and accommodation.

Sea Runner Guide Service puts together half- and full-day fly-fishing trips from Juneau. Instruction is included. You can also arrange a trip with them through the downtown-based fly-fishing store and outfitter **Juneau Flyfishing Goods**. Rates (5 hours, $300/trip for 2 people; 8 hours, $450/trip for 2 people) include snacks, drinks, and instruction.

Bear Creek Outfitters and **Juneau Sportfishing & Sightseeing** will put together custom fishing charters, including accommodation and transportation. Rates vary; you may need to guarantee a minimum number of people.

Check with the visitor center for more fishing options.

For contact information for outfitters and tour operators listed in this chapter, see sidebar on pages 130–31.

HIKING

From Downtown

The **Perseverance Trail** (4 hours), the original gold-mine access road, has evolved into Juneau's most popular hike. It is of special interest to those with a passion for gold rush history. Follow the Juneau Walking Tour (page 110, see #10a) to Basin Road and continue to the end of the road, to Last Chance Basin. The trail is easy to moderately difficult, with a 700-foot elevation gain. The trail leads through the remains of the old AJ Mine and on to the remains of the Perseverance Mine in Silverbow Basin. There's a lot to see. Bring along the Last Chance Basin walking-tour map, available at the Centennial Hall Visitors Center or Juneau–Douglas City Museum. The trailhead for the much more challenging **Mount Juneau Trail** is nearby (3 hours). With its 3,576-foot elevation gain, it should be attempted only by experienced, fit hikers.

The hike up **Mount Roberts** (6 hours from trailhead, 6th and Nelson Sts), while strenuous, is beautiful (see Juneau Walking Tour, page 109, #9). The trail to the upper tramway level is 2.7 miles one way, with 1,800 feet of elevation gain. You can go farther—to Gastineau Peak (3 miles, 3,666 feet up) and on to the summit of Mount Roberts (4.5 miles, 3,819 feet up). Although this trail is not particularly difficult, it's all uphill and best attempted by those in good condition. Don't expect to have the trail to yourself; this hike is very popular with residents. As it passes through rain forest and alpine meadows, the view just keeps getting more spectacular. The 9-mile round trip takes the better part of a day for most people, but you can shorten the time to a half day by taking the tram up or down one way. If you take it up, you'll have to pay the full fare, but if you've hiked up, you can ride the tram down for $5—or for free, if you've got a receipt showing you spent $5 or more at the tramway complex.

With a Car

To reach the **Herbert Glacier Trail** (4–5 hours, plus 1.25 hours for transportation), park in the parking area at mile 26.5 of the Juneau Veterans Memorial Highway. This 9.2-mile round-trip hike, with an elevation gain of 100 feet, is suitable for most hikers. The trail goes through lush forest and has excellent glacier and waterfall views.

The trailhead for the **Peterson Lake Trail** (5 hours, plus 1.25 hours for transportation) is at mile 23.5 of the Juneau Veterans Memorial Highway. From here, it is 4.2 miles to the USFS Peterson Lake Cabin. The hike is strenuous, so allow enough time. Just north of the trailhead is the Peterson Creek bridge, where you can see salmon spawning in late summer. Watch for bears.

Sheep Creek (5–6 hours, plus 20 minutes for transportation) is an easy hike (6 miles round trip) through a scenic historical landscape that includes mining relics, as well as wildflowers and wildlife. The trailhead is 4 miles south of Juneau along Thane Road. There's an 800-foot elevation gain.

Mendenhall Glacier

The trailhead for the **West Glacier Trail** (5–6 hours) is at the end of the Skaters Cabin Road parking area. The moderately difficult trail rises 1,300 feet. From this vantage point, hikers have good views of glacier ice falls, called seracs. Gulls nest here in early summer; trails are sometimes closed to protect them.

From the East Glacier Loop Trail, the **Nugget Creek Trail** adds another 7 miles round trip to the 3 miles round trip on the East Glacier Loop to reach the Nugget Creek trailhead (7–8 hours from visitor center). The elevation gain is about 500 feet. The trail ends at the Vista Creek shelter. The first part of the trail is lovely, becoming brushier and more challenging after the first 1.5 miles.

Guided Hikes

Gastineau Guiding has a **Guide's Choice** hike (4.5 hours; $73/adult, $45/child; daily, times vary) that includes 3.5–4 hours of hiking to various destinations. Hike includes transportation, water, snack, and poncho. A trip to **Herbert Glacier** includes a 4-hour hike, a hip pack, walking stick, water, snack, and lunch (7 hours; $89/adult, $54/child; Fri, Sat noon). For both hikes, participants should be comfortable hiking 3.5 hours at a stretch; good footgear is a must. A bit less strenuous is an early morning **Mount Roberts** tram trip and hike (4.5 hours; $79/adult, $49/child), with 4 hours of hiking and tram fare included.

Above & Beyond Alaska offers a Mendenhall Glacier hike (10 hours; $450; June–Sept, Mon–Fri at 8am). The trip includes transportation, helicopter flight, gear, and training. Although no experience is required, participants should be in good condition. Their Ocean to Ice

Day Adventure (10 hours; $490) includes whale watching, sea kayaking, a helicopter flight, and a glacier trek. Transportation, lunch, and gear are provided. Participants should be moderately fit.

KAYAKING

Alaska Boat & Kayak has a **Tongass wildlife kayak trip** (6 hours; $170; May–Sept daily 9am, 2pm). Price includes transportation, gear, and a hearty snack. No experience is required. The **Taku Glacier kayak** (10 hours; $250) requires a moderate level of fitness but no prior kayaking experience. The **Ocean to Ice Sea Adventure** ($490, including lunch; June–Sept) combines 3 hours of kayaking with a helicopter ride to the icefield and a 2-hour glacier hike using crampons and mountaineering gear. No experience is required.

In a kayak trip through the **Channel Islands** north of Juneau (6–7 hours; $114.45; mid-May–mid-Sept 9:30am) with native-owned **Goldbelt Tours**, you can view wildlife and the Chilkat Mountains. Transportation, gear, a snack, naturalist interpretation, and native storytelling are included. No experience is required.

For kayak rentals, see Two Days or More, below.

TWO DAYS OR MORE

KAYAKING

Alaska Boat and Kayak has kayaks for rent (single: $45/day; double: $60/day) and skiffs ranging from 16 feet ($130/day, up to 5 passengers) to 27 feet ($300/day, up to 6 passengers). Transport and delivery fees vary. They also offer kayaking and boating classes ranging from a few hours to all day, and will help plan multiday kayak trips (3–10 days). Among the destinations are Admiralty Island (5 days; $640), Gustavus to Juneau (10 days; $1,040), Taku River and Taku Glacier (5 days; $520), Tracy Arm (6 days; $680), and Endicott Arm (5 days; $670).

ADMIRALTY ISLAND

Admiralty Island, Alaska's fifth largest, at 1,709 square miles, draws more visitors each year, but compared to other Inside Passage destinations, it qualifies as virtually undiscovered—and unexploited. **Admiralty Island National Monument** and **Kootznoowoo Wilderness** take up most of the island. Logging and development have been minimal, so it's not surprising that the island supports not only one of the densest populations of brown bears in the world but also its largest congregation of nesting bald eagles. Sitka black-tailed deer are common, as are loons, great blue herons, and mergansers. Local sea mammals include humpback whales, orcas, sea lions, and seals.

At its closest to Juneau, Admiralty Island is 20 miles and a 30-minute floatplane ride away. Along with popular day-trip flights to the island's Pack Creek, there are opportunities to spend a few days on the island. The island's largest community, **Angoon**, with a population of 572, has a few lodges and B&Bs, as well as regular air and ferry service, but it's not really equipped for tourism. A multiday trip here is best suited to those who want a wilderness experience.

One such getaway, the **Cross-Admiralty Canoe Route**, is 25 miles of connected lakes and portages extending from Mitchell Bay on the west coast to Mole Harbor on the east coast. Several USFS cabins are available along the way. Canoe route maps and cabin information are available from the Forest Service. At the north end of the island are three other USFS cabins, connected by a lake and trail. See Bear Watching and Flightseeing under One Day, pages 134–35, for information on outfitting a trip to the island. For cabin rental information, see the introduction.

GLACIER BAY NATIONAL PARK & PRESERVE

Glacier Bay, 66 miles northwest of Juneau, runs north of Icy Strait, which separates the northern tip of Chichagof Island from the mainland. To the west of the bay is the Fairweather mountain range, whose tallest peak, Mount Fairweather, is 15,300 feet. Tidewater glaciers descend from the icefields into the bay. Although the mountains and glaciers appear to have been here for millennia, Glacier Bay is new. Just over 200 years ago, when Captain George Vancouver sailed through, Icy Strait was barely navigable, thickly covered in ice, and what is now Glacier Bay was merely an indentation in a glacier 4,000 feet thick and 20 miles wide. Less than a century later, when naturalist John Muir visited in 1879, the glacier had become a deep, two-pronged bay, and in the 125 years since, it has changed almost as much again. The glaciers are still retreating at an extraordinary pace.

What has caused the retreat? A so-called "Little Ice Age" occurred about 4,000 years ago, resulting in increased glaciation in this area. It ended in the mid-1700s; the melting continues to this day. As the glaciers retreat, land long pressed down below tons of ice is springing back and rising from the water in the process called "glacial rebound." Rebound is occurring throughout Alaska, but nowhere as fast as in Glacier Bay and the nearby town of Gustavus.

The area's human history predates the Little Ice Age. Tlingit elders have inherited stories about villages that were wiped out when glaciers suddenly advanced. Other tales of great floods are thought to describe the catastrophic natural consequences of sudden thaws, when previously icebound lakes drained in minutes, releasing millions of gallons of ice water onto the land.

Access

An excursion to Glacier Bay National Park is high on the agenda of many Alaska visitors. However, severe restrictions on the number of cruise ships (just two per day), tour boats, and charter and private vessels allowed in the park make it essential to plan your visit well in advance. The closest town to the bay is **Gustavus**, population 258. **Alaska Airlines** (907/225-2145, 800/426-0333; *www.alaskaair.com*) has frequent flights (31 minutes) between Juneau and Gustavus. **LAB Flying Service** and **Wings of Alaska** also offer scheduled service between Juneau and Gustavus. Four times a week, May to September, the **Glacier Bay ferry** runs from Auke Bay Marina to Gustavus; ferries return from Bartlett Cove to Auke Bay Marina ($138/adult, $70/under 12). For times and details, see One Day, page 133–34. **TLC Taxi** provides service around Gustavus, including from the Gustavus ferry dock to Glacier Bay Lodge ($10), and they also offer tours ($60/hour).

Accommodations

The closest accommodation to Glacier Bay is **Glacier Bay Lodge**, the only hotel within the park (see page 148). Gustavus has several lodges and B&Bs that offer comprehensive services (food, dining, and tours). For details, contact the **Gustavus Visitor Association** (907/697-2285; *www.gustavus.com*).

Park Activities

Visiting **National Park Headquarters** in Bartlett Cove and attending a free naturalist program are recommended. Wildlife in the park includes porcupines, wolves, ducks, and, increasingly, moose. (Wolves were recently reintroduced and do not yet appear to look on moose as a food source. Consequently, the moose population has been growing unchecked.) Birdlife, among the richest in Alaska, includes bald and golden eagles, ravens, owls, loons, sandhill cranes, puffins, murres, marbled murrelets, and herons.

NATURE: One of the best ways to see **Glacier Bay** is on the comfortable, lodge-operated **Baranof Wind** (907/264-4600, 888/229-8687) cruise (8 hours; $159.50/adult, $79.95/ages 2–12). A hot lunch and snacks are included. Expect to be chilly. Long underwear, gloves, hat, and scarf are advised. The parade of wildlife includes sea otters, humpback and minke whales, orcas, Steller sea lions, harbor seals, puffins, marbled murrelets, brown bears, and mountain goats. The boat makes stops to drop off or pick up kayakers. Tours usually go up Tarr Inlet to Margerie Glacier, sticking around long enough to watch it calve. Weather and ice conditions affect itineraries, but with sixteen tidewater glaciers in the bay, expect to see several. Gustavus-based **Air Excursions LLC** has an **icefield flight** (45 minutes; $75) and a flight over Glacier Bay (1.25 hours; starts at $120; 3-passenger minimum). **Fjord Flying Service** also has **flightseeing trips**.

CYCLING: You can rent bikes at the lodge or from **Wolf Track Expeditions** in Gustavus, which offers mountain biking guided trips. There's a two-person minimum; prices include ferry pickup and drop-off.

FISHING: **Deep Blue Fishing Charters** has chartered fishing trips (half day, $175; full day, $250), which include lunch on the boat, bait, and tackle but not fishing license, smoking, or packing your catch. **Ripple Cove Charters** has charters (half day, $195; full day, $250) and a "mini whale watch" (2 hours; $40).

HIKING: Park rangers offer **free guided walks**, daily, that introduce local flora and fauna as well as the geology and human history of Glacier Bay. Look for elaborately carved Tlingit trail markers among the trees. In spring especially the park is colorful with berry blossoms, lupine, and chocolate lilies.

KAYAKING: In Bartlett Cove, you can **rent kayaks and take lessons** from **Glacier Bay Sea Kayaks**, with two group lessons daily, at 9am and 2pm. Kayaks can be rented by experienced kayakers (single: half day $25, full day $40; double: half day $45, full day $60). Instruction is mandatory. Outfitting, map, and route information are included. **Alaska Discovery** leads several kayaking tours in double kayaks out of Bartlett Cove, including lunch, snacks, gear, and equipment. Options include an afternoon trip (2 hours), a full-day trip ($125), and an evening trip (6:15pm; $49). No experience is required; meals and snacks are included. They also offer a selection of multiday, all-inclusive trips in Glacier Bay and Icy Strait (3–10 days).

TRACY ARM

Auke Bay Sportfishing & Sightseeing offers an extended excursion to Tracy Arm (3 days; $4,725 for 4 passengers). The cruise includes transportation; meals; fishing gear; and cleaning, processing, and shipping the catch home. Fishing licenses can be purchased aboard.

PUBLIC-USE CABINS

Nearby **Tongass National Forest cabins** are especially popular getaways for Juneau residents and should be booked as early as possible. There are nine cabins in the Juneau area and fourteen on Admiralty Island (plus two shelters). Fees are generally $35 per night.

Five Juneau-area cabins are accessible by land: The **John Muir Cabin** is 3 miles up the Auke Nu Trail (trailhead at mile 12.3 of the Juneau Veterans Memorial Highway). The **Dan Moller Cabin** on Douglas Island is accessed via a steepish 3-mile trail through muskeg from Pioneer Avenue in Douglas. The **Peterson Lake Cabin** is reached via a fairly challenging 4.3-mile trail at the west side of Peterson Lake (at mile 23.5 of the Juneau Veterans Memorial Highway). The **Eagle Glacier Memorial Cabin** is accessed via a tough 5.5-mile trek on the Amalga Trail (at mile 27.2 of the Juneau Veterans Memorial Highway). The **Windfall Lake Cabin** is accessed from the 3.2-mile Windfall Lake Trail, an offshoot of the Montana Creek Trail (at mile 26.5 of the Juneau Veterans Memorial Highway). Stays are limited to two consecutive nights. For details contact the **USFS** (*www. fs.fed.us/r10/tongass/recreation/rec_facilities/cabinlist/*). To reserve a cabin, contact **ReserveUSA** (518/885-3639, 877-444-6777; *www.reserveusa.com*).

Point Bridget State Park also has two public-use cabins, operated by Alaska State Parks. The **Cowee Meadow Cabin** is accessed 2.5 miles up the Point Bridget Trail (at mile 39 of the Juneau Veterans Memorial Highway); the **Blue Mussel Cabin** is 3.4 miles up the same trail. Both sleep up to eight people and can be rented up to three consecutive nights. Water is usually available, but check first; purify before using it. For information and booking, contact **Alaska State Parks** (907/465-4563; *www.dnr.state.ak.us/parks/cabins/south/*).

ACCOMMODATIONS

JUNEAU

Juneau accommodations range from unpretentiously comfortable inns to elegant downtown hotels.

Gold Street Inn ($$–$$$; 303 Gold St; 907/586-9863; *www.juneauinn.com*), formerly known as Cashen Quarters, is located in a historic house dating from 1914. This B&B—once a small hotel—has five recently remodeled rooms, each with bath, kitchen, and private entrance.

The **Goldbelt Hotel** ($$$; 51 Egan Dr; 907/586-6900, 888/478-6909; *www.goldbelttours.com;* &) has the best

"Friends Don't Let Friends Eat Farmed Salmon"

These warning signs are posted throughout Southeast Alaska, often to the puzzlement of visitors. Pacific salmon play a critical role in Alaska's economy; commercial and sports fisheries, canneries, and smokeries depend on their health. In recent decades, keeping wild salmon stocks plentiful and healthy has become a challenge. Canneries have closed and harvests have been restricted to prevent over-fishing. Other threats—economic and environmental—are posed by salmon farming.

Many diners find the flavor of farmed salmon bland compared with the robust taste of wild salmon, but the differences run deeper. Studies have found that farmed salmon carry more toxins, such as PCBs, than wild salmon. Accidental release of farmed salmon into the wild has resulted in interbreeding, which could alter the genetic structure of wild salmon, and—owing to conditions in fish farms, where fish are raised close together—high instances of disease that can be transferred to wild salmon. Some believe fish farming generates waste that could lead to water pollution. For these reasons, and to protect wild salmon fisheries, fish farming is illegal in Alaska.

view in town, generously sized rooms, a prime location for exploring Juneau on foot, and friendly staff—all of which make this a top choice. The spacious **dining room** serves good, hearty fare.

The **Guesthouse Inn** ($$; 1800 Shell Dr; 907/790-6435, 888/559-9846; *www.aspenhotelsak.com;* &), though catering to business travelers, welcomes vacationers, too. The swimming pool, hot tub, and guest laundry make this a prime choice for families and footsore travelers in search of affordable luxury. Rooms come with refrigerator and microwave oven. Rates include free breakfast and courtesy shuttle. Don't be alarmed at the proximity of the airport; in Juneau, there aren't enough flights and traffic to make it a problem.

Juneau International Hostel ($; 614 Harris St; 907/586-9559; *www.juneauhostel.org;* &) occupies a large, comfortable home in a hilltop residential neighborhood two blocks from the Mount Roberts trailhead and offers guests free Internet access, laundry, and a family room. It's open year-round. In summer, reservations are recommended; for parties of eight or more, they're required.

In winter, the **Westmark Baranof** ($$–$$$; 127 N Franklin St; 907/586-2660, 800/544-0970; *www.west markhotels.com;* &), a Juneau landmark, fills with legislative staff and lobbyists; in summer, it's popular with savvy tourists who like a bit of history with their stay. Rooms are on the small side, but many have great views and some have kitchens. For dining, there's the upscale **Gold Room**; for breakfast and lunch, try the cheery **Capital Café**.

GLACIER BAY

At Bartlett Cove, 8 miles from Gustavus, **Glacier Bay Lodge** ($$$; 199 Bartlett Cove Rd; 907/264-4600; *visit glacierbay.com;* &) is the only accommodation in the national park, well worth the advance booking required. Rooms are spacious; many have views. Lodge buildings are connected by boardwalks around a central lodge with an excellent **dining room**, a gift shop, and a national park visitor center. There's a ferry shuttle ($12 one way).

DINING

Juneau has a full spectrum of dining choices, from tony spots where lobbyists wine and dine clients to family-oriented establishments. Visitors will likely run out of time before they run out of good choices.

Downstairs, the **Fiddlehead Restaurant & Bakery** ($, dinner $$, Di Sopra $$$; 429 W Willoughby Ave; 907/586-1042; *www.thefiddlehead.com*; Fiddlehead: Mon–Fri 7am–9pm, Sat–Sun 8am–9pm; Di Sopra: dinner only) offers healthy food that's hearty enough to keep you energized through a morning of kayaking. Breads are baked on the premises. Lunch and dinner menus include burgers, pasta, and meat and seafood entrées along with vegetarian pastas, salads, and veggie burgers. Upstairs, the **Di Sopra** offers upscale, Italian-accented cuisine with plenty of seafood choices.

Hangar on the Wharf ($$; 2 Marine Wy, Ste 6; 907/586-5018; daily 11am–10pm) is noisy, full of tourists, and fun. Watch floatplanes arrive and depart as you sip a local microbrew and dig into a plate of butter clams or fresh salmon.

Whenever the **Hot Bite** ($; Auke Bay Boat Harbor; 907/790-2483; summer 11am–7pm, winter 11am–3pm) is open, this joint is jumping. On the menu are halibut burgers, fish-and-chips, a few veggie options, hamburgers, hot dogs, soups, old-fashioned fountain drinks, and smoothies—try a blackberry shake. Dine in or take out. Parking is limited; if you stay too long in a 30-minute slot, you'll be ticketed—but lines move fast.

New owner Joan Deering has made **Paradise Lunch & Bakery** ($; 245 Marine Wy; 907/586-2253; summer daily 7am–3:30pm, winter Mon–Fri) a top pick for a quick meal or snack between activities. Everything, including croissants, is homemade except for the cheesecake, which is outsourced. Eye the snappy cowgirl-and-musical instrument ambience while you wait. Try wraps and salads for lunch; save room for a shortbread tart.

Twisted Fish Company ($$; in Taku Smokeries Bldg, 550 S Franklin St; 907/463-5033; daily 11am–10pm; &) offers good Alaskan seafood with turf options. Pizzas, burgers, and wine by the glass are good deals. Try seafood pasta or steamer clams in a mushroom and tomato broth, served with knobs of Parmesan bread. The young waiters are personable, and there are a lot of local diners and noise—but it's cheerful noise.

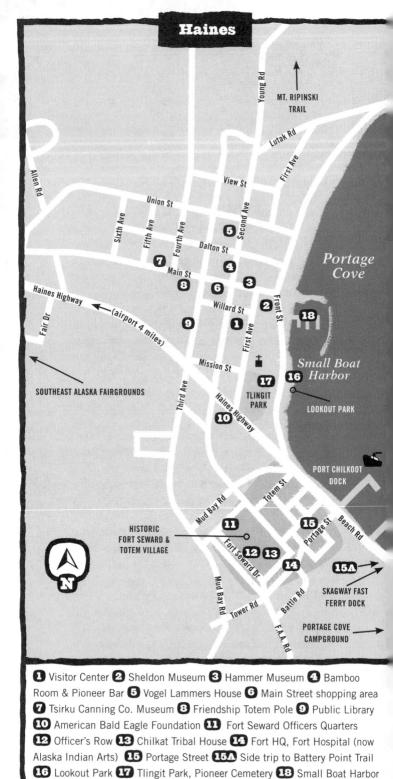

Haines

MT. RIPINSKI TRAIL

Young Rd

Lutak Rd

First Ave

View St

Union St

Allen Rd

Sixth Ave

Fifth Ave

Fourth Ave

Second Ave

Dalton St

5

7

4

8 **6** **3**

Main St

Willard St

2 Front St

1

First Ave

9

Haines Highway ← (airport 4 miles)

Fair Dr

Mission St

17 **16**

TLINGIT PARK

LOOKOUT PARK

Haines Highway

10

Third Ave

Portage Cove

18

Small Boat Harbor

SOUTHEAST ALASKA FAIRGROUNDS

PORT CHILKOOT DOCK

Totem St

Mud Bay Rd

HISTORIC FORT SEWARD & TOTEM VILLAGE

11

Fort Seward Dr

12 **13**

14

15

Portage St

Beach Rd

15A

SKAGWAY FAST FERRY DOCK

Mud Bay Rd

Tower Rd

Battle Rd

F.A.A. Rd

PORTAGE COVE CAMPGROUND

N

1 Visitor Center **2** Sheldon Museum **3** Hammer Museum **4** Bamboo Room & Pioneer Bar **5** Vogel Lammers House **6** Main Street shopping area **7** Tsirku Canning Co. Museum **8** Friendship Totem Pole **9** Public Library **10** American Bald Eagle Foundation **11** Fort Seward Officers Quarters **12** Officer's Row **13** Chilkat Tribal House **14** Fort HQ, Fort Hospital (now Alaska Indian Arts) **15** Portage Street **15A** Side trip to Battery Point Trail **16** Lookout Park **17** Tlingit Park, Pioneer Cemetery **18** Small Boat Harbor

Chapter 4

HAINES

Haines lies halfway down the east side of the long, narrow Chilkat Peninsula, just 14 miles from Skagway, situated to the northeast on Taiya Inlet. A short ferry ride separates the two cities, which are also joined by scenic highways—but despite how close these two towns are by water, 360 miles of road are needed to link them by land. With its position on the peninsula, Haines has miles of gorgeous waterfront and two superb state parks, with great hiking, fishing, and kayaking within minutes of town. The highway also connects Haines to the world's largest protected wilderness, a UNESCO World Heritage Site encompassing thousands of miles of U.S. and Canadian regional and national parks.

In Haines, people live life at an exotic pace in today's world: slow. It's no accident that *Outside Magazine* put Haines on the cover of its August 2004 issue featuring the best small U.S. towns to live in. Haines not only offers the best of small-town American life, it's encircled by glaciated mountain peaks, forested hills, and pristine waters.

Some blame the water; others claim that Haines lies on a mystical convergence of magnetic forces—but however explained, Haines is special. The residents are a closely knit, sometimes fractious family, with its share of internal strife but a family nonetheless. What unites them is love of their community. This is a town that came together to build a spiffy playground for its children in just five days. It has one of Alaska's finest public libraries and some of its best schools. If you visit on a day when a wedding is taking place, you'll likely find half the town deserted. Celebrating neighbors' milestones is important here. A major annual event is the Southeast Alaska State Fair. Absolutely everyone goes. Rain is confidently expected; in fact, it's a tradition. (Residents are still scratching their heads over the sunny fair of 2004 when temperatures topped 90°F.)

Despite the town's abundant appeal, in recent years cruise ships have bypassed Haines. But for many visitors, including cruise passengers who find their way here from Skagway, that's a plus. Shops in Haines tend to be small, locally owned operations, and the town is rarely swamped with visitors. Your chances of getting a feel for what life in the forty-ninth state is like are better here than just about anywhere else along the Inside Passage. Haines shows you what happens after the tourists go home.

HISTORY

The Chilkat Peninsula is the historic home of the Chilkat Tlingit, whose name for the area was *Dei Shu* ("End of the Trail"). Before white settlers arrived, Klukwan was the major village, and Haines was the site of a summer fish camp. Klukwan Tlingit were keepers of important trade routes to the Canadian interior and as far south as Oregon; the gateway to the interior was guarded by the Tlingit as first Russians and then Americans established trading relationships with them. In 1879 a Presbyterian minister, Samuel Hall Young, and naturalist John Muir chose the site as the place to establish a mission and school for Natives, naming it in honor of a Presbyterian dignitary.

With the influx of Klondike stampeders, the Tlingit lost their trade route monopoly. In 1903, after the gold rush and several chaotic years, which included border disputes with Canada, the U.S. Army set up its first permanent Alaska post at Fort Seward, named for the U.S. Secretary of State who negotiated the purchase of Alaska from Russia. The fort remained an important training base through World War II. Commercial fisheries and gold mining nearby at Porcupine were major industries.

HAINES TODAY

Like much of Southeast Alaska, Haines, population 1,715, has lost its sawmills and canneries, although commercial fishing remains important. It is still one of the primary employers, along with timber, government, tourism, and transportation.

Among major Inside Passage ports of call, Haines gets the least cruise-ship traffic, and that has had a dampening effect on the economy. Many reasons are offered for this dearth of visitors, but the reality is that Skagway, with its deepwater docks and one of Alaska's biggest tourist draws—the White Pass & Yukon Route Railway—just 14 miles away, it's difficult to make a case for docking at Haines, too, which has room for just one large cruise ship at the Port Chilkoot Dock in Fort Seward (Skagway can handle five).

However, there is a silver lining to this cloud. The pace is slow and relaxed. And maybe it's something in the water, but there's magic afoot.

GEOGRAPHY

Haines is located on the east side of the Chilkat Peninsula, which separates Chilkoot Inlet and Taiya Inlet to the east from Chilkat Inlet to the west. Haines is 775 miles from Anchorage; 250 miles from Whitehorse, Yukon Territory, by road; 14 miles west of Skagway; 90 miles north of Juneau by water; and 965 miles north of Seattle.

CLIMATE

Average annual precipitation is 48 inches (snowfall is 122.6 inches). In peak season, Haines's average high temperatures run in the mid-60s (June, 64.2°F; July, 66.3°F; August, 65.6°F).

Average Temperatures (°F)

	May–Oct	Nov–Apr
High	60.0	36.6
Low	45.3	26.0

Average Precipitation (inches)

Jan	Feb	Mar	Apr	May	June
5.4	4.6	2.9	2.5	1.5	1.4

July	Aug	Sept	Oct	Nov	Dec
1.4	2.3	5.2	9.2	6.2	5.4

Average Hours of Daylight

Jan	Feb	March	Apr	May	June
6	8	10.5	13.5	16	18

July	Aug	Sept	Oct	Nov	Dec
19	17	14	11.5	8.5	6

ACCESS

Alaska ferries connect Haines to other Southeast Alaska communities year-round (see the introduction, page 5). A shuttle ferry connects Haines and Skagway (see Wheels & Keels, below). **LAB Flying Service** (907/766-2222, 800/426-0543; *labflying.com*), **Wings of Alaska** (907/586-6275; *www.wingsofalaska.com*), and **Skagway Air Service** (907/766-3233; *www.skagwayair. com*) offer scheduled and charter service to and from Juneau and Skagway. Clipper, Holland America, Silversea, CruiseWest, and Princess cruise lines include Haines on some itineraries.

VISITOR INFORMATION & SERVICES

Haines Convention & Visitors Bureau (122 2nd Ave; 907/766-2234, 800/458-3579).

Alaska State Parks, Haines District (PO Box 430, Haines, AK 99827; 907/766-2292; *www.dnr.state.ak.us/parks/*).

Post Office: Between Fort Seward and downtown Haines (55 Haines Cut-Off Hwy; Mon–Fri 8:30am–5pm, Sat 1–3pm).

Alaska Public Radio Network: KHNS 102.3 FM; *www. khns.org*.

Internet Access: Haines Borough Public Library (103 3rd Ave; 907/766-2545; *www.haineslibrary.org*) has free Internet access. **Mountain Market** (3rd Ave and Haines Hwy; 907/766-3340; *mountain_market@yahoo.com*) has Internet access for a fee. (Wi-Fi access is restricted to residents only.)

WHEELS & KEELS

The Eagle's Nest Motel & Car Rental (mile 1, Haines Hwy; 907/766-2891, 800/354-6009; *www.eaglesnest.wytbear. com*) has a limited number of cars for rent ($15/hour, $45/day, $270/week; 100 free miles/day, thereafter 35 cents/mile); advance reservations are a must. Vehicles may have more mileage than renters are used to encountering. The other source for car rentals ($69/day; unlimited mileage) is the **Captain's Choice Motel** (108 2nd Ave; 907/766-3111, 800/478-2345). Both permit renters to drive the Golden Circle Route. However, cars must be returned to Haines, so either you'll need to drive the Golden Circle 360 miles back to Haines or bring the rental car from Skagway to Haines on the Alaska ferry (a 1-hour trip). If you do, you'll need advance ferry reservations.

Note to Canadian visitors: The Canadian government currently does not permit Canadians who have rented a U.S. vehicle in Alaska to drive it across the border into Canada.

Haines has no public transportation, but it does have a taxi: **24/7 Taxi Service** (907/766-2676). **Haines Shuttle & Tours** (907/766-3138) meets all ferries and offers guided tours.

There is no water taxi here, per se, although two ferry systems serve Haines. For car ferry information, see the introduction, page 5. The passenger-only **Chilkat Ferry** (907/766-2100, 888/766-2103; *www.chilkat cruises.com*) makes the 35-minute run between Haines and Skagway hourly most days in summer ($25/adult one way, $45/adult round trip; $12.50/ages 3–12 one way, $22.50/ages 3–12 round trip). The Haines dock is in Fort Seward.

EVENTS

Southeast Alaska State Fair and Bald Eagle Music Festival (Fairgrounds, mile 1, Haines Hwy, 907/766-2476; *www.seakfair.org*; $7/adult, $6/senior, free/under 6): In mid-August, Southeast Alaskan inhabitants of all ages throng to the fair to meet, greet, eat, and frolic. Tradition has it that it always rains, but don't count on it. Live music is provided by local and marquee-name musicians. The usual accoutrements of any U.S.

Haines Three-Hour Must-See Itinerary

- Sheldon Museum (45 minutes)
- Fort Seward and shopping (45 minutes)
- Chilkat Bald Eagle Preserve (1.25-hour tour)
- Refueling Stop: **Local Catch** (Portage St, Fort Seward)

country fair—from prize pigs and sheep to odd food items and gadget hucksters—are on view, along with displays of prize-winning preserves and art by pre-schoolers.

Alaska Bald Eagle Festival (907/766-3094; *www.baldeagle festival.org*; $25/day adults, $20/youth, free/under 6): Long after other salmon-bearing streams and rivers have frozen over, the shallow Chilkat River remains ice free; chum salmon continue to flop upstream to spawn, and bald eagles congregate to feast on them. This is when those photos of leafless trees covered in testy-looking bald eagles are taken. As many as 3,000 eagles have gathered on the river flats in some years. To celebrate and study this phenomenon, five days in November are given over to the appreciation of all things raptor. Guided walks by naturalists, work-shops and slide shows, live bird demos, and cultural events (including Tlingit dancing and art exhibits) are presented.

FOUR HOURS OR LESS

Beneath its normal exterior, Haines is home to quirky and fascinating people and projects, such as the Ham-mer Museum and the Tsirku Canning Co. Museum, each the product of a collector's passions run amuck. Unusual tours, like Offbeat Haines, give a flavor of what makes this community unique. A stroll through town is bound to introduce you to interesting local characters.

WALKING TOURS

Haines Walking Tour *(2 hours)*

This tour covers both downtown Haines and Fort Seward. You can cut the time in half by eliminating one. There are a few gentle hills but no stairs. For walking tour map, see page 150.

❶ Start from the attractive **visitor center** (122 2nd Ave), just south of Willard Street. The center is well staffed in summer, with ample visitor resources. Across Second Avenue are several galleries, including the **Far North, Wind Spirit**, and **Uniquely Alaskan Art**; around the corner on Willard are a few more shops.

❷ Walk up to Willard; turn right, go one block, then turn left onto First Avenue. Continue up to Main Street, where you'll find the entrance to the **Sheldon Museum**.

❸ Cross Main Street and turn left, heading away from the water. If you're lucky, you'll have a dazzling view of the Chilkat Mountains ahead. Walk up to Second Avenue. On the way, you pass the charming cottage that contains the **Hammer Museum**. On the same block, between First and Second Avenues, are two popular local hangouts: the **Fogcutter Bar** (907/766-2555) in a building dating from 1923, and **Grizzly Greg's Pizzeria** (907/766-3622), built in 1916 and at four stories still the tallest building in town.

❹ For a look at more of old Haines, turn right on Second Avenue. On the left is the red **Bamboo Room** and **Pioneer Bar**. This building began life as the Hotel de France, an upscale, circa-1900 boardinghouse with continental overtones, but by the 1930s it had devolved into a brothel and bootleg establishment. In 1953 Marty Tengs and her husband purchased the enterprise, and it's been in the family ever since, now presided over by Christy Tengs Fowler. A block north on Second, across the street, is the **Captain's Choice Motel**.

❺ At the corner of Second and Union is the Summer Inn B&B, once the **Vogel Lammers House**, built in 1912 by Tim Vogel, a member of Soapy Smith's gang in Skagway (see page 206). Turn left on Union Street (it's unmarked, the first street past the Summer Inn). The attractive **Lindholm House**, beyond the Assembly of God church, was built in 1912.

❻ Retrace your steps back on Second to Main Street, where you'll find many town businesses. Between Second and Third avenues on the right is a large gift shop: **Chilkoot Gardens**. On the second floor above the adjacent building is **Alaska Backcountry Outfitters**. Across the street is **Howser's IGA** next door to the **Babbling Book**. On the block west of Third Avenue, on the right side of Main Street, are several attractive old buildings with tiny but lovely flower gardens and, at the corner of Fourth and Main, **LAB Flying Service**.

❼ Crossing Fourth Avenue, you pass the **Alaska Sport Shop**, and then the **Tsirku Canning Co. Museum**.

❽ At Sixth Avenue, cross the street and turn down the other side of Main Street, heading to the water. Notice the **Friendship totem pole** in front of the elementary and middle school.

❾ Continue down Main to Third Avenue and turn right. You'll pass the spiffy new **Haines Public Library**. A little farther on, at the junction of Third Avenue and the Haines Highway is the popular whole-foods store and café, **Mountain Market**. Turn left onto the Haines Highway and head back toward the water. (To the right, the Haines Highway leads to the public swimming pool, on to the state fairgrounds, and eventually to the Canadian border and the Alaska Highway.)

❿ Cross the Haines Highway (carefully) and walk down to Second Avenue. Just southeast of Second is the **American Bald Eagle Foundation**. Turn right onto Second Avenue and follow it past Mud Bay Road. As you approach **Fort Seward**, the name of the road becomes Fort Seward Drive and forms the southern boundary of the Fort Seward **Parade Ground**. The fort, a National Historic Landmark, was Alaska's only military base until 1940. After World War II, it was deactivated and sold to some U.S. veterans in a business venture.

Although it did not pan out, thanks to it the fort stayed in one piece and the buildings were preserved.

11 At the perimeter of the parade ground, turn right and walk uphill. To your immediate right is the **Guard House** and, above that, the **Fire Hall**. The next three buildings, which today make up the **Hotel Halsingland**, were once the **Officers Quarters**.

12 Turn left at the top of the parade ground onto **Officer's Row**. These lovely buildings with a great view of Portage Cove housed married officers and their families. The spacious duplexes have been restored. Some are private residences; several are B&Bs.

13 When you reach the end of Officer's Row, turn left and walk down the street with the parade ground on your left. Note the buildings on the parade ground, including a replica **Chilkat Tribal House** where performances by the New Chilkat Dancers Storytelling Theatre take place, plus the **Sea Wolf Gallery**. Salmon bakes are held here in summer when cruise ships are in port.

14 On your right you pass a house with a totem pole and cannon at either side. Once the **Fort Headquarters**, today it's a private residence. The next building down is the old **Fort Hospital**. Today it's home to **Alaska Indian Arts**. At the bottom of the parade ground, continue down Portage Street. To your left are a few fort buildings, somewhat dilapidated. The largest was a **barracks** that once housed the fort's enlisted men. Nearby are public restrooms.

15 Stores, art galleries, and restaurants are located on or just off Portage Street, including the **Fireweed Restaurant**, whose entrance is along an alley to your left. **Local Catch** (907/766-3557), open in summer (hours vary), makes a great stop for an espresso and a fresh bagel; they also offer sushi and a few Thai dishes. You'll pass **Sockeye Cycle** to the left and **Wild Iris** on the right. Continue to the end of the street at Beach Road. Straight ahead is the **Port Chilkoot Dock**, the city's cruise-ship dock.

15A For an optional extension, turn right and continue on Beach Road past Orca Arts & Crafts (which rents bikes) and the **Chilkat Cruises ferry dock**, where you'll find **Just for the Halibut**. If the weather is good and time allows, you can continue on to the **Portage Cove Campground** and **Battery Point Trail**. Be sure to check your tide table first. Then return via Beach Road.

16 At the intersection of Portage Street and Beach Road, turn left on Beach Road and head back to downtown Haines. You pass attractive **Lookout Park**, with picnic tables and a stunning view.

17 Across Beach Road away from the water is **Tlingit Park**, which contains an old **pioneer cemetery** with headstones dating from around 1900. Beyond the cemetery is the rest of the park, with public toilets, picnic tables, and a well-equipped children's playground.

18 Follow Beach Road, whose name changes to Front Street, then to Main Street. Down Main Street on the right is **Portage Cove**. At the **Small Boat Harbor** is the dock from which **Alaska Fjordlines** departs for Skagway and Juneau (see page 219 in the Skagway chapter). Turn left again onto First Avenue. To return to the visitor center, turn right on Willard Street.

HISTORY & CULTURE

In one of the larger Fort Seward buildings, **Indian Arts** (15 minutes; 13 Fort Seward Dr; 907/766-2160; *www. alaskaindianarts.com*; Mon–Tues, Fri 9am–5pm, Wed–Thurs 7am–9:30pm; free)—a combination of school, museum, and art gallery— showcases the work of local Tlingit artists past and present. Masterpieces by some of Alaska's foremost Native artists, such as glassblower Preston Singletary and carver John Hagen, were created here. Works range from prints and engraved silver jewelry to carved masks, bowls, and totem poles. Those with the means can commission their own pole; everyone can watch the artists at work. Workshops are offered on traditional arts.

If hammers don't strike you as much of a tourist attraction, a trip through the **Hammer Museum** (15 minutes; 108 Main St; 907/766-2374; *pahlfam@apt alaska.net*; daily in summer—call for details; $2), in a small, charming house on Main Street, could change your mind. Try visiting when its founder, Dave Pahl, is on hand to guide you around. His passion for hammers in all their surprising variety is contagious. As a homesteader without electrical service, Pahl found that what could be accomplished without it gave him a new respect for simple tools: particularly hammers. He moved from simple collecting through eBay transactions to finally opening a museum. Ancient Roman hammers; combination hammers–and–tent pegs from the U.S. Civil War; decorated hammers; long, extendable hammers for attaching billboard posters to the sides of barns—they're all here. By far the spookiest exhibit is an ancient Tlingit stone hammer that Pahl discovered when he was excavating his basement. It was used for ceremonially killing slaves.

Inside the cavernous, nondescript building of the **Bald Eagle Foundation** (30 minutes; 113 Haines Hwy; 907/766-3094; *baldeagles.org*; summer Mon–Tues, Fri 9am–5pm, Wed–Thurs 9am–10pm, Sat–Sun 1–5pm; winter by appt; $3) is a large room full of stuffed wildlife, from tiny hummingbirds to giant brown bears. If you have literate small fry in tow, get them to match the animals to the names on the list provided to visitors. A theater shows a video about bald eagles and the annual festival held here in their honor. The best reason to visit the museum is the chance to hear its founder, Dave Olerud, expound on eagles, ecosystems in balance and imbalance, global warming, and whatever else takes his fancy. He can be spotted in his wheelchair, engaging spellbound listeners just about any day of the week. When cruise ships are in, he gives formal presentations. A small but excellent gift shop carries wildlife books and locally made arts, crafts, and goodies, with some of the best prices in Haines.

The Tlingit dancers of **New Chilkat Dancers Storytelling Theatre**, under the auspices of Alaska Indian Arts and Tresham Gregg, artist/owner of the Sea Wolf and Whale Rider Galleries, perform an hour of dances and plays at **Totem Village Tribal House** (parade ground, Fort Seward; 907/766-2540; summer Mon, Wed, Fri 5–6pm, Wed–Thurs 7:30–8:30pm; $10/adult, $5/4–14, free/under 4) when cruise ships are in town. Schedules are prone to change, so be sure to confirm times. The dark tribal house setting is suitably atmospheric for these mesmerizing performances. Recorded music is enhanced by live drumming (attendees may be pressed into service here). The stories acted out and danced are authentic, sometimes funny, and often hauntingly complex.

Sheldon Museum & Cultural Center (1 hour; 11 Main St; 907/766-2366; *www.sheldonmuseum.org*; summer Mon–Fri 11am–6pm, Sat–Sun 2–6pm; winter Mon–Fri 1–4pm; $3/adult, free/under 12) offers an excellent synopsis of local history, including a concise explanation of the complex Tlingit moiety system. Native arts from basketry to Chilkat blanket weaving to carving are well represented. The history of Alaska's Russian settlements is covered, and there is a fascinating if gruesome history of famous Alaska shipwrecks. Downstairs, more recent history is explored, including the building of the highways to the interior along the three "grease" trail routes that Tlingit traders developed and controlled, trading eulachon (also known as "hooligan" or "candlefish") oil with Tlingit and Athabascan people on the other side of the mountains until the Klondike gold rush.

Like the Hammer Museum, the **Tsirku Canning Co. Museum** (1 hour; 5th and Main; 907/766-3474; mid-May–mid-Sept; $10/adult, free/under 12 with accompanying adult) is the result of an unusual passion given free rein, and it's just as fascinating. Tours are given several times a day when cruise ships are in town. The founder, Jim Szymanski—with the support of his long-suffering wife—assembled a complete canning line here with beautifully refurbished machines that once made salmon tins, filled them with salmon, then sealed and labeled them. The story of how the machines were brought to Haines is at least as interesting as watching them at work. Factoids of salmon-canning history divulged include the fact that labels were colored red to cover up signs of rust and that the lilies that grow everywhere in Haines were the contribution of Chinese laborers brought here to work on the "slime line." Today each tin costs 25 cents to produce—more than the salmon that goes inside it. There's a small gift shop. Plans are afoot to move the museum to the now-closed cannery in picturesque Letnikof Cove.

GUIDED TOURS

Chilkat Classic Motorcars pitches its Classic Motorcars Tours (1 hour) of Haines to accessibility-challenged visitors with a fondness for old-time automobiles. If that description applies to you, you might enjoy zipping around town in a 1939 Packard, a 1948 DeSoto Woody, or another of five lovingly restored vintage vehicles.

The bus tour offered by **Chilkat Cruises & Tours**, the company that operates the fast ferry to Skagway (2.5 hours; $36), hits the town's high spots, including Fort Seward, the Sheldon Museum, and a scenic drive to Letnikof Cove.

The versatile John Katzeek, a Tlingit elder from the nearby village of Klukwan, is behind **Keet Gooshi Tours**. Katzeek puts his position and life experience to good use on van tours (3 hours; $71/adult, $44/under 12) that include Klukwan, where visitors tour a salmon smokehouse and tribal house. The tours also visit the Chilkat Bald Eagle Preserve. The word *keet gooshi* means "killer whale," Katzeek's moiety (see sidebar, page 93). This is a rare chance to visit a contemporary Tlingit community.

Rainbow Glacier Adventures, a venture of Haines photographer and tour guide Joe Ordonez, has a selection of guided tours that offer something out of the usual. **Offbeat Haines** (2 hours) visits some lesser-known attractions; the **Artist's tour** (3.5 hours) focuses on local arts and crafts, while the **Taste of Haines** (4.5 hours) tour focuses on food; the **All-American tour** (3.5 hours) is centered on things that begin with the letter "B" (including bald eagles and beer); while the **Highlights of Haines** (3.5 hours) is nature oriented. All include wildlife viewing. Ordonez will customize tours on request; call for prices.

SHOPPING

For a town with fewer than 2,000 residents and lacking much in the way of cruise-ship traffic, Haines presents visitors with remarkably good shopping opportunities. Most galleries and stores are locally owned; you won't find a giant T-shirt emporium among them. Galleries are divided between Fort Seward and downtown Haines.

Art

ALASKA NATIVE ARTISTS: Start at **Alaska Indian Arts** to get up to speed on local Tlingit arts and crafts and to purchase high-end, authentic Tlingit art. **The Far North** (111 2nd Ave; 907/766-3535) carries Eskimo art from northern Alaska and northern Canada. Ivory and whalebone carvings, objects made from whale baleen, basketry, and dolls are specialties. A few items from the interior, such as moosehair tufting, are also sold. The **Sheldon Museum** is another good source for information on Native art and carries a selection of authentic arts and crafts. Wild Iris (see below) carries Eskimo ivory.

HAINES ARTISTS: Local phenom Tresham Gregg, although not Native Alaskan, combines an encyclopedic and intimate knowledge of Native art with a wide-ranging education, artistic and worldly, and displays the impressive results in his two shops: the **Sea Wolf Gallery**, in the Fort Seward Parade Ground, and the **Whale Rider Gallery**, nearby on Portage Street (for both: 907/766-2540). The versatile artist creates wall carvings, masks and totems large and small, lamps, appliquéd jackets, and sculptures, as well as jewelry in a variety of materials.

The magnificent garden and view at **Wild Iris** (Portage St, Fort Seward; 907/766-2300) are so entrancing that you might forget to go inside. Don't. In this excellent gallery are arts and crafts ranging from lower-priced gifts, such as silkscreened T-shirts and art cards, to elaborate mosaic mirrors and jewelry. All work is created locally, except for the Eskimo ivory. **Windspirit** (109 2nd Ave S; 907/766-2858) carries an excellent array of local and Native Alaskan works, including jewelry, candles, knives, moose-hair tufting from the interior, dolls, pottery, and clothing. Handmade chocolate is on offer, too.

It's a 20-minute drive south of town but well worth the effort to find your way to **Extreme Dreams** (mile 6.5 Haines Rd, Mud Bay; 907/766-2097). The studio/gallery in an elegant building with gorgeous mountain views was designed by artist/owners John and Sharon Svenson, who sell their own and other local artists' work here. Chances are good you've seen one of Sharon's mosaic mirrors on display back in town.

Books

The small **Babbling Book** (223 Main St; 907/766-3356) carries a high-quality if limited assortment of books in most genres, along with cards, maps, periodicals, and gifts. The **Sheldon Museum** and **Bald Eagle Foundation** also sell Alaskana and books on natural history.

Several of the art galleries have Alaskana titles. For inexpensive selections in hard and soft cover selling for less than a dollar, visit the **Haines Public Library** (103 3rd Ave; 907/766-2545).

Clothing & Sundries

For outdoor clothing, try **Alaska Backcountry Outfitters** (210 Main St; 907/766-2876) and **Outfitter Sporting Goods** (mile 0, Haines Hwy; 907/766-3221). The seasonal **Lost Coast Surf Shop** (Portage St, Fort Seward; 907/766-2505, 800/539-3608) sells surfing accoutrements and a small selection of casual sportswear. Find women's clothing at **Caroline's Closet** (209 Main St; 907/766-3223). Also check out **Alaska Sport Shop** (420 Main St; 907/766-2441) in the closest thing Haines has to a mall.

Willard Street Treasures (215 Willard St; 907/766-3230) sells antiques and collectibles. It's fun to browse through what Alaska homesteaders once considered indispensable. Next door is **Chilkat Valley Arts** (209 Willard), with the same phone number. Along with beads and beading supplies, they have a good selection of jewelry for sale. Should you experience an emergency of a photographic nature, **King's Store** (104 Main St; 907/766-2336), with a photo lab, can help.

Food & Drink

Fans of whole and organic foods will find what they need at **Mountain Market** (3rd Ave and Haines Hwy; 907/766-3340), along with an excellent café. The large **Howser's IGA** (209 Main St; 907/766-2040) has an ATM as well as a lot of groceries, and is open daily for long hours in summer.

The **Dejon Delights Smokery** (off Portage Rd, Fort Seward; 907/766-2505, 800/539-3608) smokes and sells salmon and halibut, as well as salmon caviar. Unusual products include "Lookout Stout" (smoked sockeye brined in an Alaskan microbrew) and "Extra Special," a rum-cured cold-smoked salmon. There is a small assortment of locally made gifts at modest prices. The smoked fish keeps up to 10 days unrefrigerated, 6 months refrigerated, and a year in the freezer.

For something completely different, investigate **Great Land Wines** (817 Small Tract Rd; 907/766-2698,

Good Buys

Throughout Southeast Alaska, **Birch Boy Syrups** *(www.birchboy.com)* are sold; here in the Chilkat Valley is where they are made. Most are distilled from local berries, but some come from more exotic sources, such as birch and spruce tips. Although many Haines stores and galleries carry them, prices for identical products vary significantly; shop around for bargains. Some stores allow you to try the syrup first, which is recommended when you're contemplating a purchase of rhubarb pancake syrup. The Bald Eagle Foundation gift shop has a good selection for tasting.

907/766-2096). You can arrange a winery tour and free tasting (call in advance) before throwing caution to the winds and springing for one of their high-priced splits at a local liquor store or the Bamboo Room. Most wines are made from local fruits and flowers. Among the exotic offerings are Chilkat Cherry, Clover, Rose Hip, and Fireweed Flower wines. Great Lands has also experimented with vegetables, including carrot, beet, and potato wines. Their Zwiebel (onion wine) won an international competition in 2002. Really.

NATURE

First the bad news: There are not a lot of bald eagles at the **Chilkat Bald Eagle Preserve** (1 hour, plus 1 hour for transportation; 907/766-2292 or 907/766-3094) during the summer. There are always some, including nesting couples with offspring and rebellious tow-headed teens learning to fish for themselves on the Chilkat River flats. However, unless you are here in late fall or early winter, you will not see those trees packed with eagles, as featured prominently on tourist brochures. Like their human counterparts, eagles have plenty of options for salmon fishing during the summer, of which the preserve is just one. On the other hand, the preserve does offer scenic, wheelchair-accessible riverside trails to hike with interpretive signage. In late summer, bears may amble by, hunting for salmon; also expect a lot of sightings of rubber boats filled with tourists. To maximize wildlife sightings, take a float trip or hike close to dawn or dusk (see Kayaking & Rafting, page 178, and Hiking, pages 175–76).

Bear Watching

In August and September, Haines is one of the best places in Alaska for bear watching. Until recently, the **Chilkoot Lake State Recreation Site** (9 miles north of town on Lutak Rd) was a well-kept secret. It's out now, though, and visitors are seizing the opportunity to spot brown bears playing and fishing north of town along the banks of the short but beautiful Chilkoot River. When salmon are running, bears head down across the road in droves to fish close to the river's weir, which they seem to view as their personal sushi bar. Sightings are best at dusk when cars line the road's narrow shoulder and park rangers are called into service to direct traffic. As tourists stand elbow to elbow hoisting digital cameras and camcorders, the experience can feel less like communing with nature and more like attending a rock concert. What is fascinating is that the bears seem oblivious to it all; once they're in the river it's all about the salmon, and there are few sights more awesome than a sow teaching her obstreperous cubs to fish. It only adds to the pleasure to know that, unlike your visitor counterparts elsewhere in Alaska, your bear-viewing experience did not come with a $1,000 price tag or require a stomach-churning float-plane ride.

Flightseeing

Flying over **Glacier Bay** from Haines makes sense; weather is likely to be better than in Juneau or Ketchikan, where other Glacier Bay flyovers originate. Locally based **LAB Flying Service** offers tours over Glacier Bay (55 minutes; $140, 2-person minimum). **Mountain Flying Service** has three tours from Haines: a flight over the east arm of Glacier Bay (1 hour; $129), a flight over the west arm of Glacier Bay (1.3 hours; $169), and a "Pilot's Choice" tour over Glacier Bay to the Pacific and Lituya Inlet, including a possible beach landing (2 hours; $269). There's a two-person minimum. They also provide charter flights daily to local destinations. **Skagway Air Service**, most of whose trips are out of Skagway, also offers flightseeing tours of Glacier Bay from Haines (1.5 hours; $140/adult, $105/child), along with scheduled daily flights to Skagway and Juneau from Haines.

Wildlife Tours

Alaska Nature Tours offers two guided **bus tours** that bring visitors into the **Chilkat Bald Eagle Preserve** and the landscape surrounding Haines (3 hours: $55/adult, $40/under 13; 4 hours: $65/adult, $50/under 13; multiple daily departures). The focus is not just on viewing eagles. Marine life—whales, seals, porpoises, seabirds—and moose and mountain goats are also on the agenda. Seeing bears is a possibility, but if bear watching is your primary interest, you're better off taking an evening bear-watching tour. Spotting scopes help to bring the wildlife into focus. Lunch is provided on the longer tour. Both include transportation.

Prospective bear watchers who lack wheels need not despair. **Keet Gooshi Tours** offers an evening **bear-watching van tour** (2–3 hours; $40) and brings plenty of local knowledge to the task. The Twilight Wildlife Watch (2.5 hours; $50/adult, $35/under 13) from **Alaska Nature Tours** does not guarantee bear sightings but does claim a 99 percent success rate in doing so. Note that as with many wildlife-viewing excursions, time may be extended a bit—if passengers are agreeable—to maximize viewing opportunities.

ROAD TRIPS

Chilkoot Lake State Recreation Site
(20 miles/1 hour)

Starting from the visitor center, follow Second Avenue north out of town (away from Fort Seward). As you leave town bearing right, Second becomes Lutak Road.

The road hugs the water; to the right is Portage Cove. In 1 mile there's a large turnout with great views of the mountains across the water. Stop and look back the way you came for a panoramic view of Haines. As you leave Portage Cove behind, Lutak Road continues to hug Chilkoot Inlet, then rounds a point to **Lutak Inlet**. At mile 3.1 you pass an old oil-tanker dock dating from World War II. Once used as a fuel transport site by the military, the site is being dismantled and cleaned up.

Four and a half miles from Haines is the **AMHS ferry dock**, where all state ferries depart and arrive. At mile 5.2 you pass the site of an old sawmill. Haines lost its last sawmill in the late 1970s. The road becomes increasingly scenic, with several turnouts where you can park and take in the view. At mile 6.5 you pass the Salmon Run RV park and campground.

Beyond the campground, the inlet narrows, and in 2 miles you reach the tiny but gorgeous **Chilkoot River**, a rushing, shallow, but vigorous river that attracts salmon and fishers—ursine and human—in search of them. If you turn onto the Chilkoot River bridge at mile 9.2, you can drive 0.6 mile to the turnaround at the end of the road. On your left are houses facing south, down Lutak Inlet; the lucky residents have one of the best views in Southeast Alaska, which is saying a lot.

Turn around and drive back over the bridge; go right to follow the Chilkoot River up to **Chilkoot Lake**. The road is quite narrow in places, but there are several pullouts. In August and September, this is where the fishers congregate. It's along this stretch that bears amble down from the forest to fish, often with cubs in tow. A fish weir, maintained by the Alaska Department of Fish and Game, is placed across the river in summer to count the sockeye salmon coming back to Chilkoot Lake. The road ends at the **Chilkoot State Recreation Site** campground. The lake is lovely; there are several ways to get out on it (see Kayaking & Rafting, page 178).

Chilkat State Park *(16.5 miles/1 hour)*

From the visitor center, follow Second Avenue to Fort Seward. Turn right onto Mud Bay Road and follow it around the top of Fort Seward and out of town.

The road runs south along the highly scenic Chilkat Inlet, across which rise the Chilkat Mountains.

Three miles along is the trailhead for the **Mount Riley Trail**. Shortly thereafter you'll be rewarded with a view of two stunning glaciers: to the left and farther off as you face west is **Davidson Glacier**; to its right and much closer is **Rainbow Glacier**, from which a huge waterfall cascades down.

At mile 5.3 you see the picturesque red buildings belonging to the old salmon cannery. At mile 6.5 is **Extreme Dreams** (see Shopping, page 164) on the right. The road into Chilkat State Park at mile 6.7 soon becomes gravel and is steep enough to require gearing down. On the way, you pass the turnoff for the **Seduction Point Trail**. There is a park ranger cabin with a viewpoint (the deck is a great place to view the glaciers and waterfalls) near the bottom. At the end is a large, paved boat ramp, a turnaround, and room to park and get out for a spot of beachcombing.

For contact information for outfitters and tour operators listed in this chapter, see sidebar on pages 174–75.

CYCLING

Sockeye Cycle offers three short bike tours from Haines. Each requires a group of at least three and up to twelve participants. A tour of **Haines, Fort Seward, and the Chilkat River estuary** (1.5 hours; $42) runs 6 miles and requires a moderate level of fitness. A longer but easier 8-mile tour to **Chilkoot Lake** (3 hours; $90) runs along Lutak Inlet, with great scenery and wildlife. The minimum age is 10 for both trips. A tour called the "Glory Hole Bicycle Adventure" (3.5 hours; $95) runs 11 miles and requires a moderate level of fitness. This rugged trip takes you along the shore of Chilkoot Lake into the Chilkat Bald Eagle Preserve. The two longer trips include a snack.

Sockeye Cycle also has a variety of bikes, including kids' bikes, for rent ($12/2 hours; $20/4 hours; $30/8 hours; discounts for multiday rentals). Helmets and locks are included. **Orca Gifts and Mini Mart** also rents bikes ($10/5 hours; $15/day, must be returned by 9pm). Helmets and locks are included. Credit cards or cash security deposits are required in all cases.

FISHING

A generous assortment of halibut- and salmon-fishing charters are run out of Haines. Expect to pay $100 per person for 4 hours. For many more possibilities than are listed here, check with the Haines visitor center. Note that some charters advertising in Haines actually operate out of Skagway. Unless you're going there, your best bet is to stick with Haines-based charters.

Hart's Fishing Charters include fishing equipment, bait, cleaning and filleting your catch, land transportation, plus a snack. **Whale Tale Charters** offer much the same. Freshwater fishing charters are also available (the Chilkat River attracts more than just bald eagles: all five Pacific salmon species, plus Dolly Varden, swim up the Chilkat to spawn).

HIKING

From Downtown

Even if you're not here during the Southeast Alaska State Fair in August, a stroll along the Haines Highway to the simulated Klondike-era **Dalton City** and the **State Fairgrounds** (90 minutes) makes a good hike from downtown Haines. The fairgrounds are less than a mile from the visitor center; follow Second Avenue to Mission Street and turn right. The road runs into the Haines Highway. Between Third Avenue and Allen Road, you pass Haines High School, where the **swimming pool** (907/766-2666) is open to the public 6 days a week ($3.50/adult, $2.50/student, senior). To get to the fairgrounds, turn left on Fair Drive and follow it to the parking lot (both can be muddy in wet weather, so boots are recommended footwear). The Dalton City set created for the Walt Disney film *White Fang* is home to the **Haines Brewing Company** (108 White Fang Wy; 907/766-3823). Here you can test-drive a microbrew made with spruce buds, along with more conventional offerings (tours and tasting Mon–Sat 1–7pm). Nearby is the **Klondike Restaurant** (296 Fair Dr; 907/766-2477; open seasonally).

From downtown, the round-trip **Battery Point Trail** (2–3 hours) hike is 7 miles, but if you start from the

Port Chilkoot cruise-ship or fast-ferry docks, you can shave off a mile round trip. The easy, scenic hike, with no appreciable elevation gain, follows Portage Cove into Chilkat State Park. Start your journey on Beach Road in Fort Seward (see #10 on the Walking Tour, page 158, if you're coming from downtown); head away from town, with the water on your left. A little farther on the left is the tent-only Portage Cove Campground, where campers can escape from RVs on a small, pleasant knoll with a picnic area. Continue to the end of the road (motorists can drive up to this point; there's parking, but not much) and follow the "trail" sign. The trail wanders through mossy spruce forest with occasional devil's club nettles to keep you on your toes. After nearly a mile, you arrive at a fork in the trail. The right fork leads to the **Mount Riley trails**; the left goes to Battery Point, eventually coming out at a wide pebble beach. When your view is clear of trees, scan the water for whales, fishing boats, and cruise ships. In May and June, look for lupines in bloom; in August and September, be on the lookout for bears.

With a Car

The accessible **Chilkat Bald Eagle Preserve Trail** (1 hour, plus 1 hour for transportation) runs 1.5 miles through the prime Council Grounds of the preserve, 19 miles out of Haines along the Haines Highway. It's anchored at both ends with paved pullouts where drivers can park and access the trail. At the southernmost pullout are restrooms and a drinking fountain, with interpretive signs on the preserve and a 0.25-mile-long boardwalk leading to an observation platform with viewing scopes. This is a real highway, used by truckers and commuters. Shoulders are limited or nonexistent. Don't ever park in the road; always use the pullouts.

Guided Hikes

Alaska Nature Tours offers a 3-mile Chilkat Peninsula guided **rain forest hike** (4 hours; $65), suitable for anyone seven or older who is in reasonably good health and able to handle trail walking. A lunch on the beach and transportation are included.

KAYAKING & RAFTING

Deishu Expeditions & Alaska Kayak Supply offers a half-day **kayaking trip** (4 hours; $85; May–Sept) that is suitable for all, including beginners and children. Instruction and a snack are included. Destinations vary, depending on weather and where the wildlife—the focus of this journey—is. Identical trips are offered for independent travelers and as cruise-ship shore excursions. If too few people sign up for an independent trip, they may be asked to join a cruise-ship shore excursion instead.

Given how shallow the **Chilkat River** is, "float" may be too strong a word for this trip (4 hours; $79/adult, $62/ages 7–12; multiple daily departures; hotel pickup and drop-off); when water is low, rubber rafts frequently run aground and steps (literally) must be taken to get them back on their way. But though the trip features neither white water nor white knuckles, it does drift, with occasional bumps, down a lovely river in blissfully peaceful surroundings. **Chilkat Guides** does the heavy lifting and rowing, pointing out eagles, bears, and sights of interest, including the Tlingit town of Klukwan, from the water. Passengers disembark, eat a snack, then are bused back to downtown Haines. This is a good tour for less-mobile visitors and younger children.

River Adventures offers **Chilkat River jet-boat tours** (3.5 hours; several daily departures; call for prices) that are a good choice for people who want to get out on the water in the Chilkat Bald Eagle Preserve without having to get in and out of a raft. The boats can be noisy, but these locally owned tours are popular and so far none of the wildlife seems to object.

ONE DAY

NATURE

Between Memorial Day and Labor Day, **Alaska Fjord-lines** offers daily sightseeing trips to Juneau and back (10.5 hours; $139/adult, $109/ages 2–12) from Haines and Skagway to Juneau and back, leaving Haines at 9am and returning at 7:30pm. The price includes a trip to Mendenhall Glacier and onboard snacks. For details, see One Day in the Skagway chapter, page 219.

Haines Outfitters & Tour Operators

Alaska Backcountry Outfitters 210 Main St; 907/766-2876; www.kcd.com

Alaska Boat Rentals 425 Beach Rd; 907/766-2427, 800/552-9257; www.alaskaboatrentals.com

Alaska Mountain Guides and Climbing School 907/766-3366, 800/766-3396; alaskamountainguides.com

Alaska Nature Tours 907/766-2876; kcd.com/aknature/contact.htm

Alaska Sport Shop 420 Main St; 907/766-2441

Chilkat Classic Motorcars 907/766-2491; ClassicMotorcars@ChilkatGuides.com

Chilkat Cruises & Tours 142 Beach Rd; 907/766-2100, 888/766-2103; www.chilkatcruises.com

Chilkat Guides 907/766-2491; raftalaska.com

Deishu Expeditions & Alaska Kayak Supply 425 Beach Rd; 907/766-2427, 800/552-9257; www.seakayaks.com

Haines Shuttle & Tours 907/766-3138

Hart's Fishing Charters 907/766-2683; www.hartsalaskafishing.com

CYCLING

The **Chilkat Pass Bike Tour** (8 hours; $120) from **Sockeye Cycle** offers a rare opportunity to get out into Tatshenshini-Alsek Provincial Park, part of our planet's largest protected wilderness. The ride takes you across spectacular country, through alpine vegetation with nearby glaciers. The trip is classified as moderately strenuous; participants should be fit. This tour is also offered as an overnight outing (see Two Days or More, page 178). Meals are included; minimum age is 12.

For bike rentals, see Four Hours or Less, page 170.

Keet Gooshi Tours 907/766-2168, 877/776-2168; www.keetgooshi.com

LAB Flying Service 390 Main St; 907/766-2222, 800/426-0543; labflying.com

Mountain Flying Service 132 2nd Ave; 907/766-3007; lyglacierbay.com

Orca Gifts and Mini Mart across street from Port Chilkoot dock, 57 Beach Rd; 907/766-2741

Outfitter Sporting Goods Mile 0, Haines Hwy; 907/766-3221

Rainbow Glacier Adventures 907/766-3576; joeordonez.com

River Adventures 907/766-2050, 800/478-9827; www.jetboatalaska.com

Skagway Air Service 907/766-3233; www.skagwayair.com

Sockeye Cycle 24 Portage Dr, Fort Seward; 907/766-2869; cyclealaska.com

Whale Tale Charters 907/209-5874, 907/766-2945

Wings of Alaska 907/586-6275; www.wingsofalaska.com

FISHING

All-day fishing excursions start around $175 per person. See Four Hours or Less, page 171, and Two Days or More, page 178; also check at the visitor center for charter options.

HIKING

From Downtown

The popular hike up **Mount Ripinski** (8–10 hours), although not technically difficult, is best for reasonably fit and experienced hikers. To access the trail, follow Second Avenue away from Fort Seward; don't turn onto Lutak Road, but stay on Second, which becomes Young Road after Oslund Drive. Where the road forks, stay left and follow the power lines as the road gets narrower and rougher. The trailhead is on the left in front of a gate; if you've walked from downtown, you've already put in 1.5 miles. You can cut hiking time by getting a lift to the trailhead.

The trail ascends through a cross section of Southeast Alaska ecosystems, from hemlock and spruce rain forest through alpine meadows, past the tree line to bare rock. There can be snow on the trail until mid-July. From the summit, panoramic views sweep from Chilkat Mountain icefields down Lynn Canal as far as Admiralty Island, with glimpses of Taiya Inlet.

Try this hike in good weather only. Don't be tempted to take shortcuts, and do turn back if there is a sudden onset of bad weather. Bring water and a topographic map (USGS 1:63,360 series is recommended). There is a register to sign at the 3,650-foot north summit. Believe it or not, a run up Mount Ripinski is a popular annual Fourth of July event.

With a Car

Three routes lead to the summit of 1,760-foot **Mount Riley** (3.5–5 hours). Although it is possible to do this hike in a half day, it's a strenuous half day, so you might prefer to take a slower, easier route and pace yourself. Access is from the Battery Point Trail (see Four Hours or Less, page 171), from Mud Bay Road 3 miles out of Fort Seward, and from Lily Lake. Each route varies in time and difficulty. The **Battery Point access route** (5 hours) is 8 miles round trip and climbs steeply through forest and muskeg meadow. The **Mud Bay Road route** (3.5 hours) is shortest but also the hardest and steepest. It's about 6 miles round trip. The start of the trail on Mud Bay Road is well marked and there is parking. At the top of the steep first section, the trail intersects with the Lily Lake route, then zigzags up to the summit. For the 6-mile **Lily Lake route** (4.5 hours), take the well-marked FAA Road behind Officer's Row in Fort Seward to the end, about 1 mile, and turn right before you get to the city dump. Walk along the city water-supply access road, about 2 miles, to meet the trail that comes from Mud Bay Road. At the summit are gorgeous views of the Chilkat River, Lynn Canal, and Taiya Inlet.

The **Seduction Point Trail** (8–10 hours, plus 1 hour for transportation) in Chilkat State Park lives up to its enticing name. At 6.8 miles one way, it makes for a long day, but you can easily turn it into an overnight camp-out. The trailhead and parking area are located along the Chilkat State Park gravel road (off Mud Bay Road). The lovely trail starts out in forest and, after a few miles, reaches the beach, which it follows to the end of the Chilkat Peninsula: Seduction Point. The trail, without appreciable elevation gain, is not so much difficult as it is long. (It's important to use a tide table when planning your hike so be sure to take one with you.) The last stretch of beach requires a fairly low tide to negotiate. The views of the Chilkat Mountains and Davidson and Rainbow glaciers across Chilkat Inlet are magnificent. If you decide to camp out, there are several inviting coves to choose from; check with the visitor center for information.

Guided Hikes

Three guided hikes, with lunch included, are offered by **Alaska Nature Tours**: the Seduction Point Trail (4 hours; $60), Mount Riley Trail (5 hours; $70), and Mount Ripinski Trail (8 hours; $100).

KAYAKING

Although this **sea kayak day trip** (8 hours; $125; May–Sept) by **Deishu Expeditions & Alaska Kayak Supply** is a full day, it's suitable for beginners who really want to get their feet wet (so to speak) and learn to kayak. Destinations vary, depending on weather and where the marine life is hanging out. However, most trips explore the Chilkat Peninsula south of Haines.

For kayak rentals, see listing under Two Days or More, page 178.

For contact information for outfitters and tour operators listed in this chapter, see sidebar on pages 174–75.

TWO DAYS OR MORE

GENERAL OUTFITTING SERVICES

Alaska Backcountry Outfitters provides gear and clothing for hikers and climbers, skiers and snowboarders, and kayakers. They can arrange and guide multiday tours. **Alaska Mountain Guides and Climbing School** offers a variety of multiday mountaineering courses from Haines, including rock and ice climbing. The shortest are two days; the longest is three weeks. They lead a variety of mountain climbing and skiing expeditions. **Outfitter Sporting Goods** has a large assortment of clothing and gear for camping, fishing, and hunting, as does the **Alaska Sport Shop**.

CYCLING

Sockeye Cycle offers their **Chilkat Pass tour** (see One Day, page 174) as an overnight trip ($320). Camping gear and four meals are included. Participants must be age 12 or older. The company also leads several long trips, from 9 to 11 days. One follows the Golden Circle Route, one follows the old Canol Highway, and one combines ferry travel and cycle. They outfit custom trips, as well.

FISHING

Powerboats for fishing can be rented from **Alaska Boat Rentals** ($300/8 hours plus fuel; $450/day, plus fuel, for each additional day). You can pick up the powerboat in either Haines or Skagway and drop it off in the other town for an extra $50. Boats come fully equipped with fishing poles; you supply your own tackle and bait.

KAYAKING & RAFTING

Chilkat Guides offers multiday river rafting expeditions from Haines into the Yukon Territory and Glacier Bay area: a 10-day trip on the Tatshenshini River ($2,495) and a 13-day trip on the Alsek ($2,995). **Deishu Expeditions & Alaska Kayak Supply Inc**. offers **multiday kayaking trips** out of Haines. One takes you around Seduction

Point to the glaciers along the **Chilkat Inlet**. One goes to **Icy Strait** for some serious whale watching. For each, meals and camping are included; camping gear rental fees (small) are not. Levels of difficulty may vary depending on weather conditions and itinerary. An overnight trip to **Davidson Glacier** (2 days; $320) focuses on the former tidewater glacier that now empties into a freshwater lake. Hiking is included, to and on the glacier. Difficulty level is easy to moderate. **Chilkat Islands** (3–5 days; $160 per day) is a customizable trip south to these wildlife-packed islands and, usually, over to Rainbow Glacier. The final length is up to you. Difficulty level is moderate. For optimum whale-sighting possibilities, go in May or June.

For periods of one day or longer, May through September, Deishu Expeditions also rents single kayaks ($35/day for 1–2 days; $30/day for 3–5 days; $25/day for 6–10 days) and double kayaks ($55/day for 1–2 days; $45/day for 3–5 days; $35/day for 6–10 days). Kayaks come fully equipped, including navigational charts. Deposit varies depending on where you're taking the kayak. A shuttle to the launch site is available.

If you're interested in learning to be a kayak guide, Deishu Expeditions also has a training program that not only covers how to work with novice kayakers but also natural history, troubleshooting, food preparation, and more. Training trips are multiday and can be customized.

ROAD TRIP: THE GOLDEN CIRCLE ROUTE

Just a few miles north of Haines is some of the wildest, most beautiful terrain on the planet, as well as the world's largest protected wilderness. Four contiguous parks—British Columbia's Tatshenshini-Alsek Provincial Park, Canada's Kluane National Park, Alaska's Glacier Bay National Park and Preserve, and Wrangell–Saint Elias National Park and Preserve—come together here, collectively designated a UNESCO World Heritage Site.

Even if you have only a few days to work with, you can get a taste of this extraordinary wilderness by driving the Golden Circle Route, which connects Haines to Skagway by three paved highways. Though separated by just 14 water miles, the towns are nearly 360 miles apart by road. From Haines, the route follows the 150-mile Haines Highway over the Canadian border into British Columbia, then into the Yukon Territory to the small town of Haines Junction, skirting the edge of wild and beautiful Tatshenshini-Alsek Provincial Park and Kluane National Park, home to Canada's highest mountains. The national park's principal visitor center is in Haines Junction, along with amenities and services. From here, the route follows the Alaska Highway for 100 miles southeast to Whitehorse, the Yukon territorial capital with a population of 22,000. South of Whitehorse, the route leaves the Alaska Highway to follow the 109-mile South Klondike Highway along the Gold Rush route past Lake Bennett and Carcross down to Skagway. To complete the circle, from Skagway car-and passenger-ferry service is available back to Haines.

It is recommended that motorists take at least 3 days to make the trip. If you lack time to drive the full Golden Circle, consider going partway. You can drive to Haines Junction and back easily in one day, with time for a hike at Dezadeash Lake and a sumptuous dinner at the Raven (for which you'll need reservations), thanks to long summer days. Count on at least 16 hours of daylight.

A note of caution: Be sure your vehicle is roadworthy and that you have a spare tire, first-aid kit, and emergency supplies. Bring snacks and water. Keep track of what's in your gas tank: there are virtually no services for 100 miles from the outskirts of Haines to just outside Haines Junction.

At the time of writing, Americans need a birth certificate and photo ID or a passport. Although customs and immigration stations on either side of the border are tiny, long delays are rare. Still, they can happen, so factor in a half-hour wait at the border just in case. Remember that Yukon Territory and British Columbia observe Pacific time, which is an hour later than Alaska time.

Contact the following for information on Yukon destinations and driving the Golden Circle Route: **road conditions** in the Yukon (867/456-7623; *www.gov.yk.ca/roadreport/*) and **tourism information** (Government of Yukon, Department of Tourism & Culture, Box 2703; Whitehorse, YT Y1A 2C6; 800/661-0494; *www.touryukon.com*). For up-to-date information on crossing the international border, contact the U.S. border station (907/767-5540).

Haines Hwy to Haines Junction
(150 miles one way/3.5 hours)

Mile 0 of the Haines Highway is in downtown Haines. After passing the Haines airport, the highway runs to the right of the Chilkat River. The road is narrow and winding, with little or no shoulder. On a busy summer day, traffic is heavy with tourist buses and vans carrying float-trippers. Look for views of the Takhinsha mountains, rising beyond the river. Eight miles along are **two fish wheels** in the river operated by the Alaska Department of Fish and Game. These ingenious fish traps, widely used in Europe and the United States in the nineteenth century, were introduced to Alaska around 1900. The river's current rotates two baskets that turn on an axle, scooping up fish as they turn. When the fish are caught, they slide down a chute into a box in the water, which is taken out and emptied periodically. Fish are thus kept alive until retrieved from the box. Subsistence fishers in the north still use fish wheels. However, the Chilkat River's fish wheels are strictly catch and release. Fish are measured, tagged, and released for tracking.

At mile 9.4, you enter the **Chilkat Bald Eagle Preserve**. Throughout the preserve are pullouts where you can park and investigate the river. Look for the turnoff for the Tlingit village of **Klukwan** 21.5 miles from Haines (see Keet Gooshi Tours under Four Hours or Less, page 168). The highway soon crosses the Chilkat River and continues to the right of the Klehini River. At **Porcupine Crossing**, 5 miles past Klukwan, a side road off to the left leads to Porcupine Creek, site of a mini gold rush in 1898. One mile past Porcupine Crossing is the turnoff for the **Mosquito Lake State Recreation Site**, with a lakeside picnic area and campsites, a 2.4-mile drive from the highway on gravel road. Unfortunately, the site's name is well deserved.

Back on the highway, mile 31, a scenic viewpoint on the left has spectacular views; shortly thereafter you come to the eponymously named **33 Mile Roadhouse** (907/767-5510; summer Mon–Sat 7am–8pm, Sun 8am–6pm), the last chance for gas for 100 miles. It's a popular local hangout serving hearty fare. At mile 35.6, 2 miles beyond the 33 Mile Roadhouse, is a **scenic viewpoint** on the left with a paved parking area. There are interpretive signs about the Tlingit, the grease trail, and the gold rush. Views are spectacular down to the valley and west across to the mountains.

Forty miles from Haines, you cross the **international border** (907/767-5540) into British Columbia. The border station is open year-round; in summer, it's usually open 24 hours a day; otherwise, call for hours. Advance your watch one hour. Also, you're in kilometer land here; most signs are metric. A few of the prominent historic mileposts (HM) are referred to in the remainder of this section.

From the border, the road climbs up to the Chilkat Pass, growing ever more scenic. Along the way are several viewpoints. One, at **MP 48**, has sweeping views and signage on the history of the Haines Road. Just past this viewpoint, look to the east (to the right) for **Three Guardsmen Mountain** (6,300 feet/1,920 meters).

The Haines Highway is the eastern border of **Tatshenshini-Alsek Provincial Park**. The road ascends to a world of snowcapped peaks and glaciers. Near the summit there are no trees, just long, sweeping vistas. The road follows a huge U-shaped valley with numerous viewpoints where you can pull out and marvel at the majestic panorama in all directions. At mile 59, the summit of **Chilkat Pass** (3,510 feet/1,070 meters) has a double-ended paved turnout. It's well worth taking a break here. You are likely to have it all to yourself, even in summer, because this is not a highly traveled road.

From the summit, above the tree line, the landscape is otherworldly. Under good weather conditions, you can see for many miles. However, if there is a forest fire in the vicinity, visibility quickly deteriorates. You may wonder at the lone white building that can be spotted far off as you descend from the summit. It's an air strip with a white hangar. Just shy of 20 miles beyond Chilkat Pass is another viewpoint west into the provincial park; 86 miles out of Haines, you cross from British Columbia into Yukon Territory. In the Yukon, the park becomes **Kluane National Park and Reserve**.

For the remainder of the Golden Circle route, until you head down the South Klondike Highway to Skagway, you are on a high plateau, roughly 2,000 feet above sea level. At mile 93.5 is the turnoff to **Million Dollar Falls Campground**, a good place to break your journey. In addition to thirty-three campsites with kitchen shelters, there are outhouses, a playground, water (boil it first), and hiking trails. The boardwalk trail to the waterfall is especially scenic, but with stairs it's not accessible. You can fish in the Takhanne River for salmon, trout, and grayling. This is also prime brown bear country, especially when salmon are running. Be alert.

At **HM 118** is the turnoff to the Tlingit summer fish-camp community of **Klukshu**, 0.5 mile from the high-way on a gravel road. In town are a small crafts store and museum. Notice the meat and salmon caches and smokehouse. At mile 110.3 is the **Saint Elias Lake Trail-head**, with parking and an outhouse. The trail runs 2.4 miles (3.8 kilometers) one way to a pretty lake with a 400-foot elevation gain; it's also bear country.

At mile 114.5 is **Dezadeash Lake**, a large body of water almost like an inland sea; it's a popular destination for anglers fishing for grayling, trout, and north-ern pike. The campground at mile 115.6 has a gorgeous setting. There are twenty campsites, a kitchen shelter, outhouses, and a picnic area, but no drinking water. At mile 119.6 is the **Rock Glacier Interpretive Trail**. About 0.5 mile (0.8 kilometer) one way, the trail includes boardwalk.

The road flattens out after Dezadeash Lake, with long straight stretches. **Kathleen Lake Campground**, the only established campground in Kluane National Park, with all campground amenities, is at mile 130.2. You can fish for kokanee, grayling, and lake trout. Trails include the **Kokanee Trail**, an accessible 0.3-mile (0.5 kilometer) boardwalk nature trail, and the **King's Throne** (4–6 hours), rated difficult, 3.1 miles (5 kilome-ters) one way.

At mile 151.6 (**HM 1016** on the Alaska Highway) is the small town of **Haines Junction**. With a population of just 811, the town has a smattering of homes with a supermarket, a gas station, and several motels and restaurants (see pages 190–93). But the tiny town has plenty of alpine charm. Surrounded by towering, snow-covered peaks and the clear air, you may find yourself singing "The hills are alive with the sound of music."

For information of all kinds, stop in at the **Klu-ane National Park Visitor Center** (just off Alaska Hwy; 867/634-2345; May–Sept daily 8am–8pm, rest of year Mon–Fri 10am–4pm). Inside are restrooms, a the-ater, and natural-history displays. Check with staff for information on weather, bear sightings, and any recommendations. Interpretive programs are offered daily in summer for a fee. You can pick up a walking tour brochure for Haines Junction here. For essentials, groceries, postal services, and limited banking (plus an ATM), head to **Madley's General Store** (Alcan and Haines Hwys; 867/634-2200). Although Haines Junction is tiny, somehow visitors still manage to get lost in it. On your way out of town, make sure you're heading in the right direction.

You can access the **Dezadeash River Trail** from the center of town or drive to the Kluane RV Park and take the well-marked trail from there. It's a pleasant and easy 3-mile (4.8-kilometer) hike one way, with a 50-foot elevation gain, along the scenic river. About 0.3 mile along the way, an observation platform offers good area views.

Alaska Hwy to Whitehorse
(109 miles one way/2–3 hours)

Though it's the least exciting portion of the Golden Circle Route, by ordinary highway standards it's plenty scenic. For the first 30 miles, the Kluane Range remains in view (those heading west from Skagway will see the mountains better). Several viewpoints and recreation areas along the way offer the chance to stretch your legs and search for interesting wildlife.

At 5 miles out of Haines Junction, at **Pine Lake Recreation Park**, open late May to early September, you'll find a sandy beach and pretty lake (yes, it is possible to swim outdoors in the Yukon), along with a picnic area, a playground, potable water, a boat launch, and forty-two RV and tent sites. There's also an interpretive trail.

Fifty-nine miles south of Haines Junction, the **Takhini River Valley Viewpoint** has beautiful panoramic views from a viewing platform, with interpretive signs about the devastating forest fires of 1958 collectively known as the Takhini Burn. Watch for elk. About 12 miles farther you pass the **Takhini Salt Flats**. These oddities are bowl-shaped depressions in which salts rise to the surface, brought up by water from underground springs, remaining after the water has evaporated. The flats are home to *halophiles*, salt-loving plants found nowhere else in the Yukon, such as the rayless aster and brilliant red sea-asparagus. The flats are on public land and have attracted geologists, amateur and professional. Guided hikes to the area are sometimes offered. Check at the visitor center in Whitehorse.

Ten miles north of Whitehorse is the junction with Highway 2, the paved **Klondike Highway** that runs 333 miles north to Dawson City, ground zero of the Klondike gold rush.

Whitehorse

From the Alaska Highway, a road descends to Whitehorse, situated on the banks of the Yukon River with high-rises and all the amenities of a large city. The city is sheltered from the west by high bluffs. Two out of three Yukoners live in Whitehorse.

No gold was discovered in or close to Whitehorse, but it was an important stop on the way to the Klondike, allowing it to grow at a more sedate pace. This was where prospectors—who had each lugged a ton of provisions up the Chilkoot Trail, wintered on the shores of Lake Bennett waiting for the ice to break, built a boat to cross the lake, and attempted to ride the mighty Yukon River to Dawson City—often came to grief. The rapids that give Whitehorse its name drowned some gold seekers and carried away the supplies of many more.

Even a short visit to Whitehorse is enough for you to experience some of the city's unique attractions: four not-to-be-missed museums, a historic stern-wheeler, and excellent art galleries. Two nights here are recommended (see Accommodations, page 191).

Start your exploration at the **Yukon Visitor Reception Centre** (100 Hansen St; 867-667-3084; *www.tour yukon.com*; year-round; in summer 8am–8pm). The **Yukon Historical & Museums Association** offers walking tours in summer, starting from **Donnenworth House** (3126 3rd Ave; 867/667-4704; June–Aug Mon–Sat; $2). Free guided hikes (2–6 hours) are offered by the **Yukon Conservation Society** (302 Hawkins St; 867/668-5678; *www. yukonconservation.org*) to destinations such as Miles Canyon and Canyon City. Some are pitched to kids.:

HISTORY & CULTURE: At the SS *Klondike* National Historic Site (30 minutes; 867/667-3910, 800/661-0486; mid-May–mid-Sept; $5/adult, $4.50/senior, $3/ages 6–16), you can tour a stern-wheeler built in 1937 to make the run between Whitehorse and Dawson City in the then-amazingly short time of 36 hours. Its function was to carry cargo—and passengers, when space allowed. The boat, which today sits in drydock on the banks of the Yukon River, has been authentically restored. A 20-minute video on the history of Yukon stern-wheelers is also shown. There is a gift shop and restrooms.

The fascinating **Beringia Interpretive Centre** (1 hour; 867/667-8855; *www.beringia.com*; May–Sept daily 9am–6pm, June–Aug daily 8:30am–7pm; $6/adult, $5/over 54, $4/student, free/under 6) is located on the Alaska Highway above the city, close to the airport. Beringia is the name given to the huge, chilly swath of grassy tundra in the interior of Alaska and the Yukon that remained ice free while the rest of North America was glaciated during successive ice ages. As water was increasingly locked into the glaciers, sea levels lowered dramatically, uncovering this land bridge to Asia. Beringia was home to giant beavers, scimitar cats, woolly mammoths, and the people who hunted them. Exhibits, outdoor and indoor, showcase Beringia's plant and animal life. An excellent film tells the story of how the evidence of Beringia was uncovered. Recent exhibits offer chilling evidence of the impact climate change is having in the North. Visitors can try their hands at using the *atlatl*, an early hunting weapon. There's a gift shop and café.

Next door is the **Yukon Transportation Museum** (1 hour; 30 Electra Crescent; 867/668-4792; *www.yukon transportmuseum.homestead.com*; mid-May–Sept daily 10am–6pm; $4.25/adult, $3.25/over 54, $2/ages 6–12). Yukon history is also a story of transportation, and in this enormous building it is told with life-size dioramas, videos, and a fairly hair-raising set of exhibits on the history of Yukon aviation, including spectacular crashes. There's a gift shop. You can buy combined Beringia and Transportation museum tickets for $9 each. Allow at least 2 hours to tour both.

Downtown, a capsule history of the region is presented at the **MacBride Museum** (1 hour; 1124 1st Ave; 867/667-2709; *www.macbridemuseum.com*; mid-May–Aug daily Mon–Fri 10am–9pm, Sat–Sun 10am–7pm; Sept daily noon–5pm; rest of year Thurs–Sat noon–5pm; $5/adult, $4.50/senior, $4/student, $3.50/ages 5–16). First Nations and gold rush exhibits are stand-outs, along with historic films and Sam McGee's cabin.

There are frequent tours and presentations, and a gift shop is on the premises.

The tiny, picturesque **Old Log Church Museum** (30 minutes; 3rd Ave and Elliott St; 867/668-2555; mid-May–Labor Day 10am–6pm; $2.50/adult, $2/senior, student, $1/ages 6–11) began life as an Anglican church in 1901. The story of the "Bishop who ate his boots" is more than worth the price of admission.

SHOPPING: Most shops and galleries are clustered on Main Street between the Yukon River and Fifth Avenue. The museums have excellent gift shops, a good shopping bet when time is short. The one exception to the Main Street rule is **North End Gallery** (118–1116 1st Ave; 867/393-3590), which carries high-quality northern arts and crafts, from moose-tufting and scrimshaw to mammoth-ivory jewelry. The **Yukon Gallery** (201B Main St; 867/667-2391) represents Yukon artists. **Midnight Sun Gallery & Gifts** (205C Main St; 867/668-4350; *www.midnightsunyukon.com*) carries a variety of Yukon-made arts and crafts, but it's the homemade fudge that lands it on this list. Across the street, **Paradise Alley** (206 Main St; 867/456-4228) sells good quality gifts from outside and within the Yukon.

Mac's Fireweed Books (203 Main St, 867/668-2434; *www.yukonbooks.com*) carries all genres, with special emphasis on northern First Nations, and Klondike and natural history.

Coast Mountain Sports (208A Main St, 867/667-4074) carries outdoor wear and gear for any sports you're likely to engage in here. For ordinary apparel, try **Hougen's Department Store** (3rd and Main St; 867/668-6842), which also carries traditional Yukon souvenirs.

When caffeine is required, try **Midnight Sun** (4th Ave and Black St; 867/633-4563), which roasts its own beans, or the **Java Connection** (3125B 3rd Ave; 867/668-2196). Also see Dining, page 193.

NATURE: **Takhini Hot Springs** (867/633-2706; *www.takhinihotsprings.yk.ca*) makes a fun half-day excursion. Access is off Highway 2. Retrace your route on the Alaska Highway to the junction with Highway 2, the Klondike Highway, and take it north to Takhini Hot Springs Road; follow it to the resort, where you can bask in the waters ($6.50/adult, $6/youth, $5/child). There's also a licensed restaurant, trail rides, and a campground.

To experience magnificent Miles Canyon from the water, take a **tour of Schwatka Lake** on the small MV *Schwatka* or join a flightseeing tour based here (off Miles Canyon Rd; 2 hours; 907/668-4716, 867/668-4716; *www.yukon-wings.com*; boats: June–early Sept multiple daily departures; $25; flightseeing: call for details).

South Klondike Hwy
(100 miles one way/3 hours)

The highway down to Skagway is a scenic and historical gem. The road was built in two parts. The section between Whitehorse and Carcross dates from World War II; the spectacularly hair-raising section from Carcross to Skagway dates from 1978. Although locals routinely make the trip in under 2 hours, visitors should allow time for scenic and historic stops along the way. Check gas before leaving Whitehorse; there are a few service stations along the way, but not many.

From Whitehorse, continue south on the Alaska Highway for 10 miles to the junction with the South Klondike Highway. After you turn onto this highway, the landscape is at first heavily forested. About 25 miles after the junction is a turnout that overlooks beautiful **Emerald Lake**. A complex mix of sediments and light waves creates a rainbowlike effect. Six miles farther along is the **Carcross Desert**, billed as the world's smallest. It may also be the most charming, with its tiny, shimmering white sand dunes, all that's left of an old glacial lake. A few gnarled and stunted lodgepole pines, spruce, and kinnickinnick struggle to gain a foothold—a kind of bonsai Death Valley. There is a pullout with an interpretive sign.

A mile farther, 33 miles past the Alaska Highway junction, is **Carcross**, a historic town with faded charm. The name is a contraction of Caribou Crossing, named for the caribou herds that once crossed the narrows separating Nares from Bennett Lake. Today Carcross has a population of about 400, but in early 1898, while the stampeders wintered over and built boats to carry them up to the Klondike, the population topped 10,000. The Caribou Hotel dates from 1898; the old White Pass and Yukon Route train station dates from 1910. The prospectors most often credited with starting the Klondike gold rush are buried in Carcross:

Skookum Jim Mason, Kate Carmack, and Tagish Charlie. At the **Visitor Reception Centre** (in old train station; 867/821-4431; mid-May–mid-Sept daily 8am–8pm) are displays on local history. Pick up a walking guide and spend a half hour exploring some of the town's historic buildings, or head across the street from the center to **Watson's General Store** (867/821-3501) for ice cream. You can cross the Narrows, the tiny Natasaheenie River, by a footbridge.

Back on the South Klondike Highway, the road hugs Windy Arm of **Tagish Lake**; there are several scenic turnouts along the way. The highway climbs over 1,000 feet from Carcross (which has an elevation of 2,175 feet) to **White Pass** (3,292 feet). About halfway to Skagway, the highway crosses the border into British Columbia. The road becomes increasingly scenic, with many turnouts from which to marvel at the constantly changing mountain views. **Log Cabin**, a Chilkoot Trail National Historic Site 71 miles past the Alaska Highway junction, is the site of a town, no signs of which now remain, that sprang up to supply the gold rush miners. It is now just a pullout with detailed interpretive signs and the spiffiest outhouses in the Yukon: miniature, picturesque log buildings, sturdy and clean.

Just beyond Log Cabin is the start of **Tormented Valley**, a beautiful but desolate no-man's-land of strange little lakes, dwarf stunted trees, and rocky outcroppings that extend for miles. Turnouts and viewpoints provide an opportunity to observe this haunting environment. Five miles on, at tiny **Fraser**, is the Canada Customs border station (867/667-3943), open 24 hours a day in summer. Travelers headed for Skagway must drive another 15 miles to the U.S. border station. The true international border is at the crest of White Pass. Set your watch back an hour for Alaska.

From the summit down to the U.S. border station is the most spectacular stretch of the highway. (This is also where to make sure your brakes are in good working order.) The White Pass & Yukon Railway line runs along the east side of the Skagway River Gorge, with the road on the west side. You may be able to glimpse the train chugging along across the gorge. Frequent paved turnouts with interpretive panels highlight the gorge, waterfalls, and the beautiful Captain William Moore Suspension Bridge. Seven miles beyond the summit, across the canyon to the east, is Pitchfork Falls. A mile later is the **U.S. border station** (907/983-3144, 907/983-2325), open 24 hours daily in summer. Delays, although not the norm, are possible. Adults must have photo ID and proof of citizenship: a birth certificate or passport. From the border station, the road descends rapidly to the Skagway River.

ACCOMMODATIONS

HAINES

The charms of Haines are reflected in its limited but excellent accommodations, distributed between Fort Seward and downtown.

Bear Creek Cabins & International Hostel ($; 5 Small Tracts Rd, near Fort Seward; 907/766-2259) has charming tiny cabins, dorms, and tent sites along with kitchen facilities, a coin laundry, and a small store. You can rent bikes and book tours; showers are free for guests.

A stay at the large and comfortable downtown **Captain's Choice Motel** ($–$$; 108 2nd Ave N; 907/766-3111; *www.capchoice.com;* &) includes continental breakfast. There's a guest laundry, and hotel staff can arrange fishing charters and sightseeing tours. The **Bamboo Room** (see Dining, below) offers room service.

Hotel Halsingland ($–$$; Fort Seward; 907/766-2000, 800/542-6363; *hotelhalsingland.com;* &) occupies three buildings that once served as accommodations for Fort Seward's officers. Many rooms feature tile fireplaces, claw-foot bathtubs, and fabulous views. Rooms with shared baths are a bargain. There's a superb **restaurant** and bar.

HAINES JUNCTION

Alcan Motor Inn ($; at Haines and Alaska Hwys; 867/634-2371, 888/265-1018; *www.yukonweb.com/tourism/alcan/*) lacks the charm and grace of the Raven, but it's perfectly comfortable. Two rooms have kitchenettes; all have air conditioning.

For many years, Yukon visitors and diners in search of a first-class boutique hotel have found their way to the wonderful European-style **Raven** ($$$; 181 Alaska Hwy; 867/634-2500; *www.yukonweb.com/tourism/raven/*). Outside is a lovely flower garden; inside are twelve spacious units with satellite TV and a small, elegant gift shop. The inn's German expat owners, Hans and Christine Nelles, serve guests a superb breakfast with homebaked breads for a modest additional fee.

WHITEHORSE

Whitehorse has two inexpensive hostels—**Beez Kneez Bakpakers** ($; 408 Hoge St; 867/456-2333; *www.bzkneez. com*) and **Hide on Jeckell** ($; 410 Jeckell; 867/633-4933; *www.hide-on-jeckell.com*)—located close together in a fairly drab residential area, a good mile from downtown. Both offer laundry, bikes for day use, coffee, equipped kitchens, and high-speed Internet access.

Edgewater Hotel ($$–$$$; 101 Main St; 867/667-2572; *www.edgewaterhotel.yk.ca*) is popular with Northerners; one secret is the air conditioning. Standard rooms are not large, but suites with kitchens are available. On the premises are a casual café and the **Cellar**, an upscale restaurant. The central location is ideal if you don't have a car. If you do, there's parking.

Yukon Inn ($; 4220 4th Ave; 867/667 2527, 800/661-0454; *www.yukoninn.yk.ca*) is a 5-minute drive from downtown, with spacious, comfortable rooms and a good restaurant, the **Moose Café**, on the premises. Some rooms have kitchenettes and Jacuzzis.

DINING

HAINES

The charms of Haines are reflected in its limited but excellent dining offerings.

Don't be misled by the exotic name; the **Bamboo Room** ($$–$$$; 2nd and Main; 907/766-2800, bar 907/766-3443; *www.bambooroom.net*; year-round daily 6am–late evening) specializes in standard Alaskan fare. Stick to the generous portions of fresh seafood, especially halibut, or, for the teenagers in your party, the hearty burgers.

Alaska's State Bird?

Haines has just about everything going for it, including good weather, so you know there has to be a catch.

It's mosquitoes. Sometimes sardonically referred to as Alaska's state bird (that's actually the willow ptarmigan), mosquitoes here can be ferocious. June and July are the worst months, and twilight is insect prime time. Breezy open areas close to salt water are the most likely to be bug-free. Trails in the Alaska Bald Eagle Preserve can be especially buggy. Haines's warm, relatively rain-free summers are no help. (Note to Ketchikan visitors: When you're tempted to curse at another downpour, remember the upside; mosquitoes are rarely a problem in a rain squall.) Bring bug juice, wear light- (but not bright-) colored clothing that covers up your extremities, and keep in mind that if we are afraid to venture out, the bugs win.

It takes a little perseverance to locate **Fireweed** ($; on Blacksmith Rd, in Fort Seward; 907/766-3838; *fireweedrestaurant@yahoo.com*; summer only 11am–till they feel like closing) in Fort Seward off Portage Street, but it's worth the effort. Fresh baked breads and pastries, pizza, and hearty soups are good bets; there are also excellent vegetarian selections.

The name says it all. **Just for the Halibut** ($; Chilkat fast-ferry terminal, 142 Beach Rd, Fort Seward; 907/766-2100; *www.chilkatcruises.com*; summer Mon–Fri 11am–7pm, Sat–Sun 11am–5pm) has a small menu that includes hearty fast food and a salad or two, along with baked goods and espresso drinks. But you know what to come for . . . **Mountain Market** ($; 3rd Ave and Haines Hwy; 907/766-3340; *mountain_market@yahoo. com*; year-round Mon–Fri 7:30am–7pm, Sat–Sun 9am–3pm; ﹠) is not only a great whole-foods market but its café makes a perfect stop for breakfast or lunch. You'll encounter plenty of locals, along with visitors, collecting breads and pastries, sandwiches and wraps. Vegans, vegetarians, and carnivores are all well served.

HAINES JUNCTION

Upstairs at the **Raven** ($$$; 867/634-2500; 181 Alaska Hwy; *www.yukonweb.com/tourism/raven/*), the inn's first-rate restaurant, with a spacious deck and view of the Kluane Mountains, is open to the public for dinner featuring a small German-accented menu. The restaurant has garnered fans across the world. It's not uncommon for Haines residents to drive up just for dinner.

Village Café & Bakery ($; Kluane and Logan Sts; 867/634-2867; *www.junctionbakery.com*; May–Sept daily 7am–9pm), across from the Kluane National Park Visitor Center, feels like the town's center of gravity. Order from the counter or choose from the deli case; eat in or dine out on the spacious deck. Breads are made fresh (try a pepperoni cheese dog or a sourdough pizza); there are fountain drinks, beer, and wine. They'll make up sack lunches. Weekly salmon bakes feature live music.

WHITEHORSE

Klondike Rib and Salmon BBQ ($$$; 2116 2nd Ave; 867/667-7554; late May–mid-Sept daily 11am–10pm) is one of Whitehorse's busiest dining establishments, serving up caribou, muskox, bison, and arctic char along with more traditional meats and fish. It's a favorite of large tour groups, so reservations are recommended. Prices and portions are substantial.

Sam 'n' Andy's ($–$$; 506 Main St; 867/668-6994; *www.yuk-biz.com/samnandys/*; Mon–Wed 11am–10pm, Thurs–Sat 11am–11pm, Sun 4:30–10pm) is a popular Mexican restaurant in a pleasant house, offering excellent food at low to moderate prices with friendly and efficient service. Dine inside or out in summer.

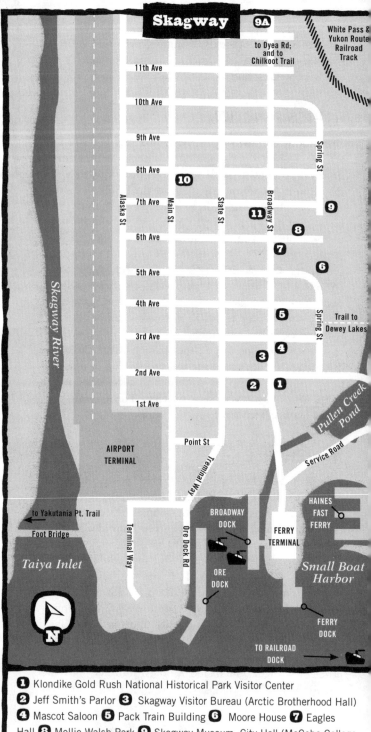

Skagway

9A

White Pass & Yukon Route Railroad Track

to Dyea Rd; and to Chilkoot Trail

11th Ave
10th Ave
9th Ave
8th Ave
7th Ave
6th Ave
5th Ave
4th Ave
3rd Ave
2nd Ave
1st Ave

Alaska St
Main St
State St
Broadway St
Spring St

10
11
9
8
7
6
5
4
3
2 **1**

Trail to Dewey Lakes

Skagway River

Pullen Creek Pond

AIRPORT TERMINAL

Point St

Terminal Way

Service Road

to Yakutania Pt. Trail

Foot Bridge

Taiya Inlet

Terminal Way

Ore Dock Rd

BROADWAY DOCK

FERRY TERMINAL

HAINES FAST FERRY

Small Boat Harbor

ORE DOCK

FERRY DOCK

TO RAILROAD DOCK

N

1 Klondike Gold Rush National Historical Park Visitor Center
2 Jeff Smith's Parlor **3** Skagway Visitor Bureau (Arctic Brotherhood Hall)
4 Mascot Saloon **5** Pack Train Building **6** Moore House **7** Eagles
Hall **8** Mollie Walsh Park **9** Skagway Museum, City Hall (McCabe College
Building) **9A** Side trip to Gold Rush Cemetery and Lower Reid Falls
10 The White House **11** Skagway Inn Garden

Chapter 5

SKAGWAY

Just 14 miles from Haines, Skagway couldn't be more different from its neighbor. Whereas Haines savors its slow pace, Skagway relishes busy summer days when up to 18,000 visitors descend on it. Yet the tourists and the businesses that exist to serve them have not diluted Skagway's authenticity; it retains its distinctive personality. Perhaps the secret is that what you see in Skagway is the real thing: Klondike-era buildings, the White Pass & Yukon Route Railroad, even hordes of tourists taking it all in. Skagway was welcoming tourists almost as soon as the gold rush was over. Skagwegians have always known they have something special and are more than happy to share it with the world.

History comes alive throughout Skagway. Despite its wild and lawless past, with a plethora of bars, brothels, and the scofflaws who patronized them, Skagway never suffered a catastrophic fire. Today, the National Park Service carries on the task of restoring historic Skagway, and many old buildings are open to the public.

Although the disproportionate ratio of visitors to residents can be a challenge, if the crowds get to you, escaping couldn't be easier. Skagway is unique among Southeast Alaska towns in that it is as flat as a pancake; bikes, a major mode of in-town transportation, can get you out on the historic South Klondike Highway in no time. Terrific hikes and scenic drives can be accomplished in four hours or less. The dry weather (Skagway gets just 30 inches of rain a year) is icing on the cake.

HISTORY

The White Pass and nearby Chilkoot Pass were carefully guarded Tlingit trade routes for centuries until the late 1800s, when prospectors and adventurers began to lay their own plans for exploiting trade routes. William Moore and his son, Bernard—members of a Canadian surveying party—hoped to develop a workable trail over the White Pass using these routes. Dreaming of building a town to be called Mooresville at the water's edge, Moore homesteaded what would become the town of Skagway and hatched big schemes, but the Klondike gold strike put an end to his dreams. In 1896 Skookum Jim, a Dyea Tlingit who had shown the surveyors the trail over White Pass, struck gold in the Klondike with Tagish Charlish and George Carmacks. After news of the strike got out and the first shipments of gold had arrived in Seattle, any hope of controlling the passes was lost. By fall 1897, the townsite was swamped by hordes of prospectors. Attempts to control the passes by means of toll roads also failed in the chaos.

Soon the trail over the White Pass was full of clueless prospectors, trying by the thousands to lead overburdened horses up the dangerous route. The Canadian government required each prospector to bring one ton of supplies to survive the harsh Yukon winter. The pack animals died in droves, and the route became known as "Dead Horse Trail." The route from Dyea—the Chilkoot Trail—proved marginally easier.

The Royal Canadian Mounted Police, which had arrived to establish order at the international border, briefly came to Skagway—to claim it as Canadian territory, it was feared. Their presence was a cause of concern to Americans; U.S. buffalo soldiers were sent up in 1899 to establish a post in Dyea to make it clear to Canada which nation owned the town.

The toll road was sold to railroad developers; soon train tracks ran down the center of Broadway, which was lined with stores, a post office, a school, churches, saloons, and brothels. From the start, Skagway was a rollicking town, with a population in 1898 of 10,000. It was a nearly lawless world. Criminal gangs found easy pickings. Jeff "Soapy" Smith, a fairly inept confidence man, employed simple tricks to part miners from their money. Bilked once too often, a mob led by town surveyor Frank Reid confronted and shot Smith who, before expiring, delivered a fatal gunshot to Reid, who died a week later. Both men are buried in Skagway's Gold Rush Cemetery.

In 1900 Skagway became Alaska's first incorporated city. After the gold rush (the prospectors who made it to the Klondike discovered that claims had been staked to all of it at least a year earlier), Skagway slowly shrank, but the railroad kept the town alive.

Martin Itjen, a local character of humble origins, first rose to the challenge of drawing tourists up to Skagway, developing the town's first tourist street-car. He offered guided tours, bought Soapy Smith's remains, and created a museum. His efforts paid off. The 1920s saw a tourism boom. When tourism flagged during the Great Depression, Itjen sought to draw visitors back with PR stunts. He paid a visit to Mae West in 1935, a celebrated photo op in which he invited her to "come up to Skagway."

America's entry into World War II brought the U.S. Army to Skagway; the railroad was used to support the building of the Alaska Highway. After the war, the army left, but the railroad continued to run, moving ores from and supplies to the Yukon. No road over the White Pass to the interior was built until the early 1970s. A cross-border effort, the South Klondike Highway was completed in 1978.

Mine closures in the Yukon led to the 1982 closure of the White Pass & Yukon Route Railroad, an economic disaster for Skagway. But in 1988, the train was reinvented as a summer tourist attraction between Skagway and the summit of White Pass. The 1980s saw yet another resurrection of the Skagway economy, this time led by cruise ships.

SKAGWAY TODAY

In winter Skagway's population drops below 900, then it triples to more than 2,500 in summer when hordes of tour guides, retail clerks, waiters, and hotel staff are hired to serve the even larger hordes of visitors: the figure in 2004 was close to 1 million. Housing is in perennially short supply, and many summer residents camp in tents. This annual expansion and contraction takes a toll, and making a go of a year-round business in Skagway is a challenge. There are stresses on a small community that is utterly transformed for a few months each year into a metropolis. Yet Skagway's historic roots are firmly planted in the tourist-boom economy. It's a town that knows how to weather big changes and, in fact, to relish them. Primary employers are tourism and transportation.

GEOGRAPHY

Skagway is located at the head of Taiya Inlet. It is connected by road to Whitehorse, Yukon Territory (100 miles), Anchorage (819 miles), and Haines (360 miles). It is 14 miles east of Haines by water, 93 miles north of Juneau, and 974 miles north of Seattle.

CLIMATE

Annual precipitation is 26.5 inches; snowfall is 49.9 inches. Average summer high temperatures in Skagway are the highest among the destinations in this book, running in the upper 60s (June, 66.2°F; July, 68°F; August, 65.8°F).

Average Temperatures (°F)

	May–Oct	Nov–Apr
High	60.8	36.1
Low	44.2	24.3

Average Precipitation (inches)

Jan	Feb	Mar	Apr	May	June
2.2	1.9	1.4	1.5	1.5	1.1
July	Aug	Sept	Oct	Nov	Dec
1.1	2.2	4.1	4.5	3.0	2.3

Average Hours of Daylight

Jan	Feb	Mar	Apr	May	June
6	8	10.5	13.5	16	18
July	Aug	Sept	Oct	Nov	Dec
19	17	14	11.5	8.5	6

ACCESS

Alaska car ferries serve the communities of Skagway, Haines, and other Inside Passage destinations year-round (see the introduction, page 5). A shuttle ferry connects Skagway and Haines in summer. **Skagway Air Service** (907/983-2218; *www.skagwayair.com*) and **Wings**

of Alaska (907/983-2442; *www.wingsofalaska.com*) offer scheduled and charter service between Skagway and nearby communities.

VISITOR INFORMATION & SERVICES

Skagway Convention & Visitors Bureau, ANB building (2nd and Broadway; 907/983-2854; *www.skagway.com*).

Post Office: 641 Broadway; 907/983-2330; Mon–Fri 8:30am–5pm.

Alaska Public Radio Network: KHNS 102.3 FM.

Internet Access: The **Skagway Public Library** (769 State St; 907/983-2665; *spl@aptalaska.net*; Mon–Fri 1–9pm, Sat–Sun 1–5pm) offers Internet access free with signup. **Seaport Cyber** (336 3rd Ave; 907/983-3174; *www.sea portel.com*) provides Internet access ($5/hour) and maintains three Wi-Fi hot spots: at the AMHS terminal, at 336 Third Avenue, and at Garden City RV Park.

WHEELS & KEELS

Sourdough Car & U-Haul Truck Rental & Bike Rentals (907/983-2523, 907/209-5026; *sourdoughrental@yahoo. com*) has car rentals ($50/day for compact, $99/day for SUV or van; discounts for weekly rentals; no mileage charged for day rentals, 125 miles/day for longer rentals; $26 for airport or dock pickup). **PB Cruisers** (326 3rd Ave; 907/983-3385; *www.aptalaska.net*) rents cars only ($60 in summer, $50 in winter). You can take them only as far as Whitehorse; driving the Golden Circle route is prohibited. **Avis Rent A Car** (2nd and Spring in Westmark Hotel annex; 907/983-2247; *www.avis.com*; May–Sept; rates vary) rents cars for local use only. **Note**: Canadian citizens are not permitted to bring a rented U.S. car into Canada. If you are Canadian and carless, your best bet is to join a guided tour.

Known by its acronym **SMART**, **Skagway Municipal and Regional Transit** (907/983-2743) is a bus that shuttles around Skagway, stopping at prime tourist destinations in town. **Dyea Dave** (907/209-5031) offers taxi service between Skagway and Dyea.

The passenger-only **Chilkat Ferry** (907/766-2100; *www.chilkatcruises.com*; $25/adult one way, $45/adult

Skagway Three-Hour Must-See Itinerary

- Historic guided walking tour; Klondike Gold Rush National Historical Park (1 hour)

- A quickie tour up to White Pass (1.25 hours)

- Shopping (45 minutes)

- Refueling stops: **Sweet Tooth Café** (closes at 2pm) or **Sabrosa**

round trip; $12.50/ages 3–12 one way, $22.50/ages 3–12 round trip) shuttles between Haines and Skagway, making the 35-minute run almost hourly in summer. The Skagway dock is at the small boat harbor; the Haines dock is at Fort Seward.

EVENTS

Buckwheat Ski Classic (Mountain Shop; 907/983-2544, *packer@aptalaska.net*): Named for its founder, Buckwheat Donahue, Skagway's colorful director of tourism, this annual cross-country ski race, held on a weekend in late March, draws amateurs and professionals. It doesn't just tolerate unskilled participants, it encourages them. Tracing the White Pass route followed by prospectors in 1898, like the gold rush it partly celebrates, it's a cross-border affair open to American and Canadian adults and kids with plenty of entertainment, including the "Miss Buckwheat" baby beauty pageant.

Fourth of July (Skagway Chamber of Commerce; 907/983-1898; *chamber@aptalaska.net*): The city celebrates the glorious Fourth with a cluster of events over several days. It starts with a softball tournament that takes advantage of the long hours of daylight. On the Fourth, a parade, contests, and races, including a rubber-ducky race, occur. The festivities conclude on July 8 with a wake for Soapy Smith, who died on this date in 1898.

Klondike International Road Relay (Sport Yukon; 867/668-4236; *info@sportyukon.com*): Held on a weekend in early September, this race covers 110 miles from Skagway to Whitehorse over 2 days and a night. Entrant countries, sometimes as many as 162, field teams of six to ten runners.

FOUR HOURS OR LESS

Skagway is a pleasure to explore on foot; it's neither hilly nor sprawling, just four blocks wide and twenty-three blocks long. Shopping can be a bit daunting. Lining Broadway, the main thoroughfare, are gigantic retailers from elsewhere. It takes a bit of effort to find local arts and crafts, but they are here, too. And it's a lot easier than it looks to leave the crowd behind; in half an hour you can be away from the hustle and bustle, marveling at the view from Yakutania Point or Lower Dewey Lake.

WALKING TOURS

Skagway Walking Tour
(1.5 hours; add 1.5 hours for optional extension)

Before starting your tour, pick up a *Skagway Walking Tour* brochure, which identifies the dozens of gold rush–era buildings throughout Skagway. Brochures are available at the national park visitor center (2nd and Broadway; 907/983-2921) and the Skagway Convention & Visitors Bureau. For this walking tour, refer to the map on page 194.

❶ Start from the **Klondike Gold Rush National Historical Park Visitor Center**, in the old White Pass and Yukon Route Railroad depot that dates back to 1898. Train tracks once led from here up Broadway on the way to White Pass. Cross to the other side of Broadway for a look in the **Martin Itjen Residence**, dating from 1901, now the park's Trail Center, dispensing information and permits for the Chilkoot Trail. Itjen was first in the city's long line of enthusiastic tourism promoters.

❷ Head up Broadway to Second Avenue; turn left and walk half a block for a quick look at the dismal **Jeff Smith's Parlor**. Dating from 1897, this was Soapy Smith's saloon, from which he operated his various cons. It was moved to its present location in 1964.

❸ Returning to Broadway, cross Second. On the corner is the 1898 **Red Onion Saloon**, moved to its present location in 1914. During the move, it was inexplicably made to face backward; thus, the staircase that once led to an upstairs brothel around the back is now out front in full view. The Red Onion is still a bar, and a popular stop for tourists, where you can listen to live jazz from lunchtime on while you sip a microbrew.

On the same block as the Red Onion is Skagway's most distinctive building: the **Arctic Brotherhood Hall**, now housing the city of **Skagway's Convention & Visitors Bureau** visitor center under the savvy leadership of Buckwheat Donahue, a passionate advocate for the city, its history, and its residents, past and present. Itself a tourist attraction, the AB Hall was once a fraternal order, a men's club with charitable leanings. The quirky building with its rustic-Victorian, driftwood-covered exterior, dates from 1899. The façade, said to contain 20,000 pieces of driftwood, was the brainchild of an early AB member, Charley Walker.

On Broadway, you encounter the big names in international cruise–oriented jewelry retailing, along with some locally owned galleries (see Shopping, page 208). At the northwest corner of Third and Broadway is the **Golden North Hotel**, built in 1898. Through 2002, it was Alaska's oldest operating hotel, complete with antique furnishings, a brew pub, a restaurant, and a resident ghost. Today, it's another T-shirt emporium. The graceful lines of the building and its golden dome adorn many photos of Skagway.

❹ Cross Broadway at Third Avenue to visit the 1898 **Mascot Saloon**. You may have noticed that saloons were prominent in historic Skagway; during the boom years, there were seventy. One of three adjacent buildings owned by the National Park Service, the saloon is fully restored, with historical displays, and is open to the public.

❺ Continue up Broadway past the 1900 **Pack Train Building**, the tallest of Skagway's historic buildings, once barracks for buffalo soldiers. Turn right on Fourth Avenue to view the old **St. James Hotel** behind the hardware store, now a weathered warehouse. Also on Fourth is the trailhead (across the tracks) for the **Dewey Lakes trails**.

❻ Return to Broadway and walk up to Fifth Avenue. On the west (left) side of the street you pass the bright-blue **Kone Kompany**, Skagway's ice cream (and fudge) parlor. Turn right on Fifth to see the fairly dreary **Moore Cabin** (between Broadway and Spring Sts), built in 1887 by the same William Moore who once dreamed of being the patriarch of Mooresville. Nearby is the more elegant **Moore House** (1897), built by Moore's son, Bernard, and refurbished with authentic period decor; the downstairs is open for touring. Adjacent to the Moore House, an old icehouse is being resuscitated by the Park Service.

❼ Return to Broadway and walk up to Sixth Avenue. On the right is **Eagles Hall**, where the **"Days of '98 Show" with Soapy Smith** has been entertaining audiences, reportedly since 1927, with mock gambling, melo-drama, and vaudeville.

❽ Cross Sixth and turn right to visit **Mollie Walsh Park**, with a playground and signage that describes the tur-bulent life of the young woman who ventured up north with the stampeders in 1897 and opened a restaurant on the Chilkoot Trail.

❾ From the park, follow the path to see the remains of **Pullen House**, once an important hotel operated by Harriet "Ma" Pullen, another female stampeder and successful entrepreneur. The hotel closed in the 1950s, a decade after her death. All that is left of it today is an ancient chimney. Follow the path across **Pullen Creek**—full of spawning salmon in August, a grisly but mesmerizing sight—to the old **McCabe College building**, a handsome granite edifice dating from 1899. It was intended to serve as a Methodist school but soon ran into financial difficulties and closed in 1901; thereafter it served as the district courthouse. A recent addition houses the **Skagway Museum** and **City Hall**.

❾Ⓐ Optional extension: From here, you can return to Broadway and walk up to the **Gold Rush Cemetery and Lower Reid Falls**. It's a little over a mile one way, but flat all the way to the cemetery. Alternatively, walk up to Twenty-third Avenue and turn left to cross the Skagway River and visit **Jewell Gardens**, adding another 0.5 mile to the hike.

10 From the Skagway Museum, walk up Spring Street to Eighth Avenue and turn left. As you cross Broadway, look down Broadway to Seventh Avenue. This area was once Skagway's thriving **red-light district**. Prostitutes' "cribs" (tiny shacks in which they plied their trade) lined nearby streets and alleys. (To see inside a real crib, from Eighth and Broadway visit **Sourdough Car Rentals** on 6th between Broadway and State Sts; the crib was moved there from the red-light district.) Continue on Eighth Avenue to State Street, one block west of Broadway. Between Eighth and Ninth are **Haven** and **You Say Tomato**. In the other direction, between Seventh and Eighth, is the public library. Go on to Main Street to take a look at the 1902 **White House**, restored and now a B&B. One of Skagway's original stately homes, it served as a hospital during World War II.

11 Walk down Main Street to Seventh Avenue and turn left to return to Broadway. At the intersection of Seventh and Broadway, on your right is the flourishing garden belonging to the **Skagway Inn**. Turn right on Broadway and head south five and a half blocks to the national park visitor center.

Guided Walks

On the **Klondike National Historical Park Walking Tour of Skagway** (45 minutes), you can see seventeen buildings owned by the Park Service. Some, like the old Mascot Saloon and the Moore House, have been restored. Rangers lead multiple free tours daily in summer (at 9am, 10am, 11am, 2pm, 3pm); reservations are required. Reserve a spot at the **national park visitor center** (2nd and Broadway; 907/983-2921; *www.nps.gov/klgo/pphtm*; May–Sept daily 8am–6pm, Oct–April daily 8am–5pm).

HISTORY & CULTURE

The buildings of the **Klondike Gold Rush National Historical Park** (20 minutes) are not reproductions but the real thing. Many landmark buildings, such as the Golden North Hotel with its distinctive cupola, have been converted into generic T-shirt and jewelry stores, but you can still get a feel for their provenance by visiting the **national park visitor center** in Skagway's old White Pass & Yukon Route Railroad depot and the buildings purchased and restored by the Park Service, as well as attending one of the 45-minute daily presentations. Park rangers are on hand to answer questions and give talks; videos are shown in the tiny theater. Here is where to book a free historical walking tour (see Guided Walks, above). The bookstore carries a large selection of Klondike-related books and Alaskana titles.

Only a third of the park is in Skagway. One part is located in Seattle, Washington, and the other in Dyea, 9 miles from Skagway at the start of the Chilkoot Trail. Park rangers give free daily tours of the **Dyea Townsite** (1.5 hours; in summer at 2pm). You'll need to provide your own transportation to Dyea or call a taxi. The park also administers the U.S. portion of the Chilkoot Trail. To obtain information and permits for the Chilkoot (see Two Days or More, page 224), visit the Trail Center, located in the historic Martin Itjen House across the street from the national park visitor center.

Corrington Museum of Alaskan History (30 minutes; 5th and Broadway; 907/983-2580; daily in summer; free), tucked away in a bustling retail establishment, is a genuine museum, offering a capsule history of Alaska, with emphasis on its northern indigenous people. Exhibits include delicate Eskimo ivory artworks and baleen baskets.

The **Skagway Museum & Archives** (30 minutes; 7th and Spring; 907/983-2420; *www.skagwaymuseum.org*; mid-May–Sept daily 9am–5pm; winter hours vary; $2/adult; $1/student, free/under 13), a few blocks off the beaten Broadway tourist path, is still a short walk and well worth the effort. View eclectic displays ranging from Alaska Native artifacts (note the Tlingit war canoe and Yupik rain parkas) to antique gaming machines and other Klondike-era exhibits. Children will enjoy a treasure hunt and hands-on exhibits that include stereoscopes, whale baleen, and wildlife skeletons. Among several videos shown is an interesting one about Skagway during World War II. There is a small gift shop and well-stocked bookstore.

In the **"Days of '98 Show with Soapy Smith"** (1 hour; 6th and Broadway; 907/983-2545; *daysof98@aptalaska. net*; May–Sept; mid-May–mid-Sept several times daily; evening shows: $16/adult, $8/ages 3–15; matinees: $14/adult, $7/ages 3–12), the tale of the fatal encounter of outlaw Soapy Smith, who briefly ran Skagway, and Frank Reid, the courageous town surveyor who took on the job of standing up to him, is acted out in song and dance in the Eagles Hall. A chance to try out mock gambling starts out evening performances. The show is fun, mildly bawdy, but suitable for kids.

On the **Klondike Gold Dredge Tour** (1.5 hours, plus 30 minutes for transportation; mile 1.7 South Klondike Hwy; 907/983-3175; *www.klondikegolddredge.com;* call for times; $34/adult, $24/child), you'll see a giant, floating gold dredge built in 1936 in Seattle and barged up the coast to Skagway, where it was dismantled and shipped up to Dawson City. Among Klondike-era artifacts, these dredges have to be the weirdest. Half machine, half building, they extracted gold from vast quantities of earth using a long line of buckets that scraped up soil and dumped it into sluice boxes, into which water was pumped to separate the gold from the dirt and gravel, which was then dumped back out. This one's twenty years of service were followed by forty years of quiet rusting until it was sent back down to Skagway and refurbished as a tourist attraction. Although it makes little sense (Skagway wasn't a placer mining site), visitors can pan for gold here, too. An interesting video is shown. There is a gift shop. Transportation is included in the tour.

The **White Pass & Yukon Route Railroad** (907/983-2217, 800/343-7373; *www.whitepassrailroad.com*) is the star attraction of Southeast Alaska tourism, and for good reason. The **train trip** (3–4 hours; mid-May–mid-Sept, Mon–Fri 8:15am, 12:45pm, 4:30pm; $89/adult, $44.50/ages 3–12; steam train: Sun 12:45pm; $135/adult, $67.50/ages 3–12, free/under 3) is simply beautiful and perhaps the best way, short of hiking the Chilkoot Trail, to get a sense of the challenges that faced the army of inexperienced prospectors who dashed up here to strike it rich in the Klondike. Trains chug up the east side of the Skagway River canyon to the summit of White Pass, going through two tunnels and over absolutely hair-raising trestles. The long trains and the curves in the track make it easy to snap photos of your train on the move. The tracks pass the Gold Rush Cemetery and the Denver Caboose (see Two Days or More, page 223). Out of Skagway, the views are all on the left side. If you're making a round trip, you'll have a good view one way. An audio narration recounts the history and points of interest.

On weekdays, the engines are vintage diesels. On weekends a steam engine takes their place and longer tours are offered (see One Day, page 221). All trains are wheelchair accessible. On Sundays, June through August, a steam engine replaces the diesel engine, and passengers get to cross the international border into British Columbia at Fraser Meadows. You'll need proof of citizenship (passport or birth certificate).

Important note: Because of an agreement between the railway and cruise lines, cruise-ship passengers are not allowed to get on or off the train at the cruise-ship dock unless they purchased their tour as a cruise-ship shore excursion. Some passengers book independently anyway, to save money, and simply walk between the cruise ship and the depot. This may not be an option for those with limited mobility. Also, if you purchase your ticket independently, you'll need to keep track of time. Some train departures and arrivals, while designed to accommodate cruise-ship schedules, cut times close. It's not uncommon to see cruise-ship passengers dashing madly to the cruise ship dock because they were not permitted to disembark from the train there. Leaving an extra half hour at either end is recommended.

GUIDED TOURS

Thanks to the constant stream of visitors in and out of Skagway, there are almost limitless guided tours available. For other options, check with the visitor center.

Those with tight schedules can still work in a tour through locally owned **Frontier Excursions**, which offers three **sightseeing "budget tours."** There's a "Summit photo bus" low-key drive (1.25 hours; $20) to White Pass and back, with time for photos. Two other short tours are offered: a city tour (1.5 hours; $23) and a narrated summit tour (1.5 hours; $25).

Guided city tours (2 hours) on distinctive yellow buses are offered by **Skagway Street Car Company**. **Creation Tours** offers a tour with a Tlingit focus (2.5 hours;

$38.50/adult, $17.50/under 12) that includes a drive up the Klondike Highway. Frontier Excursions has a tour of town and the summit (2.5 hours; $38.50).

You can drive yourself to the scenery and historic spots on a Frontier Excursions narrated "Chilkoot Jeep Stampede" (3 hours; $75; up to 4 people/jeep). As the name suggests, their "Yukoner" trip (3.5 hours) takes you up to the pass and into Canada. You'll need to bring proof of citizenship and photo ID.

SHOPPING

Visitors who don't come via cruise ship may want to keep track of when the ships are due to arrive and leave (the Skagway visitors center has this information). Regardless of posted hours, when the ships are in, just about every establishment in town is open for business; when the ships leave, so do tired shopkeepers.

Art

ALASKA NATIVE ARTISTS: If your heart is set on a baleen basket or Eskimo ivory carving, **Corrington's Alaskan Ivory** (5th & Broadway; 907/983-2580) can help you out. **A Gathering of Spirits** (456 Broadway; Haines phone: 907/766-3535), with the same owner as the Far North gallery in Haines (see page 163), specializes in Eskimo art, ivory carving, basketry, and jewelry.

RUSSIAN ARTISTS: Small, unusual, and moderately priced items are offered at **the Rushin' Tailor** (Broadway between 6th and 7th; 907/983-2397; *www.rtailor.com*), which has an eclectic assortment of gifts from Russia and Alaska, including clothing, in two connected store-fronts. The Quiltalaska half should appeal to needlecrafters.

SKAGWAY ARTISTS: The work of Skagway artists is the specialty at **A Fine Line** (551 Broadway; 907/983-3654). And yes, Skagway does have a locally owned jewelry store (see Good Buys, below). **Skagway Artworks** (555 Broadway; 907/983-3443) sells the work of Alaska Native artists as well as area jewelers, glass artists, and visual artists. For a wide, if more generic selection of Skagway souvenirs, head to **Richter's** (Broadway between 2nd and 3rd; 907/983-2424, 877/983-2424).

Good Buys

Throughout Alaska and the Yukon, cheap gold-nugget jewelry manufactured abroad is offered for sale as "Klondike souvenirs," often at prices that might make Soapy Smith blush. In Skagway, you can buy the genuine article at **Taiya River Jewelry** (Broadway between 2nd and 3rd; 907/983-2637). Local owner Casey McBride and his partner, Marcia Cook, design about half the jewelry they sell here, as well as fill custom orders. Many of their designs incorporate gold nuggets as well as more traditional metals and gems. Original pieces start around $100.

Books

Small though Skagway is, readers don't lack for options. The dedicated bookstore is **Skaguay News Depot & Books** (264 Broadway; 907/983-3354). Though tiny, it has an intelligent and diverse selection of Alaskana, Klondike history, Native Alaska history, kids' books, and newspapers from the United States and Canada. **Dedman's Photo Shop** (Broadway between 3rd and 4th; 907/983-2353) carries books, including many Alaska titles. Also check out the city and national park museum gift shops.

Clothing & Sundries

You know you're in a tourist town when the only clothing stores double as gift shops. Skagwegians shop online or up in Whitehorse. For visitors, the most affordable casual-clothing option may actually be the enormous **Skagway Outlet Store** (Broadway between 6th and 7th; 907/983-3331). This gift emporium, open seasonally, sells bargain-priced cotton T-shirts, shorts, sweatshirts, and accessories (if you don't mind clothing that proclaims Alaskan flora and fauna) alongside the *ulus* and key chains. For quality clothing, try **Klothes Rush** (Broadway and 5th; 907-983-2370, 800/664-2370; and at State and 5th; 907/983-3562; *www.klothesrush.com*).

Skagway Hardware Store (Broadway and 4th; 907/983-2233; *www.skagwayhardware.com*) has a good assortment of just about everything a small-town hardware store ought to carry, including sporting goods; they sell hunting and fishing licenses. **The Mountain Shop** (4th between Broadway and State Sts; 907/983-2544), the retail arm of Packer Expeditions, has a wide selection of outdoor wear and gear for summer and winter sports.

Food & Drink

Based in Haines, **Dejon Delights** has a Skagway outlet (5th Broadway; 907/983-2083) selling smoked salmon, trout, and other fishy fare. **The Pill Box** (3rd between Broadway and State), open twenty-four hours, is Skagway's take on the mini mart, billing itself as a purveyor of "gourmet junk food"; it's a top bet when the munchies strike.

For organic foods, baked goods and other things wholesome, try **You Say Tomato** (9th and State; 907/983-2784), next door to Haven. The only supermarket in town is the grim **Fairway Market** (State and 4th; 907/983-2220), renowned mainly for high prices; in a dreary, nearly windowless building with a small sign, it can be hard to find.

NATURE

Flightseeing

An advantage to booking a flightseeing tour out of Skagway is that weather and visibility are often better than in other Inside Passage towns.

BY AIRPLANE: Skagway Air Service offers a chance to see the Chilkoot Trail and Lake Bennett from above, on a **Gold Rush Tour** (45 minutes; $90/adult, $70/child). If weather allows, the trip includes a Juneau icefield fly-over. Several flights a day give visitors a bird's-eye view of the **Glacier Bay area** (1–3 hours). Skagway Air also offers a shorter tour (1.5 hours; $140/adult, $105/child); passengers in groups of two or more who don't have reservations will be accommodated if there is room. **Mountain Flying Service** (based in Haines) offers three tours from Skagway: a trip over the east arm of Glacier Bay (1 hour; $159), one over the west arm of Glacier Bay (1.3 hours; $209), and a "Pilot's Choice" tour over Glacier Bay to the Pacific and Lituya Inlet, including a possible beach landing (2 hours; $299). They also provide charter flights daily to local destinations; there's a two-person minimum. Also see Flightseeing in the Haines chapter, pages 167–68.

BY HELICOPTER: Two tours by **TEMSCO Helicopters** combine **glacier flyovers with landings**. The shorter tour (1.5 hours; $199) flies over Taiya Inlet to Dyea; it includes 20–25 minutes on the ice—landing is in the Valley of the Glaciers. The longer "Pilot's Choice" tour (2 hours; $299) includes two ice landings; itineraries vary but generally include Ferebee Glacier, Chilkat Glacier, or Meade Glacier. Each tour includes safety briefings and outfitting with glacier gear. An additional tour (2 hours; $399) combines glacier flightseeing with the chance to try some **mushing** on the Denver Glacier.

Wildlife Tours

Some of Southeast Alaska's best whale-watching can be found in the stretch of water from Taiya Inlet into Lynn Canal.

Chilkoot Charters offers multiple **daily cruises** (2 hours; $79). **Dockside Charters** also has a cruise (2 hours; $79, 3-person minimum). Children under 12 pay half when traveling with a paid adult. Other discounts apply. **Fishfull Think-N** offers a wildlife excursion (2 hours; $75; minimum 3 people); children under 13 are half price when tour is booked via their Web site.

ONE OF A KIND

The expansive organic **Jewell Gardens** (1 hour; State and 9th Sts; 907/983-2112; *www.jewellgardens.com*; May–Sept; $8.50) is a delight to visit. Its creator, Charlotte Jewell, has crafted a unique and magical attraction in Alaska's officially designated "Garden City." The patchwork of beautifully laid out beds surrounds a little mountain with a bonsai evergreen forest through which a miniature electric train runs. The garden is not merely decorative; among the flower beds are the giant vegetables that Alaska's brief but intense and light-filled summers produce, along with items not usually associated with northern climates: apricot, apple, and cherry trees; raspberries and strawberries; roses and fuchsias. A large gift shop, new in 2004, sells a wide assortment of garden-related gifts (which can be hard to come by in Southeast Alaska). High tea is served in the garden-side tearoom. Tours are offered as cruise-ship shore excursions, and independent travelers can call and book tea and a tour as well. When the berries are ripe, visitors are encouraged to try them. The luscious fruits and vegetables are already supplying local stores and restaurants.

Horseback Riding

On a **Chilkoot Horseback Adventure** (2 hours, plus 1.5 hours for transportation; 907/983-3990; *www.chilkoot horseback.com;* May–Sept, 4 departures daily; $129), participants are brought by van to Dyea where the ride through historic Dyea and the surrounding area begins. Transportation, a snack, and all gear are included. No experience is required, but riders must be at least 4 feet 10 inches tall and weigh less than 250 pounds.

ROAD TRIPS

Dyea *(18 miles/1 hour)*

This 9-mile drive that twists and corkscrews through an increasingly wild landscape is not for the faint-hearted. The narrow dirt road often runs just inches from Taiya Inlet. Yet the views of the inlet and back to Skagway's harbor are staggeringly beautiful. Some of Skagway's most charming homes are carved into the hillside above the hurly-burly of traffic. When cruise ships are in port, the road gets fairly heavy use by vans bringing hikers and boaters to Dyea; passing a vehicle going in the opposite direction can be quite a feat. Once safely in Dyea, you can join a national park guided tour of the old townsite, hike a mile or two up the Chilkoot Trail, or just wander around the beautiful campground and play Poohsticks from the bridge crossing the Taiya River while you collect yourself for the trip back to town.

White Pass *(mileage varies/4 hours)*

If you have only a half day, you can still drive the most scenic and historic portion of the South Klondike Highway up to the Canadian border and beyond. It's 14.4 miles to the summit of White Pass and the international border. Canadian Customs in Fraser, British Columbia, is a total of 22.5 miles from Skagway. Five miles beyond Fraser is Log Cabin. There are numerous turnouts with interpretive signs and views of the canyon, mountains, and—if you time it right—the White Pass & Yukon Route Railroad on its way. On weekends, the train is hauled by a steam engine, making for a terrific photo op. To cross the border, you'll need proof of citizenship (birth certificate or passport) as well as your driver's license. See Golden Circle Route in the Haines chapter, page 179, for details.

For contact information for outfitters and tour operators listed in this chapter, see sidebar on pages 216–17.

CYCLING

Sockeye Cycle offers tours that include stops for wildlife viewing. All gear is included. On their **Dyea Bicycle Adventure** (2.5 hours; $72; minimum age 10; 3–12 people), cyclists are bused to Dyea to tour the old townsite by bike for 6 miles and learn about local plants and wildlife. The trip is rated as easy. The moderately strenuous **Klondike Bicycle Tour** (2.5 hours; $72; minimum age 14; 3–12 people) combines a sightseeing trip by van up to the 3,292-foot White Pass with a 15-mile bike ride down the South Klondike Highway. The **White Pass Train & Bike Tour** (4 hours; $152; minimum age 14; 4–12 people) combines Skagway's most popular attraction, the train, with the opportunity to bike 15 miles down the highway to town. This way you get to experience the extraordinary scenery from both sides of the deep gorge. Difficulty is rated moderate.

For bike rentals, see One Day, page 219.

FISHING

For all of these salmon fishing charters, fishing licenses and tags (if needed) are available on board but cost extra. **Chilkoot Charters** has a 3.5-hour charter ($135/person, up to 6 people). Charters are also available from locally owned **Choctaw Lady Charters**. **Dockside Charters** has two charters (3.5 hours, $135; 7 hours, $225). **Fishfull Think-N** also has a charter (4 hours; $135; minimum 2 people).

You can **rent poles and bait** for lake, river, and shore fishing at **Fishfull Think-N**, which also offers sightseeing excursions.

HIKING

From Downtown

The hike to **Gold Rush Cemetery and Lower Reid Falls** (1.5–2 hours), with a 50-foot elevation gain, makes a good extension of the Skagway walking tour (starting from 9a in the Walking Tour, page 204). The cemetery is in a tranquil forest, and most of the grave markers consist of painted wooden headstones, periodically repainted. All date from a ten-year period: 1898 to 1908. Few people buried here lived past the age of forty. A meningitis epidemic and the town's tainted water supply took an especially harsh toll on children and young adults. The nefarious Soapy Smith and his nemesis, town surveyor Frank Reid, are buried here. Reid merits the graveyard's largest monument.

If you're coming from downtown, it's an easy 3-mile walk, round trip, from First and Broadway. Follow Broadway to Fourteenth Avenue, then turn left and walk one block to State Street. Turn right on State and take it to the end of town (Twenty-third Avenue). Crossing the railroad tracks, follow the gravel road that skirts the railroad maintenance yard to the right. To the right, train tracks run parallel to your road. You need to cross the tracks one more time to reach the Gold Rush Cemetery. Vigorous Lower Reid Falls is a short hike up a pretty path, well marked, from the graveyard.

The easy hike to **Yakutania Point and Smuggler's Cove** (1.5–2 hours) is popular with joggers, and by using the exercise stations along the earlier portion of the trail, you can turn it into a workout. There are several excellent picnic spots along the way, plus pit toilets. From Broadway, go west on First Avenue to Main Street and turn left. Walk around Skagway's airport terminal (on your right) and cross the footbridge at the mouth of the Taiya River (in August it's full of spawning Dolly Varden, which do not die after spawning). On the far side of the bridge, go left passing the exercise stations. The trail narrows before you reach Yakutania Point, where you'll find picnic tables, a picnic shelter, and a pit toilet. This makes a great spot from which to gaze back at Skagway's harbor, watching the ferries and cruise ships and helicopters from a serene distance. From Yakutania Point, the trail continues through rain forest for a little less than 0.5 mile, quite hilly and a bit rough in places, but well marked, to Smuggler's Cove, which is hidden and well protected. There is another picnic shelter, tables, and a pit toilet.

It is a short but fairly steep hike to **Lower Dewey Lake** (1–2 hours), with a 500-foot elevation gain; hikers who are moderately fit should have no difficulty. Head up Broadway from First to Fourth Avenue, and follow Fourth Avenue east. Wend your way between the barracks-like buildings, and cross first a bridge and then the railroad tracks. Signs and markers point out the trail. Where the trail branches, go right, stopping to catch your breath and marvel at the view periodically. A 2-mile trail circles Lower Dewey Lake. Hiking just to the lake and back should take less than an hour; if you walk around the lake, add an additional hour.

There are two ways to access **Icy Lake** and **Upper Reid Falls** (3 hours). Follow the access route to Lower Dewey Lake (see above), but instead of following the trailhead, go left on the power company maintenance road. Or simply go to Lower Dewey Lake and follow the trail north to Icy Lake. The 6-mile round trip has an 850-foot elevation gain. The trail beyond Lower Dewey Lake runs through hemlock and spruce forest. The trail gets muddy around Icy Lake.

The 7-mile round trip hike to **Sturgill's Landing** (4 hours) starts from the south end of Lower Dewey Lake (see above). The trail runs south through evergreen forest and gets boggy as it goes down toward the beach.

There are picnic tables and a pit toilet. The trail ends up at the rocky, driftwood-strewn beach on Taiya Inlet.

With a Car

On a **Chilkoot Trail day hike** (4 hours), visitors who don't have time to hike the entire trail can still hike the first 2 miles to get a taste of what Klondike prospectors experienced in 1898. If you want to hike the full trail or a shorter trek that crosses into Canada, a three-to-five-day trek, you'll need to get a permit. (See Chilkoot Trail in Two Days or More, page 224.) The trailhead is 9 miles out of Skagway at the Dyea campground. The trail is rough and fairly steep at first, with plenty of rocks and tree roots to scramble over. The spruce and hemlock forest interspersed with cottonwood and alder is beautiful. In about a mile, the trail levels out

---

Skagway Outfitters & Tour Operators

Alaska Fjordlines 907/766-3395, 800/320-0146; alaskafjordlines.com

Alaska Mountain Guides & Climbing School 907/766-3366, 800/766-3396; www.alaska mountainguides.com

Chilkoot Charters 907/983-3400, 877/983-3400; www.chilkootcharters.com

Choctaw Lady Charters 907/983-3305; 907/723-0605 cell

Cree-ation Tours 240 4th Ave; 907/983-2575; www.creeationtours.com

Dockside Charters 907/983-3625, 877/983-3625; www.members.aol.com/dockside/products.htm

Fishfull Think-N 907/983-2777, 907/723-0316; www.fishfullthinkn.net

Frontier Excursions 7th and Broadway; 907/983-2512, 877/983-2512; www.frontierexcursions.com

somewhat. Wildlife in the forest includes bald eagles (fishing on the adjacent Taiya River) and bears. Driving the narrow road to the trailhead in Dyea is an adventure best left to drivers with nerves of steel. If you don't count yourself as one, **Frontier Excursions** offers a **drop-off and pickup service** ($20/person). They'll pick up anywhere in Skagway, including the cruise-ship dock, and drive you to and from the trailhead.

Guided Hikes

Combine a hike up the first 1.8 miles of the **Chilkoot Trail** with a float down the tranquil **Taiya River** with **Skagway Float Tours** (4 hours; $80/adult, $60/under 13). The hike is strenuous, but short and beautiful, giving visitors a taste of what it might have been like to haul 2,000 pounds of provisions up in winter. The trip includes transportation to and from Dyea. Sturdy shoes or boots are a must.

Klondike Water Adventures 907/983-3769; www.skagwaykayak.com

Mountain Flying Service based in Haines, 132 2nd Ave; 907/766-3007; flyglacierbay.com

Packer Expeditions 4th between Broadway and State Sts; 907/983-2544; www.packerexpeditions.com

Skagway Air Service 907/983-2218; www.skagwayair.com

Skagway Float Tours 907/983-3688; www.skagwayfloat.com

Skagway Small Boat Harbor 907/983-2628; skgboat@aptalaska.net

Skagway Street Car Company 270 2nd Ave; 907/983-2908; www.skagwaystreetcar.com

Sockeye Cycle 5th Ave off Broadway; 907/983-2851; www.cyclealaska.com

TEMSCO Helicopters 907/983-2900; www.temscoair.com

Wings of Alaska 907/983-2442; www.wingsofalaska.com

KAYAKING & RAFTING

Klondike Water Adventures offers guided tours (2.5 hours; $75) from the small boat harbor on Taiya Inlet. Sea kayakers paddle out to the **Taiya Inlet coastline**, in two-person kayaks, with a naturalist guide. The trip includes transportation and a snack.

A **Taiya River float trip** (2.5–3 hours; $70/adult, $50/under 13) combines the scenic drive to Dyea at the Chilkoot trailhead with a gentle river float offered by **Skagway Float Tours**. A dinner float can be arranged as well, which adds a barbecue to the float trip. Groups can vary in size from two to ten.

Deishu Expeditions offers half-day kayak trips from Haines (see Two Days or More in the Haines chapter, page 178) that are open to everyone, but their Skagway-based trips are open only to cruise-ship passengers as shore excursions.

ONE DAY

HISTORY & CULTURE

Every Saturday in summer, a round-trip excursion by **steam train to Lake Bennett** (8.5 hours; $160/adult, $80/ages 3–12, free/under 3; June–Aug Sat 8am) is offered by **White Pass & Yukon Route Railroad** (907/983-2217, 800/343-7373; *www.whitepassrailroad.com*). After you disembark at Lake Bennett, you'll have 2 hours for a box lunch and walking tour with a park historian. Because this trip crosses the international border into Canada, you'll need to bring photo ID and proof of citizenship (birth certificate or passport). These popular trips regularly sell out; advance reservations are essential.

GUIDED TOURS

Several **van trips** (5–6 hours) bring passengers from Skagway over the White Pass into the Yukon as far as Carcross, Canada. Lunch is included for each trip by **Frontier Excursions**. One, the **Yukon & Sled Dog Tour** ($165) includes a visit to sled dog kennels (with petting time built in) and a ride with Yukon Quest mushers. For $175, you are whisked to the Yukon scenery in an SUV. In a van, a similar Yukon trip costs $99.

NATURE

Between Memorial Day and Labor Day, daily **sightseeing day trips** (12.25 hours; $139/adult, $109/ages 2–12) from Haines and Skagway to Juneau and back, offered by **Alaska Fjordlines**, leave Skagway at 8am and return at 8:15pm. Transportation between the Auke Bay terminal and downtown Juneau, a trip to Mendenhall Glacier, and onboard snacks are included in the price. There's a narrated tour aboard the 65-foot catamaran and pauses for wildlife viewing along the highly scenic route. Humpback whales, seals, Steller sea lions, and bald eagles are usually encountered. Once deposited in downtown Juneau, passengers are given walking maps and turned loose for 3 hours of unguided sightseeing and shopping before being whisked off to Mendenhall Glacier for an hour and then returned to the boat.

ROAD TRIPS

The drive up to the **White Pass** and across the border into **Carcross**, Canada, is spectacular (4–16 hours). If you are prepared for a long day, you can even drive all the way to **Whitehorse** and back (16 hours). But if all you have is 4 hours, it's still worthwhile (see Golden Circle Route, page 179). You'll need to bring proof of citizenship (passport or birth certificate) along with your driver's license.

CYCLING

Sockeye Cycle rents bikes in Skagway, including tandem bikes ($12/2 hours, $20/4 hours, $30/8 hours). Multiday rental discounts are available. **Sourdough Car Rentals & Tours** (907/983-2523, 907/209-5026; *sourdough rental@yahoo.com*) rents mountain bikes ($10/day, $50/week).

FISHING

Chilkoot Charters offers halibut-fishing excursions (8 hours; $240; 6 people maximum), departing at 7:30am, returning at 3:30pm. License fees are not included; a sack lunch is. They also arrange custom salmon and halibut fishing charters. **Dockside Charters** offers salmon or halibut fishing (7 hours; $225; 6 people maximum); snacks are included. **Fishfull Think-N** also has a **charter** (8 hours; $195; 3 passengers minimum); online booking discounts apply. To arrange a custom fishing trip, contact the harbormaster at the **Skagway Small Boat Harbor** (see Skagway Outfitters & Tour Operators, page 217).

HIKING

From Downtown

A difficult and strenuous climb on the **Skyline Trail** (8–12 hours), 10 miles round trip with a 5,000-foot elevation gain, rewards hikers with fabulous views of **AB Mountain**. Two competing theories explain where the name AB Mountain comes from. According to one, the letters stand for "Arctic Brotherhood." The other asserts it's the result of a pattern of snowmelt that creates the letters "A" and "B" on the mountainside each year, and proponents have photos to prove their case. The trailhead is on the Dyea Road. Pedestrians can reach it by heading west on First Avenue across the Skagway River footbridge and on to the Dyea Road. The trail is not particularly hard to follow until you get to the tree line. Thereafter, the way is marked with rock cairns that can be impossible to see when visibility is poor. Attempt this hike only in good weather and turn back if conditions deteriorate.

The full hike to **Devil's Punchbowl** (8–10 hours) can be shortened to just reaching **Upper Dewey Lake** (6 hours). The trail begins at Lower Dewey Lake (see Four Hours or Less, page 215). It is a steep and strenuous 6-mile round trip with a 3,000-foot elevation gain and fabulous views of town. Hikers emerge in muskeg meadow by Upper Dewey Lake, with a small, very basic public cabin where you can stay overnight (if no one else is there already). If you decide to press on, the trail from Upper Dewey to Devil's Punchbowl, a tiny but deep lake, takes about 4 hours for the 5-mile round trip with an additional 600-foot elevation gain and yet more gorgeous views.

By Train

Two excellent hikes near Skagway are accessed from the **White Pass & Yukon Route Railroad**, which regularly stops to drop off and pick up hikers. You'll need advance reservations for this flag-stop service. Trains automatically stop to let out passengers with reservations. (Part of the fun is taking the train 6 miles to the trailhead and getting off under the gaze of wondering passengers with noses pressed to the glass.) For the return journey, be at the trailhead at least 15 minutes prior to the pickup time and the train will stop for you. Only the train between Skagway and Fraser, British Columbia, makes these stops, so don't be alarmed if other trains pass you by.

The hike to **Denver Glacier** (10 hours) is not a particularly difficult climb until the end. Because of avalanche danger, it should be avoided in spring. The trail begins next to the Denver Caboose Cabin (see Two Days or More, page 223). From the trailhead it's a 4- to 6-mile round trip, depending how far you go on the glacial moraine. There is a 1,200-foot elevation gain. The trail heads east before the tracks cross the Skagway River, then follows the river upstream and turns south after Elway Falls. It's a lovely hike, but toward the end it can be hard to make out the trail. (Flag-stop train service; departure: 8am and 12:30pm; pickup: 11:45am and 3:55pm at milepost 6; $27/round trip.)

The hike to **Laughton Glacier** (10 hours) can be easily turned into a multiday trip, thanks to a nearby Forest Service cabin (see Two Days or More, page 223). The trailhead is 14 miles north of Skagway. The 3.5-mile round trip has an elevation gain of 200 to 600 feet, depending how far you go beyond the cabin, which is 2 miles from the trailhead. The trail to the cabin is easy and beautiful, crossing several streams. Chances of running across bears and moose are good. About a mile beyond the cabin is Laughton Glacier. Hiking to and on the glacier is more difficult; use caution.

(Flag-stop train service; departure: 8am and 12:30pm, pickup: 11am and 3:15pm at milepost 14; $54/round trip.)

Guided Hikes

Packer Expeditions leads three guided day hikes. All these hikes are best attempted by hikers in good condition. Appropriate footgear is a must (boots or shoes with ankle support), and hikers should dress in layers, because temperatures can vary significantly along the way. Hiking gear—if needed—fanny packs, water, snacks, and lunch are included. Tour leaders have emergency medical technician training.

The **Helicopter–Laughton Glacier Hike-Train** (5.5 hours; $258) is a demanding trip, so only very fit hikers should attempt it. However, it offers a great opportunity to combine flightseeing with a glacier hike and a trip on the White Pass & Yukon Route Railroad. Starting with a helicopter flight to Glacier Station at White Pass, hike 4 miles round trip to Laughton Glacier, then return to Skagway with a 1-hour train ride.

The **Denver Glacier Hike-Train** (8.5 hours; $127.50) combines a trip by train to the Denver Caboose and a hike to the Denver Glacier. A minimum of five hikers, age 13 or older, is required. The hike is offered mid-May through September.

For the **Laughton Glacier Hike-Train** (8.5 hours; $135), hikers take the train to the trailhead and hike up to the glacier and back.

KAYAKING

Combine a White Pass & Yukon Route train trip with the opportunity to kayak on **Lake Bernard**, in British Columbia (4.5 hours; $159), on an excursion with **Klondike Water Adventures**. The trip up is by train. You're then whisked to the lake for an outing (no experience necessary) in two-person kayaks. The lake is highly scenic, and wildlife is usually in evidence. The trip back is in a van on the South Klondike Highway. Because you'll be crossing the international border, be sure to bring photo ID and proof of citizenship (birth certificate or passport). Transportation and a snack are included.

For contact information for outfitters and tour operators listed in this chapter, see sidebar on pages 216–17.

TWO DAYS OR MORE

HIKING & CLIMBING

Serious trekkers and climbers can get outfitted at **Alaska Mountain Guides & Climbing School**. In addition to leading Chilkoot Trail trips, they offer many multiday, and sometimes multisport (climbing, kayaking, skiing), classes and adventures. Options range in length from a few days to three weeks, including guided mountain climbing and trekking trips to destinations such as **Mount Fairweather** (15,300 feet).

Packer Expeditions leads guided hikes along the entire **Chilkoot Trail**. Groups are no larger than ten. Packer will also create custom multiday hikes.

USFS Cabins

You can transform a hike to Laughton or Denver glaciers into an overnight trip with a stay at one of the two U.S. Forest Service cabins in the Skagway vicinity. They are quite popular in summer, so you'll need to book in advance as far as possible (up to six months).

By far the most fun is the **Denver Caboose**, retired from years of service and transformed into accommodations for six people (four single bunks and one double). With amenities typical of other USFS cabins, it is located at the Denver Glacier trailhead (see One Day, page 221) close to the White Pass & Yukon Route Railroad, which provides access to and from the caboose. If you're traveling with kids, be sure they understand that the train tracks can be dangerous. The train makes multiple trips up to White Pass daily. The **Laughton Glacier Cabin**, with two single and two double bunks, is located 2 miles up the Laughton Glacier Trail (see One Day, page 221). Both cabins are $35 per night for a maximum of ten nights in summer. For information on renting USFS cabins, see the introduction, page 15.

Chilkoot Trail

Each year, hundreds of hikers follow in the footsteps of centuries of Tlingit traders and thousands of gold rush prospectors, making the 33-mile journey from the trailhead in Dyea up the Chilkoot Trail to Bennett. The trail, running through what was designated the Klondike Gold Rush International Historical Park in 1998, crosses the international border and is jointly managed by the United States and Canada. On and off the trail, it is not unusual to find gold rush–era artifacts; these must be left in place. Think of the trail as a kind of living museum.

Apart from its historical interest, this is a highly scenic hike. Starting at sea level in lush temperate rain forest, it rises to alpine tundra above the tree line to 3,525 feet, then drops to boreal forest. Hikers often encounter black and brown bears and bald eagles at lower altitudes and arctic ground squirrels, hoary marmots, and mountain goats at higher levels. Toward the end of the trail, moose, wolves, and more bears are plentiful.

There are a number of designated campsites along the route, plus several warming shelters. Park rangers and wardens are stationed in summer at the Dyea trailhead, Sheep Camp, Chilkoot Pass, and Lindeman City. At the end of the hike, you will be required to clear Canada customs, so you'll need to bring proof of citizenship (birth certificate or passport) and photo identification.

Hikers are encouraged to make this trip late in the summer, July and August, when avalanche dangers are past. Most hikers choose to follow the historical path from Dyea rather than the other way around. Not only is it the traditional route, it is easier on the knees to go up the steep sections rather than down. At least a moderate level of fitness and backpacking experience are strongly recommended.

Hikers must register and obtain permits in Skagway before heading out, unless they are simply making a day hike on the U.S. side of the border. Canada limits hikers coming across the border to fifty per day.

Groups can be no larger than twelve people, and only one such group (nine to twelve individuals) per day is allowed. Permits (Canadian dollars: $50/adult hiking entire trail, $35/adult hiking only Canadian side, $15/adult hiking only U.S. side; children 5–16 half price; reservations $10/hiker) are required for all people using the Canadian portion of the trail and for anyone spending a night camping anywhere on the trail. The hike is not suitable for very young children, but older, fit youngsters regularly make the full hike. Although advance reservations are strongly encouraged, some slots are left open for impromptu travelers.

The **Chilkoot Trail Center** (in Martin Itjen House, Broadway between 1st and 2nd Aves, Skagway; daily in summer 8am–5pm) is staffed by park rangers who are your best source of information on hiking the Chilkoot. Here you can pick up the *Hiker's Guide to the Chilkoot Trail*, check out current trail conditions, and purchase your permit. For further information, check with the **Klondike Gold Rush National Historical Park** (see Four Hours or Less, page 205) and the **Chilkoot Trail National Historic Site of Canada** (867/667-3910, 800/661-0486; *www.parkscanada.pch.gc.ca*).

To get to and from the trail requires transportation. **Frontier Excursions** has a **trail drop-off service** for a minimum of two hikers (from Skagway to trailhead, or reverse, $10/person; from Log Cabin to Skagway, $20/person; from Carcross to Skagway, $35/person). Reservations are recommended for Dyea drop-offs; they are required for Log Cabin and Carcross.

Another option is to take the **White Pass & Yukon Route Railroad** back from Lake Bennett to Fraser or Skagway, the "Chilkoot Trail Hikers Special" (from Lake Bennett to Fraser: $35/person one way Fri, Sun; $45/person one way Sat; from Lake Bennett to Skagway: $65/person Fri, Sun; $80/person Sat). Advance purchase is required. Be sure to carry proof of citizenship (birth certificate or passport) and photo ID.

ROAD TRIP: GOLDEN CIRCLE ROUTE

Skagway to Haines *(360 miles/3 days)*

This route, allowing you to make the round trip from Skagway through British Columbia and the Yukon Territory on beautiful paved mountain roads, is described more fully in Two Days or More in the Haines chapter, page 179.

Haines

An overnight or longer trip to the nearby town of Haines is easily accomplished via the Chilkat Fast Ferry or by one of the air carriers that offers multiple daily flights between Haines and Skagway. Don't assume that just because Haines is only 14 miles from Skagway the two destinations are similar; they are as different as two towns could be. For kayakers and cyclists, Haines offers a wider selection of trips. See the Haines chapter for details.

Whitehorse

The **White Pass & Yukon Route Railroad** offers a round trip to Whitehorse (4 hours one way; $95/adult one way; $47.50/ages 3–12 one way), capital of Canada's Yukon Territory. Travelers go by train to Fraser, British Columbia, where they are transferred to a bus for the remainder of the journey to Whitehorse. Trains leave Skagway at 8am, Alaska time, daily between mid-May and mid-September, arriving in Whitehorse at 1pm, Pacific time (note that Yukon, which observes Pacific time, is an hour later than Alaska time). Buses depart Whitehorse daily at 1pm and arrive in Skagway at 4:30pm. Advance reservations are a must. You'll need to bring acceptable identification for the border (passport or birth certificate and photo ID).

ACCOMMODATIONS

When it comes to accommodations, Skagway is challenged. Legions of summer visitors, followed by a severe drop in the town's winter population, make running a hotel more than a little difficult. Not surprisingly, there are frequent turnovers. But a few excellent hostelries remain.

Alaska Sojourn Hostel ($; 8th and Main Sts; 907/983-2030) is an attractive building in a residential neighborhood, with bunks and a private family room. There is a kitchen to use. A courtesy shuttle runs between 7am and 9pm. No curfews or lockouts apply.

Sergeant Preston's Lodge ($–$$; 6th and State Sts; 907/983-2521, 866/983-2521; *www.sgt-prestonslodges-kagway.com*) has mostly spacious, moderately priced rooms and a location away from the noise yet within an easy walk of downtown, making this a top accommodation choice. It's just a block from the Haven (see Dining, below). There's a courtesy shuttle.

Westmark Inn Skagway ($–$$; 3rd and Spring; 907/983-6000, 800/544-0970; *www.westmarkhotels.com*; May–Sept; &) is the town's largest hotel, close to Broadway but on a quiet side street. It has plenty of comfortable rooms, but you must book in advance. They often fill up with cruise-tour passengers in summer. There's a dining room and a courtesy shuttle.

DINING

The dining picture in Skagway is brighter than the accommodations scene. Cities whose economies revolve around tourism are not always culinary standouts; Skagway is a welcome exception.

Glacier Pizza ($; 363 2nd Ave; 907/983-2411; summer: call for hours) offers young, perpetually hungry temporary summer help a top-notch pizza parlor. This popular hangout fills the bill and offers free delivery.

Haven ($; 9th and State Sts; 907/983-3553; *www.haven-cafe.com*; year-round; &), a fine café, is next door to You Say Tomato, Skagway's whole-foods store. Terrific soups and freshly made foccacia sandwiches are specialties, along with sumptuous desserts, coffee drinks, and shakes. A good bet for vegetarians.

Yes, But Where Did It Spawn?

In the 1990s, savvy Alaska seafood market-ers started identifying and marketing salmon according to their river of origin, the one they were returning to spawn in when hooked. Voila! A decade later, the arrival of the first Copper River king salmon in spring is a Pacific North-west culinary event for foodies, along the lines of France's November Beaujolais Nouveau wine ritual. Whether a salmon from the Copper River tastes better than one from the Stikine is open to question; luckily, the superb flavor of wild king salmon is not.

Sabrosa ($; Broadway and 6th; 907/983-2469; sea-sonally 8am–8pm) includes superb halibut chowder, hearty Mexican fare, and genuine Thai food among its specialties. Vegetarians and vegans will find many options, from entrées to desserts.

Skagway Fish Company ($$; in red bldg above small boat harbor; 907/983-3474; 11am–11pm; &) is crowded, noisy, and smoky, dominated by a big central bar. Come here for the excellent fish-and-chips, microbrew, and the chance to strike up a conversation with some-one new.

Stowaway Café ($$$; 205 Congress Wy; 907/983-3463; Mon–Fri 11am–3:30pm, daily 4–10pm; &), next door to the Skagway Fish Company, is superb but more subdued, well worth a splurge. Wasabi salmon is a standout; leave room for one of the heavenly chocolate desserts.

ACKNOWLEDGMENTS

Among the many Alaskans who generously contributed their time and expertise to this project, several merit special mention. In Skagway, Buckwheat Donahue shared his impressive local knowledge and doughnuts. In Ketchikan, the ever-resourceful Sandy Meske smoothed my path in so many ways. In Juneau, Carol Scafturon, an island of serenity in a sea of visitors, answered a myriad questions and offered valuable hiking tips. Also in Juneau, Sharon Gaiptman helped me plumb the mysteries of the Alaska Marine Highway System. Joanne Wiita at the Goldbelt Native Corporation and Kathy Miller at the Sealaska Heritage Institute shared the rich history and culture of the Tlingit people. My profound thanks to all.

In Seattle, my gratitude goes to the incomparable editorial team at Sasquatch Books in Seattle, especially managing editor Heidi Schuessler and associate editor Heidi Lenze. And at the top of my list, love and thanks to Mike, Nick, and Emily, who kept the home fires lit.

BIBLIOGRAPHY

GENERAL

BAUER, ERWIN, AND PEGGY BAUER. *Glacier Bay: The Wild Beauty of Glacier Bay National Park.* Seattle: Sasquatch Books, 2001. This book offers a visual introduction to the park and its inhabitants.

BERTON, PIERRE. *The Klondike Fever: The Life and Death of the Last Great Gold Rush.* New York: Alfred A. Knopf, 1958. Written by the great Canadian author and son of a Klondike prospector, this classic brings the exciting era to life.

CARLTON, ROSEMARY. *Sheldon Jackson: The Collector.* Juneau: Alaska State Museums, 1999. This is the biography of the Presbyterian minister whose collection formed the basis for the museum's exhibits.

CLIFFORD, HOWARD, ED. *Soapy Smith, Uncrowned King of Skagway.* Seattle: Sourdough Enterprises, 1997. Learn the story behind the legendary bad guy who inspired Skagway's first tourism boom.

COATES, KEN, AND BILL MORRISON. *The Sinking of the Princess Sophia: Taking the North Down with Her.* Fairbanks: University of Alaska Press, 1991. The story of the maritime disaster near Juneau in which 353 people died makes compelling reading.

DAUENHAUER, NORA MARKS, AND RICHARD DAUEN-HAUER, EDS. *Haa Shuká, Our Ancestors: Tlingit Oral Narratives.* Seattle:University of Washington Press, 1987. This book is a fascinating combination of literature and history.

FORD, COREY. *Where the Sea Breaks Its Back: The Epic Story of Early Naturalist Georg Steller and the Russian Exploration of Alaska.* Seattle: Alaska Northwest Books, 1992. Ford's account of Steller's journey with the second Bering expedition to Alaska in 1741 is an enthralling read.

JETTMAR, KAREN. *Alaska's Glacier Bay: A Traveler's Guide.* Seattle: Alaska Northwest Books, 1997. A comprehensive guide to the bay, this book includes history, geology, flora, and fauna, and comes with photos and map.

MCPHEE, JOHN. *Coming into the Country.* New York: Farrar, Straus and Giroux, 1991. The vivid account of Alaska's journey to statehood has become a classic.

MERGLER, WAYNE, ED. *The Last New Land: Alaska Past and Present.* Seattle: Alaska Northwest Books, 1996. An anthology of writings on Alaska, this extensive collection ranges from creation myth to contemporary memoir.

The Milepost. Augusta: Morris Communications. This annual guide to Alaska's highways and communities includes Inside Passage roads.

MORGAN, MURRAY AND E.A. HEGG. *One Man's Gold Rush*. Seattle: University of Washington Press, 1995. The work of the great Klondike gold rush photographer, E. A. Hegg, powerfully conveys the grueling journey of thousands of prospectors.

MURPHY, CLAIRE RUDOLF, AND JANE G. HAIGH. *Gold Rush Women*. Seattle: Alaska Northwest Books, 1997. Fascinating stories of twenty-three women who played important roles in the Klondike and Fairbanks gold rushes are brought to life with archival photos.

O'CLAIR, RITA, ROBERT ARMSTRONG, AND RICHARD CARSTENSEN. *The Nature of Southeast Alaska*. Seattle: Alaska Northwest Books, 1997. This guide offers a comprehensive introduction to the region's flora and fauna.

PEDERSEN, GUNNAR. *The Highway Angler*. Fairbanks: Fishing Alaska Publications, 1999. A primer for anglers offers tips on where and how to fish in Alaska.

RABAN, JONATHAN. *Passage to Juneau: A Sea and Its Meanings*. New York: Pantheon Books, 1999. Raban's celebrated account describes a journey up the Inside Passage in the context of the waterway's rich history of exploration.

RICKS, BYRON. *Homelands: Kayaking the Inside Passage*. New York: HarperPerennial, 1999. Journalist Ricks has written a vivid memoir of a five-month kayak trip.

SAMUEL, CHERYL. *The Chilkat Dancing Blanket*. Norman: University of Oklahoma Press, 1982. What's behind these complex and beautiful blankets is detailed in this book.

SHEARAR, CHERYL. *Understanding Northwest Coast Art: A Guide to Crests, Beings, and Symbols*. Seattle: University of Washington Press, 2000. This straightforward guide illuminates the language and symbolism of totem poles.

STEWART, HILLARY. *Looking at Totem Poles*. Seattle: University of Washington Press, 1993. A noted expert offers a survey and analysis of more than 100 totem poles.

WOLFE, ART, AND NICK JANS. *Alaska*. Seattle: Sasquatch Books, 2000. Beautiful photos and text introduce readers to the landscapes and wildlife of the state.

ALASKA NATURAL HISTORY ASSOCIATION BOOKLETS

Carved History. This guide explains the Sitka National Historical Park's totems and their history.

For God and Tsar: A Brief History of Russian America, 1741–1867. A succinct illustrated account, the booklet covers Russian history and trade, as well as the Russian Orthodox Church.

INDEX

O

P